Walt Whitman and Emily Dickinson

Agnieszka Salska

WALT WHITMAN and EMILY DICKINSON

Poetry of the Central Consciousness

upp

University of Pennsylvania Press/Philadelphia/1985

Library of Congress Cataloging in Publication Data
Salska, Agnieszka.
Walt Whitman and Emily Dickinson.
Rev. ed. of: The poetry of the central consciousness. 1982.
Bibliography: p.
Includes index.
1. American poetry—19th century—History and criticism. 2. Whitman, Walt, 1819–1892—Criticism and interpretation. 3. Dickinson, Emily, 1830–1886—Criticism and interpretation. 4. Self in literature. I. Salska, Agnieszka. Poetry of the central consciousness. II. Title. III. Title: Central consciousness.
PS321.S35 1985 811'.3'09353 84-17286
ISBN 0-8122-7946-8 ISBN 0-8122-1203-7 (pbk.)

Printed in the United States of America

Designed by Adrianne Onderdonk Dudden

Permission to reprint primary material in the text is hereby acknowledged from the following sources:

Quotations from Walt Whitman are reprinted by permission of New York University Press from:

Walt Whitman: Leaves of Grass, Reader's Comprehensive Edition edited by Harold W. Blodgett and Sculley Bradley. Copyright © 1965 by New York University.

Walt Whitman: Prose Works 1892 edited by Floyd Stovall. Copyright © 1963 by New York University.

Walt Whitman: Daybooks and Notebooks edited by William White. Copyright © 1978 by New York University.

Walt Whitman: The Correspondence edited by Edwin Haviland Miller. Copyright © 1961–1977 by New York University.

The poems of Emily Dickinson are from *The Poems of Emily Dickinson*, edited by Thomas H. Johnson, Cambridge, Mass.: The Belknap Press of Harvard University Press, copyright © 1951, 1955, 1979, 1983 by the President and Fellows of Harvard College, and are reprinted by permission of the publishers and the Trustees of Amherst College. Poems copyright 1914, 1929, 1935, 1942 by Martha Dickinson Bianchi; copyright renewed © 1957, 1963 by Mary L. Hampson are reprinted by permission of Little, Brown, and Company.

Quotations from the letters of Emily Dickinson are reprinted by permission of the publishers from *The Letters of Emily Dickinson*, edited by Thomas H. Johnson, Cambridge, Mass.: The Belknap Press of Harvard University Press. Copyright © 1958 by the President and Fellows of Harvard College, Copyright © 1914, 1924, 1932 by Martha Dickinson Bianchi.

Quotations from Ralph Waldo Emerson are reprinted by permission of the publishers from *The Journals and Miscellaneous Notebooks of Ralph Waldo Emerson*, edited by William H. Gilman et al., Cambridge, Mass.: The Belknap Press of Harvard University Press.

Quotations from Edgar Allan Poe are reprinted by permission of the publishers from *The Collected Works of Edgar Allan Poe*, Volume I, *Poems*, edited by Thomas Ollive Mabbott, Cambridge, Mass.: The Belknap Press of Harvard University Press, Copyright © 1969 by the President and Fellows of Harvard College.

Contents

Abbreviations

Quotations from *The Complete Works of Ralph Waldo Emerson*, Centenary Edition, ed. Edward Waldo Emerson (Boston: Houghton Mifflin, 1903–4) are identified by the volume and page number (e.g., 1 : 88).

Emily Dickinson's poems, quoted from *The Complete Poems of Emily Dickinson*, Variorum Edition, ed. Thomas H. Johnson (Cambridge, Mass.: Harvard University Press, Belknap Press, 1955), are identified by their numbers in the edition.

C — *The Correspondence of Walt Whitman*, ed. Edwin Haviland Miller, 6 vols. (New York: New York University Press, 1961–1977).

D — *Walt Whitman: Daybooks and Notebooks*, ed. William White, 3 vols. (New York: New York University Press, 1978).

J — *The Journals and Miscellaneous Notebooks of Ralph Waldo Emerson*, ed. William H. Gilman et al., 16 vols. (Cambridge, Mass.: Harvard University Press, 1960–82).

L — *The Letters of Emily Dickinson*, ed. Thomas H. Johnson and Theodora Ward, 3 vols. (Cambridge, Mass.: Harvard University Press, Belknap Press, 1958).

Letters — *The Letters of Ralph Waldo Emerson*, ed. Ralph L. Rusk, 6 vols. (New York: Columbia University Press, 1939).

LG — *Leaves of Grass*, Comprehensive Reader's Edition, ed. Harold Blodgett and Sculley Bradley (New York: New York University Press, 1965; reprinted in paperback by W. W. Norton, 1973). The numbers following the notation *LG* are the page and line numbers.

PW	*Walt Whitman: Prose Works*, ed. Floyd Stovall, 2 vols. (New York: New York University Press, 1963).
Slater	*The Correspondence of Emerson and Carlyle*, ed. Joseph Slater (New York: Columbia University Press, 1964).
Traubel	Horace Traubel, *With Walt Whitman in Camden*, vols. 1–2 (New York: Appleton, 1908); vol. 3 (Philadelphia: University of Pennsylvania Press, 1953); vol. 4 (Carbondale: Southern Illinois University Press, 1964).
UPP	*The Uncollected Poetry and Prose of Walt Whitman*, ed. Emory Holloway, 2 vols. (1921; reprint, Gloucester, Mass.: Peter Smith, 1972).

Preface

THIS study was inspired by my unhesitating, though by no means original, recognition that the work of Emily Dickinson and Walt Whitman is the best there is in American poetry of the nineteenth century. From a historian's point of view, the fact that the two artists lived in approximately the same time and occupy major positions in the history of American poetry could be considered sufficient ground for a comparative study. That they shared more or less the same historical and geographical space must mean that they faced similar intellectual and aesthetic issues. Still the relationship between the two poets has always seemed far too disturbing to be explained by a strictly historical approach.

The artists' names were brought together early; in 1891 Arlo Bates connected Dickinson with Whitman. What is even more significant, as Klaus Lubbers points out in *Emily Dickinson: The Critical Revolution*, is that linking Dickinson's name with that of Walt Whitman at that early date called attention to the problematic development of American literature (54). Following Bates the association resurfaced consistently until in the introductory chapter of Harold Bloom's *Wallace Stevens: The Poems of Our Climate*, published in 1977, Whitman and Dickinson figure as archetypes of "American poetic stances." Surprisingly, however, except for Albert Gelpi's chapters in *The Tenth Muse: The Psyche of the American Poet* and Karl

Keller's section on Whitman and Dickinson in *The Only Kangaroo Among the Beauty: Emily Dickinson and America*, no extensive comparative study of the two poets has been produced.

My approach to a comparative study is via Emerson. In the light of the scholarly work on American Romanticism since Mathiessen's *American Renaissance*, such an approach scarcely needs apology or even explanation. The debt of each of the poets to Emerson has been pointed out and argued for, although more remains to be done, especially in the case of Dickinson. In *Emerson and the Orphic Poet in America* Richard Allyn Yoder gives what seems to me the most concise and clear outline of the Emersonian background of the two poets. While Emerson's inclusiveness stands behind the opposition of Whitman's public and Dickinson's private concerns, it also remains a source of their convergence. Like Emerson, the two younger artists structured their poetic experience by "the recognition of ME and NOT ME." Thus, they moved between "the hope of Orphic apocalypse" and the predicament of the mind "unable to pierce an inch into the central truth of nature" (174–75).

My intent is to investigate comparatively "the structure of each poet's imagination," to use Northrop Frye's helpful phrase, and to indicate some of the aesthetic consequences of their diverging responses to essentially one vision—that of the central consciousness, the vision of the artist's mind as solely responsible for organizing the universe. The notion of the central consciousness which I propose as my key naturally associates with Henry James's postulate of a central intelligence as the organizing center of a work of art. The similarity lies in the recognition that it is the perceiving consciousness which ultimately structures what it perceives. The difference is that James treats such a central consciousness primarily as a compositional device, a principle of unity. It is this, but also much more for both Whitman and Dickinson. For them the significance of the recognition remains first of all philosophical. Using the central consciousness deliberately as a principle of unity for the work of art, James separates the existential quest for order from the act of constructing order of a literary work. Neither Whitman nor Dickinson is willing to make such radical division. Although Dickinson accepts more readily than Whitman the proposition that the order of life and the order of art are not identical, she treats the order of art as coextensive with experience because it offers a chance of transcendence, of personal salvation. The artist must thus become a quester for order—aesthetic, of course, but more vitally existential and metaphysical. And the self appears as the main protagonist in the drama of the quest which makes the poem.

In the course of my work I became indebted to many scholars who explored the territory earlier. Only a few can be mentioned here. Among the monograph studies of Whitman, Gay Wilson Allen's works were invaluable, as any student of Whitman knows. Howard Waskow's *Whitman: Explorations in Form* proved both stimulating and helpful. No Dickinson scholar can leave the debt to Thomas H. Johnson unacknowledged, nor can any serious work proceed without Jay Leyda's *The Years and Hours of Emily Dickinson* and Richard Sewall's *The Life of Emily Dickinson*. As for practical criticism of Dickinson's poetry, I am grateful for Charles Anderson's, David Porter's, and Robert Weisbuch's work. Roland Hagenbüchle's penetrating articles clarified many of my own insights. From the list of indispensable tools the concordances—Edwin Harold Eby's to Whitman and Stanford Patric Rosenbaum's to Dickinson—should not be omitted.

My more immediately personal debts are too many to list. I would, however, like to thank friends and colleagues in both Europe and the United States who cheerfully copied articles, sent books, invited me to poetry symposiums, answered my letters, generally encouraged me, and particularly offered their homes and hospitality when I needed a library larger than I could find in Poland. I also incurred a debt to friends and colleagues who read the manuscript, a debt that can only be appreciated by those who themselves have profited from similar services of friendship and knowledge. And, last but not least, the University of Łódź granted a timely leave of absence and assisted me financially, while a fellowship from the American Council of Learned Societies and the helpful hospitality of the English Department of the University of Pennsylvania made the final revisions possible. The result testifies but inadequately to much help, generosity, and sympathetic interest on both sides of the Atlantic.

1 / Whitman, Dickinson, and American Literary Individualism

SINCE F. O. Mathiessen's monumental work[1] it has become commonplace to say that American literature really begins in "the age of Emerson." Charles Feidelson has shown further how American artists of the period moved beyond the literary practices of contemporary Europe to usher in modes of expression characteristic of modern literature. They "anticipated modern symbolism because they lived in the midst of the same intellectual forces: mid-nineteenth-century America was a proving ground for the issues to which the method of modern literature is an answer. They envisaged the symbolistic program to an extent that few of their English contemporaries even thought possible. . . ."[2]

Nevertheless, the student of American Romantic poetry finds his position somewhat embarrassing since he must claim preeminence for figures whose significance for their own times was problematic. Although Emerson enjoyed considerable popularity and, more importantly, exerted a profound influence upon his contemporaries, neither Whitman nor Dickinson was a major force in defining the aesthetic climate of his times. Whitman's case is well known; his overarching ambition and pathetic efforts at self-publicity seem only to have increased the bitter uncertainty of his later years. Dickinson, apart from a handful of poems, did not publish at all during her lifetime, so, in a sense, her work does not belong to her times. The contemporary poetic scene was unquestionably dominated by Longfellow, who was widely read and admired on both sides of the Atlantic.

Yet today Longfellow seems a poet of mostly historical importance, almost comparable in his fate to Freneau or Bryant. His affinity with the previous generation of American Romantics is indicated by the title "the American Tennyson" often bestowed on him in analogy to the labels "American Wordsworth" or "American Walter Scott" given to Bryant and Cooper. As inaccurate as these critical shortcuts are, the labels do signal that the artists they sought to describe had looked back to an established way of writing and that an unambiguous derivative strain ran through their works. It is only too easy to speak of Whitman's poems as a concoction of assorted philosophical and political ideas expressed in the rhetoric of itinerant gospel preachers, but no unequivocal label of the sort mentioned above could be attached to his name. The very multiplicity of his alleged sources, ranging from the Neoplatonists to Hegel, to Italian opera, and the Eastern religions, puts in question the crucial significance of any of them. D. Mirsky expressed something of the bewildered attitude of a European intellectual facing the paradox of Whitman when he wrote in 1935:

> The individual quality of Whitman's poetry derives in good part from the strange and even weird combination that we find in it of originality and inspired daring, in a choice of themes never before treated by poets, with a provincial naiveté that is utterly incapable of beholding itself through the eyes of others. Out of this provincialism comes a break with the culture of the past and the poet's obstinate depiction of himself as prophet and preacher. . . . If on the one hand Whitman is a brother spirit to Dante and Goethe, his other affinities would include such individuals as Brigham Young, leader of the Mormon sect, and the founder of "Christian Science," Mrs. Eddy.[3]

It was, of course, not the quality of his sources that made Whitman such an outstanding phenomenon. The difference between Longfellow's eclecticism and that of Whitman or Emerson cannot be explained by referring to the materials they utilized but must be viewed in the context of their Weltanschauung and the aesthetic formulas developed to accommodate the vision.

Although Longfellow, Whitman, and Dickinson were born

within a span of little more than two decades (Longfellow in 1807, Whitman in 1819, and Dickinson in 1830), anthologies of modern American poetry, if they include the nineteenth century, begin with selections from Whitman and Dickinson,[4] never from Longfellow. The dividing line of relevance for our own times seems firmly established between Longfellow and the two younger poets. Longfellow belongs to a different phase of American Romanticism and has more in common with Washington Irving than with either Whitman or Dickinson. Underlying his effort to give America its "usable" literary past (very much like Washington Irving's attempt in *The Sketch Book*) in poems such as *Evangeline* (1847), *The Song of Hiawatha* (1855), *The Courtship of Miles Standish* (1858), or *The New England Tragedies* (1868) was the conviction that America lacked sufficient native resources. If the United States was to have any literature of respectable standards, the artist had no choice but to import what was missing and graft it upon the texture of American life.

Longfellow's conception of the American artist's role corresponds to the "negative" stage of American Romanticism, which seldom seems interesting to a critic today, except historically. Having as yet no sense of native values on which to build, American artists of this stage engaged in testing the relevance and adaptability of transatlantic impulses. As Benjamin T. Spencer writes in *The Quest for Nationality: An American Literary Campaign*:

> Throughout the ante-bellum decades American artists were thus obliged by the influx of foreign books constantly to assess the relevance of dominant European practices to the American scheme. Through this process they formulated, as it were, a kind of negative definition of American literature; through it they were able to see what American literature might be by perceiving first of all what it could not and should not be. . . . The next desideratum was to proceed beyond this negative definition and to discover American counterparts to which the imagination could legitimately respond.[5]

In two chapters dealing with the period from 1815 to 1860, "Transatlantic Realignments" and "Cisatlantic Impulses," Spencer throws light on two processes continuing within American Romanticism: the first that of sifting and selecting compatible European directives, the second that of tapping and assessing the native resources. The two processes occurred parallel in time and simultaneously came to a climax in what was aptly called "the flowering of New England."[6] In American Romantic poetry, the work of Longfellow crowns the one while that of Whitman and Dickinson brings to fulfillment the other. We only need to remind ourselves that *The Song of Hiawatha* and *Leaves of Grass* came out in print in the same year. The important difference is that the poetry of Longfellow appears now an end product while that of Whitman and Dickinson constitutes both a peak and a new beginning.

Longfellow could draw from any corner of European literary tradition because he believed that in doing so he was, on the one hand, alleviating the poverty of American tradition and, on the other, reestablishing the sadly thin connection between the European heritage and his native culture. He spent his creative energy adding all he could to what must have seemed to him an almost empty store of American literary tradition, for his idea of culture was that of accretion. Culture, and literature with it, was a sort of treasury of accumulated values which each generation was called upon to enrich. Mellowed by years and perhaps by the memory of Longfellow's kind visit, Whitman himself expressed understanding of the brahmin poet's aims: "I shall only say . . . what I have heard Longfellow himself say, that ere the New World can be worthily original, and announce herself and her own heroes, she must be well saturated with the originality of others, and respectfully consider the heroes that lived before Agamemnon" (*PW*, 286).[7]

The liberating essence of Emerson's idea of culture was that he conceived of it as an emanation of the inner wealth of the individual. While Longfellow believed that the individual and society starved without a rich cultural tradition and considered such tradition essential for the nourishment of man's inner life, Emerson reduced the role of a cultural heritage to that of a catalyst useful only in releasing creative energies. Stimulated properly, man would proceed to build his own world, his own culture. Instead of relying on the resources accumulated in the past, everyone must build his own system of values; instead of adding to the treasury of literature, each generation must rewrite it for itself.[8]

It is difficult to overestimate Emerson's role as "the liberating god" of national expression for, with the publication of *Nature*

(1836), *Essays* (1841), *Essays, Second Series* (1844), and *Poems* (1847), he certainly assisted in the birth of what today appears the classic period of American literature. He set the American artist free from the subtly enslaving, humiliating power of the past when he declared: "Each age, it is found, must write its own books; or rather each generation for the next succeeding. The books of an older period will not fit this" (1:88). "They are for nothing but to inspire" (1:89). He laid foundations for a new concept of the literary form when he shifted emphasis from the perfection of the finished *objet d'art* to the redeeming value of the creative process:

> Yet hence arises a grave mischief. The sacredness which attaches to the act of creation, the act of thought, is transferred to the record. The poet chanting was felt to be a divine man: henceforth the chant is divine also. The writer was a just and wise spirit: henceforward it is settled, the book is perfect; as love of the hero corrupts into worship of his statue. Instantly, the book becomes noxious: the guide is a tyrant. (1:88–89)

Finally, and most basically, he helped the American artist accept his surroundings as adequate nourishment for his art. "The American Scholar" implies no sense of handicap; on the contrary, it firmly asserts the American artist's resources: nature, books, and the active life. While advising caution in the use of books for "genius is always sufficiently the enemy of genius by over-influence" (1:91), the essay praises unreservedly the influence of untamed nature which Washington Irving wanted so desperately to "civilize" by filling it with legendary figures; it advocates the artist's engagement in the busy daily life whose materialistic narrowness offended Cooper. Throughout the essay Emerson demonstrates how ample the native influences are, yet he mentions only these three elements. But—and this is the crux of the matter—nature, books, and daily life were all there was for the American artist to fall back upon. That he could do so without a sense of privation was Emerson's concern and merit.

In 1831 Edgar Allan Poe wrote "Israfel," a poem permeated with frustration at the wide gap dividing the artist's ambition from his actual achievement. Disappointment seemed to Poe inevitable since the artist remained bound to a reality which was neither ideal nor even challenging:

Yes, Heaven is thine; but this
  Is a world of sweets and sours;
  Our flowers are merely—flowers,
And the shadow of thy perfect bliss
  Is the sunshine of ours.

If I could dwell
Where Israfel
  Hath dwelt, and he where I,
He might not sing so wildly well
  A mortal melody,
While a bolder note than this might swell
  From my lyre within the sky.[9]

Whitman's commitment to the American scene needs no demonstration. But the recluse Dickinson also shares Emerson's program when she comes to deal with her cultural situation:

The Robin's my Criterion for Tune—
Because I grow—where Robins do—
. . . .
Without the Snow's Tableau
Winter, were lie—to me—
Because I see—New Englandly—
The Queen, discerns like me—
Provincially—

(285, c. 1861)

Like Poe, Dickinson recognizes the artist's bond with her surroundings. The speaker of this poem, however, does not feel deprived or even limited as she notes what her particular environment has to offer: robins, buttercups, nuts in October, and snows in winter—nature's bounty provided by the changing seasons. Taking full cognizance, and so possession, of her world makes the speaker a queen in her province, equal to the British monarch. The difference is perhaps one of the extent of power but not of essence. The provincialism that Mirsky points to has been made into an aesthetic program as it was earlier made into a religious and political one.

It is perhaps of some interest to learn that in 1827 the aging Goethe urged the Americans to create their own literature along Emersonian lines:

> Amerika, du hast es besser
> Als unser Kontinent, das alte,
> Hast keine verfallene Schlösser
> Und keine Basalte.
>
> Dich stört nicht im Innern,
> Zu lebendiger Zeit,
> Unnützes Erinnern
> Und vergeblicher Streit.
>
> Benutzt die Gegenwart mit Glück!
> Und wenn nun eure Kinder dichten,
> Bewahre sie ein gut Geschick
> Vor Ritter—Räuber—und Gespenstergeschichten.[10]

Whether he knew the poem or not, Emerson proclaimed the roads open for the American artist to travel in the direction indicated by Goethe. And Holmes recognized fully the weight of the 1837 Phi Beta Kappa address when he called it "our intellectual Declaration of Independence."

Emerson's success as "the liberating god" should be measured by the remarkable achievements of the writers immediately influenced by him.[11] Among others, the group included such, at first sight, glaringly opposed figures as Whitman and Dickinson. Seeking to place them within the same intellectual and aesthetic climate, we should take a closer look at the impulses stimulating the complexities of Emerson's vision. Calling the period the "American Renaissance," Mathiessen addresses the analogy between the creative transformation of the classical tradition in the European Renaissance and the way European heritage and influence were made use of in mid-nineteenth-century American literature. Connections with Europe and especially with European Romanticism remained multiple and vital; they were, however, most effective in invigorating indigenous tendencies.[12]

Although Romanticism as a period in the history of ideas and expression proved so resistant to definitions that at least one leading American scholar advised that the term be used only in the plural,[13] there has been a persistent tendency in scholarship to recognize this time of the major intellectual revolution as possessing perhaps a difficult but certainly identifiable unity.[14] On the whole, eminent students of the period incline today toward locating its main significance in the changed view of the individual. To quote Howard Mumford Jones:

> The human being became at once more lonely and more independent, more unpredictable and more filled with emotion, more likely to look for the satisfactions of life here and now and less likely to be put off either by promises or by assurances that class and status were more blessed than self-fulfillment.[15]

Man is no longer identified with the sum of his history or the position in society he occupies but becomes an autonomous entity, an inviolable end in himself. In the corresponding philosophical context, the change is from a philosophy of being to a philosophy of mind and, on the literary level, from a poetry and poetics of imitation to one of exploration.[16]

For a long time now scholars of American literature have pointed to the radical emphasis American Romantic writers placed on the centrality and heroic dimensions of the self. This approach underlies such classical studies of the period as F. O. Mathiessen's *American Renaissance* or Richard Lewis's *The American Adam* as well as later books in the cultural history, such as Quentin Anderson's *The Imperial Self* or Sacvan Bercovitch's *The Puritan Origins of the American Self*. The important historical fact about American Romanticism is that it came to flower not in reaction to a previously dominant way of thinking, but as a climax in a relatively long and conscious effort to create both a national literature and a sense of national identity.[17] Thus, it was little shaped in its tone and scope by defensive stances. As B. T. Spencer points out, the most significant criticism of neoclassical principles in America came not from a young, unknown, and rebellious poet but was the work of Edward T. Channing, a Harvard professor of rhetoric and a teacher of both Emerson and Thoreau.[18] Romanticism in America did not have to spend energy fighting against previously established modes of thought and expression. On the contrary, it was substantially reinforced in its nationalistic and individualistic tendencies by the native religious and political traditions. According to Lawrence Buell, three factors account for the literary preoccupation with the self in America: the ideology of individualism which encouraged interest in the careers of single persons; a strong habit of religious self-examination which produced countless pious diaries and conversion narratives; and the influence of the Romantic movement "under whose auspices was first produced in America a literature worthy of the name."[19]

Just how radical American Romantics could be in their formulations of the principles of individualism is easily discerned in Emerson's tone when he speaks of self-reliance. Confronted with the conflict between the demands of man's social existence and the imperative of self-reliance, Emerson affirms the pre-social man—the child and the youth—not because he is closer to "the intimations of immortality" but, first of all, because he remains free of the net of dependencies into which the adult unavoidably falls:

> Infancy conforms to nobody; all conform to it; so that one babe commonly makes four or five out of the adults who prattle and play to it. . . . The nonchalance of boys who are sure of a dinner, and would disdain as much as a lord to do or say ought to conciliate one, is the healthy attitude of human nature. . . . Society is a joint-stock company in which the members agree, for the better securing of his bread to each shareholder, to surrender the liberty and culture of the eater. The virtue in most request is conformity. Self-reliance is its aversion. . . . Nothing is at last sacred but the integrity of your own mind. . . . No law can be sacred to me but that of my nature. (2: 48–50, *passim*)

Emerson is ready, at least in his earlier years, to tear man out of his social and historical context,[20] to establish him as his own purpose, authority, and law. The center of Emerson's philosophy is, thus, an explicit and often extreme formulation of what Professor Jones judges to be the core of Romanticism, at least for our own times.

On the other hand, the peculiar blend of religious and political aspiration, of public and private concerns, has been widely and readily recognized as a characteristically American attitude—the kind of ambition in the light of which a saint was necessarily a leader of his community and the newly founded colonies were Israel led out of captivity into the Promised Land of America. Political and patriotic aspects of Puritan theocracy were pointed out by Perry Miller,[21] and more recently Sacvan Bercovitch has shown how the growth of the

American self involved centrally the fusion of religious and social virtues:

> The concept of "Americanus" [as reflected in the tradition of national biography] provides a distinctive pattern. Characteristically, the American hero fuses the "universal" virtues with the qualities of national leadership, and together they define him as a prophetic exemplar of the country.[22]

It is largely the recognition in *Leaves of Grass* of a process conforming to the pattern outlined above that has firmly established Whitman within the context of national literature. It is the lack of even traces of such a pattern that has consistently obscured Dickinson's place in it. And yet one cannot overlook Lawrence Buell's keen insight that each of the three traditions converging in American Transcendentalism—religious self-examination, Romantic self-consciousness, and democratic individualism—contained an ambiguous vision of the self insofar as each countered the purely individualistic impulse with its contradiction. Thus the tradition of the religious confessional valued the personal self only in relation to the paradigm of divine grace; the Transcendentalists tended to treat the individual as valuable, chiefly *sub specie aeternitatis*; and democratic individualism lent support to mass rule.[23] In the light of this observation it seems justifiable to view Whitman and Dickinson as, as it were, poles of the dilemma.

By and large Dickinson criticism has treated her as a lonely figure, biographically as well as artistically.[24] From Klaus Lubbers's extensive research on the growth of Dickinson's reputation[25] it becomes clear that even while "academic criticism" has recognized her stature and come to situate her vis-à-vis Whitman, literary historians almost to this day have trouble placing her within a systematic outline of American literature. A classic illustration of the embarrassment Dickinson has been causing is furnished by Chapter 55 of the standard and widely used *Literary History of the United States*,[26] in which she is grouped with Lanier under the evasive title "Experiments in Poetry"—an obvious attempt to bypass the question of relating the poet in a more significant way to her historical and intellectual milieu. The confusion in the recent past should be ascribed, at least in part, to the powerful impact of Mathiessen's book. Although Dickinson is mentioned there several times, she is not counted among the major artists of her time. Later studies of American Romanticism more or less follow suit, concentrating on Mathiessen's canon of the great five: Emerson, Thoreau, Hawthorne, Melville, and Whitman.[27]

Roy Harvey Pearce's *The Continuity of American Poetry*, perhaps the closest thing we have to a history of American poetry, keeps contrasting Dickinson with three other major Romantic poets: Poe, Emerson, and Whitman.[28] Pearce's idea of continuity in American poetry is, however, intimately related to the antinomian impulse and thus allows each poet to be placed in his historical and cultural context on the basis of his very individuality. While Hyatt H. Waggoner in *American Poets* insists on Dickinson's debt to Emerson (as he does on Whitman's), his discussion of the poet's development from her early fascination with Emerson's new faith to her later "almost doctrineless, but existentially meaningful faith"[29] does not seem convincing. Although both Emerson and Whitman develop from enthusiastic, radical attitudes to more subdued and sceptical visions of the self's possibilities,[30] Dickinson's ideas do not really change with time. The dilemma of the experiential reality of doubt and the psychic necessity for faith so poignantly stated in 1859 in "These are the days when birds come back" (130) presents itself with equal or greater urgency in 1882 in a poem like "Those dying then" (1551).

In *The Manuscript Books of Emily Dickinson* edited by Ralph William Franklin, the fascicles seem to have been put together on the basis of the chronology of composition, as a way of introducing order into the mass of poems Dickinson started producing in the late 1850s, rather than with a view to any narrative, thematic, or other unity or progression. The voices of the poet, her concerns and moods within a single packet, are many and varied. Even the fascicles from the difficult year 1862 mix moods, stances, and themes, though they certainly demonstrate increased preoccupation with loss and suffering and with the art of poetry. Fascicle 17, for example, contains the poems "I would not paint—a picture—" (505) and "She sights a Bird—she chuckles—" (507) but also "It was not Death, for I stood up" (510) and "I felt my life with both my hands" (351); it has the playful "A Bird, came down the Walk—" (328) neighbor the powerful "The Soul has Bandaged moments—" (512). Fascicle 18 contains an equal variety of themes and tones. There is in it the serene "It's thoughts—and just One Heart—" (495), the erotic "I tend my flowers for thee—" (339), the amazed "Within my Garden, rides a Bird" (500), while the precise, disciplined "After great pain, a formal feeling comes—" (341) is placed not far from the melodramatic "At least—to pray—is left—is left" (502). In fact, almost any fascicle can be used as evidence for the argument that Emily Dickinson is much better viewed as a poet of "nows," shifting stances, alternating moods, arriving at only inconclusive conclusions.[31]

On the whole, the recognition of Dickinson's artistic rank seems to have come earlier than the mapping of her position in her own times and in the history of American literature. So much so that even her relatively recent critic, Robert Weisbuch, feels it necessary to justify his conviction that Dickinson belongs to American Romanticism as "legitimately" as Whitman does. Characteristically, the difficulty in placing Dickinson in her proper intellectual context lies for Weisbuch in her non-conforming to the pattern described by Bercovitch:

> Dickinson's identity with the American Romantics is somewhat obscured by her own lack of historical concerns. She is far less concerned than her fellows with the idea of America and far less involved in the particular political issues of the day. . . . She nowhere speaks, as Melville does in the sunnier early years of his career, of a new American literature, totally different from and greater than the literature of the European past. She never feels compelled, as Thoreau does, to spend a night in Concord jailhouse to protest unfair taxes, and she never writes tracts against slavery—she never writes tracts.[32]

Among the scholars who recognize Dickinson's work as a counterbalance to Whitman's is Albert Gelpi with his *The Tenth Muse: The Psyche of the American Poet*. Gelpi applies the terms of Jungian psychology to the artists' poetry and finds that their creativity was defined by opposing yet complementary drives. Whitman was primarily moved by his sympathetic, receptive "anima"; Dickinson, by the active, intellectual "animus." In an excellent article, John Lynen compares and contrasts Whitman's and Dickinson's notions of time, seeing them as direct reversals.[33] At the European Association of American Studies conference in Heidelberg in 1976, Maurice Gonnaud read a paper on the treatment of nature by Whitman and Dickinson. According to Professor Gonnaud, the opposition between the poets should be traced to the ambivalence of Emerson's conception of nature. The paper's title, "Nature: Apocalypse or Experiment? Emerson's Double Lineage in American Poetry," points to the dialectic of faith and doubt relating their work:

> And while I take encouragement largely from the recent work done on the two poets, I remain aware that there is little originality in the very idea of linking Whitman and Dickinson in a pattern of dialectic tension. For after all, I am but returning to George Whicher's insight of 1931: "These two writers defined the poles of national feeling in their time as Franklin and Edwards defined the cleavage in American thought a century earlier."[34]

In the search for the motivations underlying Dickinson's refusal to meet in art the public concerns of her day, dramatically emphasized by the seclusion of her life, it is necessary to remember how much Romantic individualism was nourished by the heritage of extreme Protestantism. In the essay "About the Freedom of a Christian" (1520), Luther took a recognizable step toward the development of that inner self, so crucial for Romantic poetry.[35] Luther distinguished there "the inner man" from the outward and physical man, and asserted the importance of the former at the expense of the latter, provided the inner man, the soul, has faith. Luther differs from the radical Romantic individualists only insofar as he insists on the condition of knowing the word of God as the *sine qua non* of salvation.

In a more directly literary context, Goeffrey Hartman reflects:

> The question, therefore, is why the Romantic reaction to the problem of self-consciousness should be in the form of an aggrandizement of art, and why the entire issue should now achieve an urgency and explicitness previously lacking.
>
> The answer requires a distinction between religion and art. This distinction can take a purely historical form. There clearly comes a time when art frees itself from its subordination to religion or religiously inspired myth and continues or even replaces them. This time seems to coincide with what is generally called the Romantic period: the latter, at least, is a good *terminus a quo*. . . . If Romantic poetry appears to the orthodox as misplaced religious feeling ("split religion") to the Romantics themselves it redeems religion.[36]

Just as it is difficult to speak about Romanticism in general without touching upon its religious connections, it is commonly recognized that the roots of Transcendentalism in America are to be sought in the religious heritage of the country. "Transcendentalism, it must always be remembered, was a faith rather than a philosophy; it was oracular rather than speculative, affirmative rather than questioning,"[37] observes Parrington. And summing up his discussion of the sources of Transcendentalism, Rod Horton points to the tradition of strong individualism in the history of religious dissension in America:

But however much of the moral force of Puritanism underlay Transcendentalism, the student should by now be able to distinguish some of the other strains in this hybrid pseudo-philosophy. In addition to the neo-Platonism already noted, we can detect the "inner light" of the Quakers, the belief in the divine nature of man as held by the Unitarians, and more than a touch of the antinomianism of Anne Hutchinson.[38]

Talking about Whitman's debt to Emerson, Gay Wilson Allen reminds his readers that Whitman's parents were friendly with Elias Hicks, a schismatic Quaker who expanded the doctrine of "inner light" to the widest limits of religious freedom, claiming that no restrictions whatever should be placed on an individual's religious convictions. Allen concludes that "the Quakers were at least partly responsible for Whitman's belief that all physical life is dependent upon and sustained by an infinite spiritual realm about which a human being may have intuitive knowledge. It is not surprising that he later found Emerson a great stimulation to his development as a poet, for Whitman was a 'transcendentalist' by conviction before he had ever heard of New England Transcendentalism."[39]

Floyd Stovall finds that Whitman showed interest in Emerson for most of the 1840s. The future poet clipped an article entitled "New Poetry in New England" from the May 1847 issue of the *Democratic Review*, but only its first part which was devoted to Emerson's poetry. Whitman's marginal comments on the article are revealing because they show, on the one hand, a temperamental affinity with the Concord artist and, on the other, a loyalty to conventional concepts of poetic form. To the reviewer's observation that "in poetry, he [Emerson] seems to desire not art, but undisciplined, untrimmed nature," Whitman responds: "This is as one feels. One feels better satisfied with the garden trimly cut and laid out, and another (I too) enjoys the natural landscape, even barrens and shores and sterile hills above all gardens." He adds, still in connection with the same observation: "The perfect poet must be unimpeachable in *manner* as well as matter."[40] This clearly is a position quite removed from the theory behind *Leaves of Grass*. Concluding that only a thorough rereading of Emerson in the summer of 1854 finally "brought to a boil" what had been "simmering" in Whitman, Stovall asks his readers to remember that "Whitman's reading of Emerson's essays was at the end, not the beginning, of the long foreground of *Leaves of Grass*."[41] It is, I think, essential for the understanding of Whitman to recognize that at the beginning of his affinity with the Transcendentalist vision lay the fact that the demand which this philosophical doctrine put on man was in its nature identical with the demand made by Luther and all extreme Protestant dissenters after him: that man has faith so absolute that it alone becomes his salvation. It took the time of "the long foreground" for the poet to translate emotional and intellectual affinities into an aesthetic theory from which *Leaves of Grass* unfolded.

The difficulty in bringing together Whitman and Dickinson lies only superficially in her political indifference. More fundamentally, it can be located in her acceptance of doubt as a legitimate state of mind, in the attitude that led her to question whether nature was "apocalypse" or "experiment," and to put the word "experiment" as her final choice:[42]

But God be with the Clown—
Who ponders this tremendous scene—
This whole Experiment of Green—
As if it were his own!

(1333)

The fusion of faith and politics was an outcome of the assertive confidence with which the pilgrim fathers and their descendants accepted America as virtually the Promised Land, to be viewed and interpreted through the word of the Scripture. Religious doctrines became identical with political principles and political principles were sanctioned by the divine word. In such a context there developed a vision of the self as representative of the cumulative, communal potential, deriving its greatness from personal identification with the American cause. This conception of individual greatness constitutes for Bercovitch the essence of the cultural continuity from the Puritans to the Romantics: "Emerson's hero, like Mather's Winthrop, derives his greatness from the enterprise he represents." "Emerson's exhortation to greatness speaks directly to the paradox of a literature devoted at once to the exaltation of the individual and the search for a perfect community. Self-reliance builds upon both these extremes." "The representative quality of American Romantic heroism expresses the furthest reach of Mather's daring auto-American-biographical strategy in the *Magnalia*."[43]

I do not, of course, overlook the fact that the relationship between politics and Romantic poetry was crucial in both Europe and America. Nevertheless, the character of the American political scene at the time nourished rather than destroyed faith, and the distinction is important. As M. H. Abrams points out, French political radicalism derived from the sceptical, even atheistic spirit of the Enlightenment while the main current of English political radicalism had its source in the dissenting tradition of Cromwell and the Civil War. The religious roots of political radicalism are common to England and America, yet for the European Romantics, English Romantics not excepted, the political fact of paramount importance was the degeneration and fall of the French Revolution. The hope that millennium was at hand collapsed with it.[44]

For the American Romantics, the events which dominated the political scene were the triumph of the masses under Jackson and the abolitionist campaign against slavery. Although both events lent themselves to crudity and insistent propaganda, both seemed to extend the promise of the birth of a new race and helped to preserve the continuity between the Puritan vision of America as the New Promised Land, and the involvement of Emerson, Whitman, and other American Romantics with the idea of democratic America crowning the long evolution of mankind. The hope for revolutionizing social and political structures, the hope for mankind in general, was not abdicated until after the Civil War. Indeed, only too frequently has critical attention focused on the fact that Whitman derived his ambition and strength from the conviction (or illusion) that he was privileged to witness the glorious change in progress and called to give his testimony.[45]

All Abrams says about the English Romantic Bard of the early years of hope and enthusiasm can be said about Whitman,[46] practically throughout his career:

> Whatever the form, the Romantic Bard is one "who present, past, and future sees"; so that in dealing with current affairs his procedure is often panoramic, his stage cosmic, his agents quasi-mythological, and his logic of events apocalyptic. Typically this mode of Romantic vision fuses history, politics, philosophy and religion into one grand design, by asserting Providence—or some form of natural teleology—to operate in the seeming chaos of human history so as to effect from present evil a greater good.[47]

In other words, the quality of the poetic design is vitally connected with faith, with "asserting Providence—or some form of natural teleology—in the seeming chaos of human history." It is precisely this dependence which the juxtaposition of Whitman and Dickinson illustrates.

Before I turn to outline the common ground for the two poets, I should like to make clear that the dialectic of faith and doubt as reflected in literature forms a tradition going back to the Puritans. American writers, who, in the early period, were as a rule public figures first of all, seem to have had persistent trouble with integrating the representative and the personal self. The difficulty polarized their writings into private diaries or lyrical poems and homiletic, didactic works meant for publication.[48]

It is, I think, revealing to realize that Emerson's writings also fall within the polarized pattern. There is the Emerson of the essays and addresses—very conscious of his public role, holding himself responsible for the success of the national cause, and the Emerson of the *Journals*—the Emerson besieged by doubt, refusing to face squarely the facts in his biography for fear of losing faith: "If . . . the world is not a dualism, is not a bipolar Unity, but is *two*, is Me and It, then is there the Alien, the Unknown, and all we have believed and chanted out of our deep instinctive hope is a pretty dream" (*J*, 7:200). In the concluding pages of his book Sacvan Bercovitch cites fragments of

Emerson's *Journals* from the 1840s and 1850s against fragments of his essays and lectures from the same period. Inevitably, the private utterance testifies to anxiety and doubt while the public one calls for new hope and new faith.[49]

With Emerson, however, the assignation of the social and private self to essays and journals respectively cannot be unequivocal. The conclusion of "Experience," for instance, shows the speaker far removed from the representative ambition; instead, the tone is one of growing estrangement and exclusiveness, if not disgust:

> But I have not found that much was gained by manipular attempts to realize the world of thought. Many eager persons successively make an experiment in this way, and make themselves ridiculous. They acquire democratic manners, they foam at the mouth, they hate and deny. Worse, I observe that in the history of mankind there is never a solitary example of success,—taking their own tests of success. I say this polemically, or in reply to the inquiry, why not realize your world? (3 : 85)

This passage goes a long way toward denying the relevance of the public, representative self. The faith can only be kept by postponing its success (that is the acquiring of "practical power" by the representative hero) indefinitely into the future. As for now, what remains is upholding the inner self—the only harbor of integrity and truth: "We dress our garden, eat our dinners, discuss the household with our wives, and these things make no impression, are forgotten next week; but, in the solitude to which every man is always returning, he has a sanity and revelations which is his passage into new worlds he will carry with him" (3 : 85). The shape of the future depends in this essay not on immediate action but on each man's fidelity to his inner vision, since only what is shielded and tended there can be extended beyond time.

Conversely, the *Journals* often speak for the representative man. As early as 1835 Emerson resolves the dilemma into what seems clearly a Whitmanian pattern:

> There are two facts, the Individual, and the Universal. To this belong the finite, the temporal, ignorance, sin, death; to that belong the infinite, the immutable, truth, goodness, life. In Man they both consist. The All is in Man. In Man the perpetual progress is from the

Individual to the Universal, from that which is human, to that which is divine. "Self dies and dies perpetually." The circumstances, the persons, the body, the world, the memory are forever perishing as the bark peels off the expanding tree. (*J*, 5 : 229)

The tension between the private and the universal (also public) self cannot be, for Emerson, schematized as the opposition of *Essays* to *Journals*. Although critics by no means agree on the subject of Emerson's development, they unanimously admit that the sceptical tone entered the public writings only with "Experience." Both Stephen Whicher and Jonathan Bishop ascribe the fact to a spiritual crisis Emerson must have undergone around 1840. Edward Wagenknecht, on the other hand, arguing for a more static conception of Emerson's personality, points to the pessimistic overtones abundant in the early *Journals*. He maintains that "the compound vision" was almost as much a part of early Emerson as it was in his later years.[50] Nevertheless, the time came when the sceptic could no longer be confined to the privacy of the *Journals* but broke into the public utterances. Thus, one is inclined to accept Stephen Whicher's position. Undoubtedly, more effort to keep up faith went into the public writings, especially those of Emerson's early period. It would be interesting to inquire whether the infusion of the *Essays* with the pessimistic and personal element occurred parallel with the progressive formalization of the *Journals*. The editors of *Journals and Notebooks* claim in the preface to volume 7 that by 1838–1842 Emerson was taking interest in the *Journals* not only for the therapeutic relief they provided but because he had begun to recognize them as an art form. Making entries whenever he felt the need, Emerson was, in fact, writing a book of inner life which was to grow with its author and which therefore, in its fundamental program, resembles *Leaves of Grass*. If the above is true, the question of Emerson's development might also be validly considered on the aesthetic plane—as genre experimentation.[51]

Whitman's triumph is that he could move beyond Emerson's hesitant attempts and integrate the representative and the private voice within one literary form so that each could complement and sustain the other. Significantly, Whitman's *Daybooks and Notebooks* are rarely personally revealing and never intimate. They bear practically no relation to literature unless they contain drafts for later use.[52] The early poems, especially, balance the prophetic and the confessional voice to the detriment of neither.

But, as Jerome Loving has demonstrated, the difference in backgrounds notwithstanding, Emerson and Whitman had much in common in talent and temperament, especially as these reveal themselves in the works of the pre–"Experience" Emerson and the pre–Civil War Whitman. Moreover, both artists had long periods of creative gestation in professions which constrained them as well as prepared them. Both men had to rebel, outgrow, and reject their conventional occupations. The turning to the literary career was for both a major act of self-reliance. Both, too, had practiced what was to become their highest achievement: Emerson in the *Journals*, Whitman in the journalistic habit of observation, in reporting scenes of New York life, and in writing "human interest" articles for the several newspapers he worked with.[53] The farther the reader progresses in Whitman's career, the more doubt the reader may have whether the poet did not eventually neglect honesty to his inner self in the effort to achieve perfect identification with the cause. Opinions that his private life at Camden was fashioned to fit the prophetic image projected in the poems are frequent and familiar. Jerome Loving sees a further similarity in the way Emerson and Whitman developed in their later years. Forced to recognize the limitations of the self-reliant self, they both became preachers rather than visionaries. Emerson sought the support of culture for his tottering ideal of the heroic self, while Whitman relied on identification with the national cause and proclaimed himself the leader of the people on the road which, in his earlier days, he not only traveled alone but exhorted everyone to travel for himself.[54]

If, despite some objections, we can say that Whitman made his multifaceted, representative self adequately contain his private "I," Dickinson followed the opposite strategy. Self-acceptance and self-knowledge were the business of her life. She did not need the support of the representative role to ensure heroic dimensions to her innermost "I." Not only did she accept the private self as central, she claimed further that its greatness was not to be confirmed by the sublimity of any cause, nor did it rest in the security of any faith. For her the test of the self's stature was not in the noble rage of its ambition but in the actual performance in confrontation with experience.

Dickinson denied the relevance of the social self for man's spiritual biography. Just as in her daily life she almost gave up relations with the external world, she cut off the public aspect of self because it seemed distracting. If she can be compared to a Puritan diarist, she is a diarist absolutely convinced that only the inner man matters. The poems she wrote practically throughout her mature life correspond in purpose not so much to Anne Bradstreet's domestic lyrics as to Whitman's *Leaves of Grass*; they were written to record the complete man: the life and progress of a consciousness.

The Emerson texts most relevant for Whitman are the early writings: "Nature," "The American Scholar," "Self-Reliance," "The Poet." They are alive with belief in the immediate rapport, more, in the essential unity of the individual mind and the universe:

In the hour of vision, there is nothing that can be called gratitude, nor properly joy. The soul raised over passion beholds identity and eternal causation, perceives the self-existence of Truth and Right, and calms itself with knowing that all things go well. Vast spaces of nature, the Atlantic Ocean, the South Sea; long intervals of time, years, centuries, are of no account. This which I think and feel underlay every former state of life and circumstances, as it does underlie my present, and what is called life, and what is called death. (2:69)

The texts against which to read Dickinson are those beginning with "Experience" through "Montaigne: or the Skeptic" to "Fate."[55] "Fate" in particular reads in fragments like the theory of Dickinson's poems, for there the balance between the Individual and the Universal can no longer be maintained through orderly progression. Instead, it becomes a duel-like confrontation: "If the Universe have these savage accidents, our atoms are as savage in resistance. We should be crushed by the atmosphere, but for the reaction of the air within the body. . . . If there be omnipotence in the stroke, there is omnipotence of recoil" (6:24–25). Consequently all freedom is won within and is the prerogative of the inner self only: "The revelation of Thought takes man out of servitude into freedom" (6:25).

Whitman gave his loyalty to the external, physical world far more radically than Emerson. Acknowledging the fact, "the Master" could not help a note of regret: "Have you seen the strange Whitman's poems? . . . He seems a Mirabeau of a man, with such insight and equal expression, but hurt by hard life and too animal experience. But perhaps you have not read the American Poem?" (*Letters*, 4 : 531). This was written to James Eliot Cabott shortly after the publication of the first *Leaves of Grass*[56] but, as scandalized voices could be heard all around, Emerson's admiration mingled with distaste: "Our wild Whitman, with real inspiration but choked by Titanic abdomen, and Delia Bacon, with genius, but mad, and clinging like a tortoise to English soil, are the sole producers that America has yielded in ten years" (*Letters*, 5 : 87).[57]

Emily Dickinson affirmed the other pole of Emerson's vision with a radicalism equal to or even surpassing Whitman's. In her view, the self's claim to heroism was only validated by the effort of the perpetually struggling mind. She agreed with Emerson when he said that "forever wells up the impulse of choosing and acting in the soul. Intellect annuls Fate" (6 : 23). But, both through her art and through the life she chose to live, she denied the inevitability of his conclusion:

> One key, one solution to the mysteries of human condition, one solution to the old knots of fate, freedom, and foreknowledge exists; the propounding, namely, of the double consciousness. A man must ride alternately on the horses of his private and public nature, as the equestrians in the circus throw themselves nimbly from horse to horse, or plant one foot on the back of one and the other foot on the back of the other. So when a man is the victim of his fate, has sciatica in his loins and cramp in his mind; a club-foot and a club in his wit; a sour face and a selfish temper; a strut in his gait and a conceit in his affection; or is ground to powder by the vice of his race:—he is to rally on his relation to the Universe, which his ruin benefits. Leaving the daemon who suffers, he is to take sides with the Deity who secures universal benefit by his pain. (6 : 47)

Dickinson would not belittle the poignancy of personal suffering by calling in aid the belief that it is for the benefit of the universal plan. Instead, loyal to the pained self, she set out to find "with narrow probing eyes" how much power the self can wield by mastering its limitations.

Self-reliance, the view of self as autonomous and, consequently, of individual consciousness as the creative center of universe, constitutes the common starting point for Whitman and Dickinson. Even though they diverge from there to explore the far frontiers of the dialectical Emersonian vision, their respective routes come together at important intersections.

Like other Romantics, they tend to see poetry as replacing religion. Emerson's career, of course, is almost paradigmatic when it comes to redeeming religion through art. A Unitarian minister turned Lyceum lecturer, a sermon writer turned poet and essayist, a few months before leaving the ministry, he confided in his journal: "I have sometimes thought that in order to be a good minister it was necessary to leave ministry. The profession is antiquated. In an altered age, we worship in the dead forms of our forefathers" (*J*, 4 : 27; June 2, 1832).[58] This reflection shows how the development from Emerson the minister and son of ministers, to Emerson the essayist and artist aspiring to become the moral leader of his times, took shape in response to the deeply felt need for more adequate forms of answering the spiritual demands of his age. Recognizing this trait in Emerson, Carlyle wrote from Chelsea about *Essays, Second Series*:

> The work itself falling on me by driblets has not the right chance yet,—not till I get it in the bound state, and read it all at once,—to produce its due impression on me. But I will say already of it, It is a *Sermon* to me, as all your other deliberate utterances are; a real *word*, which I feel to be such,—alas, almost or altogether the one such, in a world all full of jargons, hearsays, echoes, and vain noises, which cannot pass with me for *words*! This is a praise far beyond any "literary" one; literary praises are not worth repeating in comparison. (Slater, 370)

Even more determinedly and with fewer reservations, Whitman installed himself in the role of the apostle of the new religion of man. A passage in the 1855 preface to *Leaves of Grass* completes in inflamed rhetoric Emerson's private meditation of 1832:

> There will soon be no more priests. Their work is done. They may wait awhile . . . perhaps a generation or two . . . dropping off by degrees. A superior breed shall take their place . . . the gangs of kosmos and prophets en masse shall take their place. A new order shall arise and they shall be priests of man, and every man shall be his own priest. The churches built under their umbrage shall be the churches of men and women. Through the divinity of themselves shall the kosmos and the new breed of poets be interpreters of men and women and of all events and things. They shall find their inspiration in real objects today, symptoms of the past and future. . . . They

> shall not deign to defend immortality or God or the perfection of things or liberty or the exquisite beauty and reality of the soul. They shall arise in America and be responded to from the remainder of the earth. (*LG*, 727)

It seemed obvious to Whitman at the beginning of his career, as it did later in "Passage to India," that the poet must replace the priest,[59] that poetry must offer a new interpretation of man in the universe. The announcement toward the end of his life in the preface to *November Boughs* (1888): "No one will get at my verses who insists upon viewing them as a literary performance, or attempt at such performance, or as aiming mainly toward art and aestheticism" (*LG*, 574; 11:459–61) only confirmed the persistence of ambition which had spurred him throughout his creative years.

Dickinson never sounds programmatic, on any subject. She rejected the public aspect of religion just as she did the public self—as irrelevant. But in her second letter to T. W. Higginson, she wrote about the innermost motives of her poetry: "I had a terror—since September—I could tell to none—and so I sing, as the Boy does by the Burying Ground,—because I am afraid—" (*L*, 2:404). She turned to poetry as believers do to religion, for solace and sustenance in her hours of need. It was a necessary rather than enthusiastic turning. There is little sense of gain, of prospects, opened in Dickinson's poems. Instead, they are pervaded with an acute sense of loss[60] and preoccupied with assessing the cost of the endeavor. Relatively early in her creative period (1859), the poet stated her predicament as the plight of an individual no longer capable of unquestioning faith but also desperately yearning for the comfort and security it provided:

> These are the days when Birds come back—
> A very few—a Bird or two—
> To take a backward look.
>
> These are the days when skies resume
> The old—old sophistries of June—
> A blue and gold mistake.
>
> Oh fraud that cannot cheat the Bee—
> Almost thy plausibility
> Induces my belief.

Till ranks of seeds their witness bear—
And softly thro' the altered air
Hurries a timid leaf.

Oh Sacrament of summer days,
Oh Last Communion in the Haze—
Permit a child to join.

Thy sacred emblems to partake—
Thy consecrated bread to take
And thine immortal wine!

(130)

What begins as a description of Indian summer is resolved into a dialogue between the sceptical intellect supported by the evidence of the senses and the longing heart which wants to suppress the rational faculty, to become like a child for the reward of security and religious ecstasy which the union with nature can offer. Belief, however, is unmistakably stated as yearning, as only a prayer for a state desired but not necessarily attainable, while doubt is phrased in affirmative sentences bringing irrefutable testimony of the senses.[61] The feeling of loss is an essential element of the poem's mood. Dickinson turns to poetry not because it can become a new faith, reintegrating man in his reality, but because it is the last resource—the chance for immortality as "Costumeless Consciousness" embodied in a poem.

It is not, therefore, surprising to find that when Whitman writes:

I bequeath myself to the dirt to grow from the grass I love,
If you want me again look for me under your boot-soles.

You will hardly know who I am or what I mean,
But I shall be good health to you nevertheless,
And filter and fiber your blood.

("Song of Myself," *LG*, 89 : 1339–43)

and Dickinson:

He ate and drank the precious Words—
His Spirit grew robust—
He knew no more that he was poor,
Nor that his frame was Dust—

He danced along the dingy Days
And this Bequest of Wings
Was but a Book—What Liberty
A loosened spirit brings—

(1587)

they both employ the ritual of the Holy Communion as their central image because they both conceive of their art as sacrament. The essential similarity of their attitude is not undercut by the fact that each picks a different aspect of sacrament to stress: for Whitman the sacrament means first of all a mystical union, dissolution in universal life; for Dickinson, personal spiritual nourishment. Both, however, expect their art to take over some of the functions performed by religion. The seriousness and the dignity of their poetry rest upon the expectation that art could and would rescue man from chaos.

For both Whitman and Dickinson, art takes the form of the spiritual journey of its maker. According to Harold Bloom,[62] the internalization of quest romance was a development characteristic of High Romanticism in England. For our poets, however, Emerson again provides the closest model. The idea of the artist as a spiritual and mental voyager becomes very pronounced in his writings. "Life consists in what a man is thinking all day" or "Our private theatre is ourselves," both formulations quoted by Mathiessen as unmistakably Emersonian[63] focus attention on the meandering of thought as defining the content and form of life as well as art. "Self-Reliance," whose first epigraph reads "Ne te quaesiveris extra," denounces the fetish of traveling in the world. The prejudice holding touristic experience essential for knowledge and culture must be abandoned. Man's real journeys are made within: "I pack my trunk, embrace my friends, embark on the sea and at last wake up in Naples, and there beside me is the stern fact, the sad self, unrelenting, identical, that I fled from. I seek the Vatican, and the palaces. I affect to be intoxicated with sights and suggestions, but I am not intoxicated. My giant goes with me wherever I go" (2:81–82). Emerson certainly wrote this with his own European trip in mind, during which his reactions must have been conditioned by the recent facts in his biography,[64] but his point is made unambiguously: it is within one's self that one starts and ends. Emerson's efforts, however, were not undividedly dedicated to working out corresponding aesthetic formulas. Moving between essays, journals, and poems, he only indicated directions in which to turn, the bulk of practical work he left to others. Emerson's central role in the liberation of the American artists from the traditional formal constraints consists in the impact his writings exerted on the process of breaking down the rigid genre barriers. The evaluation remains true regardless of whether *Essays* are interpreted as poetry released from the confines of rhyme and meter (Porter, *Emerson and Literary Change*) or as sermons modified through the infusion of lyricism (Buell, *Literary Transcendentalism)*. The essential fact is that categories have become liquid and consequently, the becoming, the process, matters more than the final perfect shape.

Whitman's contribution in this respect has been recognized and argued about extensively. He himself insisted on treating the body of his poetry as a totality, including new poems in successive editions of *Leaves of Grass* and deciding that the 1881 edition was the final arrangement. Whatever the nature and purpose of his rearrangements within each successive edition, they first of all reflect his own preoccupations and preferences at the given point of his career. The successive books of *Leaves of Grass* constitute stages in the growth of the author's mind more clearly than they develop toward any final structural unity.[65] What constitutes the work's backbone did not change. It was conceived as a spiritual journey through America so that discovering the resources of the self was simultaneous and identical with discovering the resources of the country, of mankind, and of the whole universe. As Charles Feidelson has observed, the poem itself became a road on which the traveler, the journey, and the surrounding reality could become one.[66]

Dickinson never worked on preparing her poems for publication. She did not put together a collection or selection of her poems; neither did she comment on her preference for arrangement. Instead, she sowed the fair copies into the famous packets and left the rest unbound. Despite attempts at interpreting the packets as separate collections, each telling "a story,"[67] it seems that since there is no hint from the poet herself, the best a critic can do is to respect the poems as she left them, as a life's work whose "inherent logic must disclose itself." The body of Dickinson's poems does not show consistency of argument, sequential development of themes, a traceable narrative line, or even major stylistic changes. If anything, as Ralph Franklin observes, there is in it a discernible movement from the initial attempt at orderly gathering of the final versions (perhaps in the hope of publication) toward increased emphasis on writing poetry as an ongoing, open process. The early fascicles contain no alternative readings. It is only later that unresolved word choices are kept in the fair manuscripts. Still later, the sown booklets are replaced by loose "sets" of sheets, presumably easier to sort through and work with. Finally, the sets become collections of "scraps": drafts, versions begun but not polished, records of the continuous effort of consciousness to articulate experience. There is also evidence of later revisions of the earlier texts.[68] It seems that with years the poetic process became more and more important for Dickinson—more vital, in fact, than its destination, the truth of the finished poem. This is as much as to say that the essence of the total work is quest, regardless of the fact that it can never be completed since there is no final truth, no final form to be reached. Similarly, Whitman's final truth always recedes beyond the horizon. Consequently, what matters for both artists is the journey itself, the effort of consciousness. Like Emerson, Whitman and Dickinson sanctify the creative process rather than worship the finished form.

Notes

1. F. O. Mathiessen, *American Renaissance: Art and Expression in the Age of Emerson and Whitman* (London: Oxford University Press, 1941).

2. Charles Feidelson, *Symbolism and American Literature* (Chicago: University of Chicago Press, 1953), 75–76.

3. D. Mirsky, "Poet of American Democracy," in *Walt Whitman Abroad*, ed. Gay Wilson Allen (Syracuse: Syracuse University Press, 1955); reprinted in *Walt Whitman*, ed. Francis Murphy (Harmondsworth: Penguin Critical Anthologies, 1969), 238–39.

4. See, for example, Richard Ellmann and Robert O'Clair, eds., *The Norton Anthology of Modern Poetry* (New York: W. W. Norton, 1973), 33.

5. Benjamin T. Spencer, *The Quest for Nationality: An American Literary Campaign* (Syracuse: Syracuse University Press, 1957), 89–90.

6. This is the title of a book by Van Wyck Brooks, published in 1936.

7. Longfellow visited Whitman most probably in the summer of 1879.

See Horace Traubel, *With Walt Whitman in Camden* (New York: Appleton and Co., 1908), 1 : 129; and Gay Wilson Allen, *The Solitary Singer: A Critical Biography of Walt Whitman*, rev. ed. (New York: New York University Press, 1967), 486. The quotation is from "Death of Longfellow," Whitman's article in *Critic*, April 8, 1882.

8. See also "The Failure of the Fathers" in Quentin Anderson, *The Imperial Self* (New York: Random House, 1971), 3–58.

9. Thomas O. Mabbott, ed., *The Collected Works of Edgar Allan Poe* (Cambridge, Mass.: Harvard University Press, Belknap Press, 1969), 176–77.

10. Quoted by Howard Mumford Jones, *Revolution and Romanticism* (Cambridge, Mass.: Harvard University Press, Belknap Press, 1974), 198. The poem was entitled "Den Vereinigten Staaten" and was sent to Zelter, July 17, 1827. See Goethe, *Sämtliche Werke*, Jubiläums-Ausgabe (Stuttgart: G. Cotta, 1902–07), 4 : 127: "America, you have it better than our older continent; you have no ruined castles and no basalt rocks. You are not inwardly troubled in your lifetime with useless memory and futile conflict. Use the present with luck! And when your children start writing poetry, may good fate save them from stories of knights, robbers, and ghosts" (my translation).

11. David Porter in *Emerson and Literary Change* (Cambridge, Mass.: Harvard University Press, 1978) discusses Emerson as the artist in whose work the tensions between the impatience to arrive at a clarification of vision on the one hand, and the need for linguistic power adequate to convey the sweep and sensuality of experience on the other, finally burst open conventional literary forms.

12. See William Charvat, *The Origins of American Critical Thought, 1810–1835* (1936; reissued New York: Barnes, 1961); and René Wellek, *Confrontations* (Princeton: Princeton University Press, 1965).

13. Arthur O. Lovejoy, "On the Discriminations of Romanticisms," *PMLA* 39 (1924): 229–53, enlarged and reprinted in A. O. Lovejoy, *Essays in the History of Ideas* (Baltimore: Johns Hopkins University Press, 1948).

14. See especially René Wellek's article "The Concept of 'Romanticism' in Literary History," *Comparative Literature* 1 (1949): 1–33, 147–72, where the unifying criteria for the practice of Romantic literature are specified as "imagination for the view of poetry, nature for the view of the world, and symbol and myth for poetic style" (147).

15. Jones, *Revolution and Romanticism*, 260.

16. I have borrowed this formulation from Armin Paul Frank's paper "The Long Withdrawing Roar: Eighty Years of the Ocean's Message in American Poetry" delivered at a symposium on "Form as Method: Types and Patterns of Poetic Knowledge," held at the University of Wuppertal in November 1978. The reference here is to a manuscript version. The paper appeared in print in Winfried Fluck, Jürgen Peper, and Willi Paul Adams, eds., *Forms and Functions of History in American Literature: Essays in Honor of Ursula Brumm* (Berlin: Erich Schmidt Verlag, 1981).

17. The story of this literary campaign is told in documents in Robert E. Spiller, ed., *The American Literary Revolution (1783–1837)*, (New York: New York University Press, 1969); and in Spencer, *The Quest for Nationality*. For the earlier period, Sacvan Bercovitch's *The Puritan Origins of the American Self* (New Haven: Yale University Press, 1975) is useful.

18. Spencer, *The Quest for Nationality*, 82.

19. Lawrence Buell, *Literary Transcendentalism: Style and Vision in the American Renaissance* (Ithaca: Cornell University Press, 1973), 265–66.

20. See also "The Failure of the Fathers," in Anderson, *The Imperial Self*.

21. Perry Miller, *The New England Mind: From Colony to Province* (Cambridge, Mass.: Harvard University Press, 1953), esp. chap. 28.

22. Bercovitch, *The Puritan Origins of the American Self*, 149.

23. Buell, *Literary Transcendentalism*, 269–73.

24. A book attempting to trace Dickinson's connections with several American writers (Emerson, Hawthorne, and Whitman among them) came out only in 1979: Karl Keller's *The Only Kangaroo Among the Beauty: Emily Dickinson and America* (Baltimore: Johns Hopkins University Press, 1979). The study, the first attempt of this kind, does not go deep enough.

25. Klaus Lubbers, *Emily Dickinson: The Critical Revolution* (Ann Arbor: University of Michigan Press, 1968). See especially chaps. 9 and 10.

26. Robert E. Spiller et al., eds., *Literary History of the United States* (New York: Macmillan, 1946). The same grouping is retained in the fourth revised edition of 1974.

27. See, for example, Feidelson, *Symbolism and American Literature*; Richard Warrington Baldwin Lewis, *The American Adam* (Chicago: University of Chicago Press, 1955; Richard Poirer, *The World Elsewhere* (London: Oxford University Press, 1966).

28. Roy Harvey Pearce, *The Continuity of American Poetry* (Princeton: Princeton University Press, 1961), 174–91.

29. Hyatt H. Waggoner, *American Poets: From the Puritans to the Present* (Boston: Houghton Mifflin, 1968), 209.

30. See Stephen E. Whicher, *Freedom and Fate: An Inner Life of Ralph Waldo Emerson* (Philadelphia: University of Pennsylvania Press, 1953). Ervin Frederick Carlisle in *The Uncertain Self: Whitman's Drama of Identity* (East Lansing: Michigan State University Press, 1973) expresses the widely accepted view that as Whitman grew older he also grew less bold and more conservative, less concrete and more abstract (45).

31. This is the way Denis Donoghue and Robert Weisbuch see her. Inder Nath Kher in *The Landscape of Absence: Emily Dickinson's Poetry* (New Haven: Yale University Press, 1974) calls her work "one long poem of multidimensional reality" (2).

32. Robert Weisbuch, *Emily Dickinson's Poetry* (Chicago: University of Chicago Press, 1975), 7, 8.

33. John F. Lynen, "Three Uses of the Present: The Historian's, the

Critic's and Emily Dickinson's," *College English* 28, no. 2 (November 1966): 126–36.

34. I am quoting here from a manuscript copy of the paper. A later version appeared in *Vistas of a Continent*, edited on behalf of the European Association for American Studies by Andreas Teut Riese (Heidelberg: Carl Winter Universitätsverlag, 1979), 123–39. The quotation in Maurice Gonnaud's paper comes from George Frisbie Whicher, "Emily Dickinson: Centennial Afterthoughts," *The Amherst Graduates Quarterly* 20 (February 1931): 94; also quoted in Lubbers, *Emily Dickinson*, 181.

35. See J. H. Van den Berg, "The Subject and His Landscape," in *Romanticism and Consciousness*, ed. Harold Bloom (New York: W. W. Norton, 1970), 57–65.

36. Geoffrey Hartman, "Romanticism and Anti-Self-Consciousness," in *Beyond Formalism: Literary Essays, 1958–1970* (New Haven: Yale University Press, 1970), 305.

37. Vernon L. Parrington, *Main Currents in American Thought* (New York: Harcourt, Brace, 1930), 3:381; see also Buell, *Literary Transcendentalism*, esp. chap. 1, where the peculiar combination of religious and aesthetic aspiration in Transcendentalism is discussed. Buell sees Transcendentalism as a continuation of, rather than a breach with, Unitarianism.

38. Rod W. Horton and Herbert W. Edwards, *Backgrounds of American Literary Thought* (New York: Appleton-Century-Crofts, 1967), 117.

39. Gay Wilson Allen, *A Reader's Guide to Walt Whitman* (New York: Farrar, Strauss & Giroux, 1970), 19.

40. Floyd Stovall, *The Foreground of Leaves of Grass* (Charlottesville: University of Virginia Press, 1974), 286–87. For Whitman's marginalia, see Richard M. Bucke, ed., *Notes and Fragments* (London: privately printed, 1899).

41. Stovall, *The Foreground of Leaves of Grass*, 305.

42. Maurice Gonnaud comments on the variants in the manuscript: "Interestingly the variants concentrate on the fifth line, and ring the changes on the words 'whole' and 'experiment' with a thoroughness which betrays the author's earnestness and nearly insuperable perplexity. Of the various nouns tried in succession, only two, 'apocalypse' and 'experiment' had been underscored in the manuscript, as if to polarize Emily Dickinson's uncertainty in her first effort at clarification." See Maurice Gonnaud, "Nature, Apocalypse or Experiment: Emerson's Double Lineage in American Poetry," in Riese, *Vistas of a Continent*, 124.

43. Bercovitch, *The Puritan Origins of the American Self*, 174, 176, 177.

44. "The militancy of overt political action has been transformed into the paradox of spiritual quietism: under such militant banners is no march, but a wise passiveness. . . . But the hope has been shifted from the history of mankind to the mind of the single individual, from militant external action to an imaginative act; and the marriage between Lamb and the New Jerusa-

lem has been converted into a marriage between subject and object, mind and nature, which creates a new world out of the old world of sense" (M. H. Abrams, "English Romanticism: The Spirit of the Age," in Bloom, *Romanticism and Consciousness*, 110, 111).

45. See, for example, the essay by Mirsky quoted earlier.

46. It was a matter of a reciprocal relationship for Whitman; the political system gave the individual a chance to realize his potential greatness while the stature of its individual members justified the system. Only toward the end of his life did Whitman feel obliged to stress individual greatness not as corresponding to but as balancing the leveling effects of democracy. Though he could then clearly see the difficulty in maintaining the delicate balance, he still believed that democracy was, first of all, a way of thinking and feeling, and that it was the task of literature to evoke such a state of mind. See also Lionel Trilling, "Sermon on a Text from Whitman," in *Walt Whitman*, ed. Francis Murphy (Harmondsworth: Penguin Critical Anthologies, 291–99), in which Trilling points to the affinity with Schiller because of the conception of art as mediating between the necessary authoritarian institution of government and the ideal of individual freedom.

47. Abrams, "English Romanticism," in Bloom, *Romanticism and Consciousness*, 103.

48. Hawthorne, the artist of unsurpassed insights into the moral dilemmas of the Puritan mind, gave a poignant study of the divorce between the public and the private self in the character of Arthur Dimmesdale. The essence of Dimmesdale's tragedy is that vindication of the public self occurs at the cost of self-acceptance. See also Agnieszka Salska, "Puritan Poetry: Its Public and Private Strain," *Early American Literature*, Fall 1984.

49. Bercovitch, *The Puritan Origins of the American Self*, 179–80.

50. Whicher, *Freedom and Fate*; Jonathan Bishop, *Emerson on the Soul* (Cambridge, Mass.: Harvard University Press, 1964); Edward Charles Wagenknecht, *Ralph Waldo Emerson: Portrait of a Balanced Soul* (New York: Oxford University Press, 1974).

51. In *Literary Transcendentalism* Lawrence Buell discusses extensively the progressive infusion of the lyrical element into the Unitarian sermon and Transcendentalist essay (chapter 4). His aim there is "to examine Transcendentalist literature . . . as an attempt to develop lyric possibilities to the fullest within the confines of an essentially homiletic mode of expression" (105). On the other hand, in chapter 10 he points out the parallel formalization of the diary: "As Alcott said of Emerson, Transcendentalist journals might better be called 'commonplace books,' if one extends that term to apply not only to passages culled from other authors but choice insights of the writer's own. Emerson's journals, as Alcott noted, are 'full of elegant sketches of life and nature. . . . He does not record the history of his facts but idealizes whatsoever he observes and writes his thought in this general form. He works like an artist from his sketches and models'" (280). David Porter (*Emerson and Literary Change*) sees Emerson's formal development primarily as a drive to-

ward "prosaicization" of verse so that eventually, Emerson, the poet, triumphs in the free rhythms and images of his prose in "The American Scholar," "Self-Reliance," and other essays of the main period (see especially chapter 8).

52. William White, ed., *Walt Whitman: Daybooks and Notebooks* (New York: New York University Press, 1978). See also a review of the *Daybooks and Notebooks* by Paul Zweig in *New York Times Book Review*, April 6, 1978.

53. Jerome Loving, *Emerson, Whitman, and the American Muse* (Chapel Hill: University of North Carolina Press, 1982), 5–22.

54. Ibid., chap. 7, 175–91.

55. "Experience" was published in *Essays, Second Series* (1844) but was possibly written as early as 1842, after the death of Emerson's son Waldo. "Fate" came out in 1860 in *The Conduct of Life*.

56. The letter is dated September 26, 1855, while the famous letter to Whitman in which Emerson greeted him "at the beginning of a great career" was written on July 21, 1855.

57. To Caroline Sturgis, October 1857.

58. However, dropping out from the ministry to take up some sort of artistic career was a fairly common practice among the Transcendentalists as is evident from the biographies of John Sullivan Dwight or Christopher Cranch (see Buell, *Literary Transcendentalism*, 42). Vivian C. Hopkins points out that Emerson spoke habitually of the creative act in religious language (*Spires of Form: A Study of Emerson's Aesthetic Theory* [Cambridge, Mass.: Harvard University Press, 1951], 9–10).

59. Compare the following comment by Jerome Loving: "In a sense, Emerson's vision attempted to restore the poet to the pulpit, but instead created a secular church and the need for a poet-priest. Ultimately, Whitman filled that role, for Emerson is more accurately described as a poet-preacher: he provided the literary vision and Whitman conducted the celebration" (*Emerson, Whitman, and the American Muse*, 18).

60. The sense of loss pervading Dickinson's poems has been observed by many critics, most notably by Charles R. Anderson in the chapter "Evanescence" in *Emily Dickinson's Poetry: A Stairway of Surprise* (New York: Holt, Rinehart and Winston, 1960); by David Porter, especially in chap. 4 of *The Art of Emily Dickinson's Early Poetry* (Cambridge, Mass.: Harvard University Press, 1966); by Roland Hagenbüchle in "Precision and Indeterminacy in the Poetry of Emily Dickinson," *Emerson Society Quarterly* 20 (1974): 33–56; and Inder Nath Kher in *The Landscape of Absence*, especially in chapter 2.

61. See Anderson's excellent discussion of this poem in *Emily Dickinson's Poetry*, 146–49.

62. Harold Bloom, "The Internalization of Quest Romance," in *The Ringers in the Tower: Studies in Romantic Tradition* (Chicago: University of Chicago Press, 1971), 13–35.

63. Mathiessen, *American Renaissance*, 8.

64. Emerson went to Europe, depressed by the death of his first wife the previous year and exhausted by the crisis which culminated in his resignation from the Second Church in October 1832.

65. For discussions of *Leaves of Grass* as an example of such "cathedral"-like structural unity, see especially James E. Miller, Jr., *A Critical Guide to Leaves of Grass* (Chicago: University of Chicago Press, 1957); Thomas Edward Crawley, *The Structure of Leaves of Grass* (Austin: University of Texas Press, 1970); and Robert David DelGreco, "Whitman and the Epic Impulse" (Ph.D. diss., University of Illinois at Urbana-Champaign; Ann Arbor: Xerox University Microfilms, No. 48106).

66. Feidelson, *Symbolism and American Literature*, 18.

67. Cf. Ruth Miller, *The Poetry of Emily Dickinson* (Middletown, Conn.: Wesleyan University Press, 1968), chap. 10.

68. Ralph William Franklin, ed., *The Manuscript Books of Emily Dickinson* (Cambridge, Mass.: Harvard University Press, 1981), x.

2 / *The Self as Persona: Identity*

WHITMAN and Dickinson never met. There is no evidence that they read each other's work. Emily Dickinson's awareness of Walt Whitman is stated in her response to T. W. Higginson: "You speak of Mr. Whitman—I never read his book—but was told that he was disgraceful—" (*L*, 2:404).[1] If the prim dismissal sounds amusing, one need only recall how far apart the two poets are in, for example, these "personal" introductions:

> Walt Whitman, a kosmos, of Manhattan the son,
> Turbulent, fleshy, sensual, eating, drinking and breeding,
> No sentimentalist, no stander above men and women or apart from them,
> No more modest than immodest.
>
> Unscrew the locks from the doors!
> Unscrew the doors themselves from their jambs!
>
> Whoever degrades another degrades me,
> And whatever is done or said returns at last to me.
> ("Song of Myself," *LG*, 52:497–504)

and

> I'm Nobody! Who are you?
> Are you—Nobody—too?

Then there's a pair of us!
Dont tell! they'd banish us—you know!

How dreary—to be—Somebody!
How public—like a Frog—
To tell your name—the livelong June—
To an admiring Bog!

(288)

Yet both the poems quoted above are founded on the assumption that the self is central, and, therefore, that whatever is experienced can only be viewed subjectively. "Subjectivity, or self-consciousness," as Harold Bloom writes, "is the salient problem of Romanticism, at least for modern readers, who tend to station themselves in regard to the Romantics depending on how relevant or adequate they judge the dialectic of consciousness and imagination to be."[2] In American nineteenth-century literature Whitman and Dickinson are the two poets most vitally preoccupied with "the salient problem of Romanticism"—self-consciousness—the obvious consequence being that both use the self as persona. For both, too, the answers given to questions about the self's nature contain important aesthetic implications.

Introducing himself by the most specific but also the socially standard identification—his name, Whitman proceeds to emphasize whatever joins the self to the surrounding world, whatever makes him like others: his neighbors, compatriots, mankind in general. The connections must establish the "I" of the poem as representative. Walt Whitman can speak for America by virtue of being "of Manhattan the son." Early in "Song of Myself" he firmly makes the same claim: "My tongue, every atom of my blood, form'd from this soil, this air,/Born here of parents born here from parents the same, and their parents the same (*LG*, 29:6–7). As the paradigm of human physiology and psyche, he can speak for mankind. Finally (and also to begin with) he is a kosmos and cosmos—a self-contained organic whole, equal to and comprising any other such whole. An even more radical phrasing of the microcosm idea comes later in the poem: "I am an acme of things accomplish'd, and I am encloser of things to be" (*LG*, 80:1148). The centrality of his experience is validated by the fact of its being rooted not only in the experience of the nation and race, but in its being immersed in the timeless flow of life. Similarly, the centrality of his consciousness is guaranteed by its participation in the spiritual principle underlying the material existence of each and all, objects and bodies. It is as if having accepted subjectivity, Whitman was constantly looking for methods of alleviating the burden by pointing to its suprapersonal dimensions.

The speaker of Emily Dickinson's poem stresses, on the other hand, that part in herself which is like no one else, and appeals to a similar sense of personal uniqueness in the reader. Her message, or rather the secret she wants to share, is precisely the realization that "I," whoever it denotes, is like nobody else—an isolated entity surrounded by the hostile "them" or by the contemptible "bog." The aristocratic exclusiveness of her tone is a strategy adopted to protect the sense of personal uniqueness.[3] So is her use of the first person pronoun—at once more impersonal because anonymous, and more intimate than Whitman's social introduction by name. The centrality of Dickinson's self and correspondingly of her consciousness is negative in its essence. Since nothing is like the self, nothing except the self is directly available to cognition. This negative approach must carry the weight of whatever contact she may be able or may want to establish.

The "Walt Whitman, a kosmos, of Manhattan the son" fragment of "Song of Myself" demonstrates how Whitman's persona derives the sense of identity first of all from the concrete, physical and environmental attributes of the self: the name, place of birth, the body and its physiology. The doors of awareness are thrown open only at the next stage:

> Unscrew the locks from the doors!
> Unscrew the doors themselves from their jambs!
>
> Whoever degrades another degrades me,
> And whatever is done or said returns at last to me.
>
> Through me the afflatus surging and surging, through me the
> current and index.
>
> (*LG*, 52:501–5)

The movement of the passage is clearly from the sensuous to the conscious being, from a preconscious, appetitive existence to the awareness of spiritual ties between the self and the world. The physical concreteness of the body is the foundation from which the spiritual self develops. In an early notebook Whitman put down what to Gay Wilson Allen does not seem to be "a borrowed idea from his reading but a truly autobiographical confession: 'I cannot understand the mystery, but I am always conscious of myself as two—as my soul and I: and I reckon it is the same with all men and women.'"[4] The striking aspect of this observation is not so much the intense self-consciousness it reveals—this, after all, is a common Romantic phenomenon[5]—but the fact that the identifying "I" refers to the physical counterpart of the soul.

In "Crossing Brooklyn Ferry" the self's individualization is explicitly connected with the moment of birth, when the nonindividual soul, "struck from the float," takes on a body to become a distinctive, separate "I":

> I too had been struck from the float forever held in solution,
> I too had receiv'd identity by my body,
> That I was I knew was of my body, and what I should be I knew I should be of my body.
>
> (*LG*, 162:62–64)

Section Five of "Song of Myself" makes a similar point when the speaker addresses the soul:

> I believe in you my soul, the other I am must not abase itself to you,
> And you must not be abased to the other.
>
> (*LG*, 32:82–83)

Here too the body identifies. The voice in the poem speaks for the fusion of co-equal though distinctive components of personality. "A kosmos," a full self, can only be realized through the complete merging of the carnal and the spiritual in man. Imaged as a sexual act, such union makes possible vision and knowledge:

> Swiftly arose and spread around me the peace and knowledge that pass all the argument of the earth,
> And I know that the hand of God is the promise of my own,
> And I know that the spirit of God is the brother of my own,
> And that all men ever born are also my brothers, and the women my sisters and lovers,
> And that a kelson of the creation is love,

And limitless are leaves stiff or drooping in the fields,
And brown ants in the little wells beneath them,
And mossy scabs of the worm fence, heap'd stones, elder, mullein
and poke-weed.

("Song of Myself," *LG*, 33:91–98)

The union is a *sine qua non* of creativity. As the vision actualizes divinity within the self, all life and other men, creatures and the humblest plants, become infused with the same divine principle. The self returns to the physical and to the natural with a new awareness.

Reflecting on the intimate relationship of mysticism and sensuality in Whitman, Roger Asselineau points out that Whitman's originality lies in his "sharp consciousness of the purely sensual source of his mystical intuitions."[6] Unlike Wordsworth, Shelley, or Emerson, Whitman never forgets that his body is "the point of origin for his mystical states." "Even in religious fervor," he said, "there is a touch of animal heat."[7] In his own words, he was "mainly sensitive to the wonderfulness and perhaps spirituality of things in their physical and concrete expressions."[8] "And if the body were not the soul, what is the soul?" asks the ending line of the first section in "I Sing the Body Electric" (*LG*, 94:8).

Professor Asselineau formulates his observation cautiously, saying that the acute awareness of the sensual origins of spiritual insights was true "at least" for the Whitman of the 1855–56 editions. However, the movement from the physical to the spiritual remains characteristic of Whitman's work throughout his life. In "Crossing Brooklyn Ferry," considered the best of the new poems in the 1856 *Leaves of Grass*, a loving tribute is paid to material objects, "dumb, beautiful ministers," for "great or small, you furnish your parts toward the soul." In "Passage to India," often regarded as Whitman's last great poem, the strategy for moving into the realm of the spirit remains very much the same; a technological achievement, the transcontinental railroad, serves as a vehicle for arriving at the certainty of spiritual communion for mankind across all time and space. The difference is that the poet does not dwell here on the "wonderfulness of things." He has a purpose beyond celebrating the boundless riches of the physical world:

A worship new I sing,
You captains, voyagers, explorers, yours,

You engineers, you architects, machinists, yours,
You, not for trade or transportation only,
But in God's name, and for thy sake O soul.

(*LG*, 412 : 36–40)

But he can only start his progress toward the spiritual by fully acknowledging the material and the physical.

In fact, as both *Democratic Vistas* and the following letter to Tennyson show, Whitman's view of civilizational progress assumed that material plenitude was a necessary basis for spiritual enrichment:

America is at present a vast seething mass of varied material human and other, of the richest, best, worst, and plentiest kind. Wealthy inventive, no limit to food, land, money, work, opportunity, smart and industrious citizens, but (though real and permanently politically organized by birth and acceptance) without fusion or a definite heroic identity in form and purpose or organization, which can only come by native schools of great ideas—religion, poets, literature—and will surely come, even through the measureless crudity of the States in those fields so far, and to-day.

(*C*, 2 : 174)

Just as the self progresses from physical to spiritual consciousness, civilizations develop from material affluence to spiritual wealth. Floyd Stovall concludes: "The direction of his [Whitman's] evolution was always from the real to the ideal and from the material to the spiritual, and it was his conviction that such was also the direction of evolution in nature."[9]

The letter to O'Connor mentioning the poet's sensitivity to "the wonderfulness and perhaps spirituality of things" mainly "in their physical and concrete expressions" was written only four years before Whitman's death. Although in "Good-bye My Fancy" (1891),[10] the emphasis rests on the continuity of the creative imagination (fancy) as distinct from the physical self, still the identifying "I" belongs to the mortal body:

Good-bye my Fancy!
Farewell dear mate, dear love!
I'm going away, I know not where,
Or to what fortune, or whether I may ever see you again,
So Good-bye my Fancy.

(*LG*, 557 : 1–5)

For Whitman, complete self-realization involves constant growth from sensuous to spiritual consciousness and, especially in the earlier poems, incessant interchange between matter and spirit. The progress toward the realm of the spirit can be thought of as a pilgrimage upward or, better, forward in time and as such it corresponds to Whitman's personal evolution. As his pride in exuberant health was curbed by the wartime illness and later complaints culminating in the paralytic stroke of 1873, his poems gave more and more emphasis to the spiritual dimensions of life.

The case is not, however, that Whitman juxtaposed body and soul for their various levels of awareness, as one critic has claimed.[11] The "either or" scheme is just not Whitman's way of thinking. His is a world of "liquid rims," and it does not follow in his view that because the soul is unlimited, the body must be limited. Whitman's work, even when he became severely incapacitated, does not convey a sense of limitation through the body. It is only in conversations with Traubel that the poet complains of the painful bodily condition: "My body is nowadays so easily shoved off its balance" (Traubel, 1 : 232). But even then he makes a point of passing over it and is likely to dwell on the continuing agility of the mind: "But I am feeling quite myself today—head, belly, all" (Traubel, 1 : 232). "I do not seem to lose my mental grip—I have myself that way well in hand; but the other me, the body has little to expect for itself in the future" (Traubel, 1 : 186).

The body does not impose restrictions or necessities on Whitman's poetic persona. On the contrary, it is a marvellous agent activating the soul and Whitman uses it to that end until it serves the purpose. When no longer capable of stimulating the soul, the body is tacitly dropped, much as the "gigantic beauty of a stallion" is dropped in Section Thirty-Two of "Song of Myself." The emphasis shifts to the realm of spirit. The body simply grows progressively less important and so less and less distinctly present in the poems. There is no conflict or abrupt change, only gradual progression toward abstraction. Already in the 1872 preface (to "As a Strong Bird on Pinions Free") Whitman insists on the religious motivation of his whole work: "When I commenced, years ago, elaborating the plan of my poems, and continued turning over that plan, and shifting it in my mind through many years, (from the age of twenty-eight to thirty-five,) experimenting much, and writing and abandoning much, one deep purpose underlay the others, and has underlain it and its execution ever since—and that has been the Religious purpose" (*LG*, 742 : 80–85). In the 1876 preface to *Leaves of Grass* and *Two Rivulets*, the note becomes even stronger: "It was originally my intention, after chanting in *Leaves of Grass* the songs of the Body and Existence, to then compose a further, equally needed Volume, based on those convictions of perpetuity and conservation which, enveloping all precedents, make the unseen Soul govern absolutely at last" (*LG*, 746 : 30nff.). Eventually, however, Whitman had to confront the realization that "the full construction of such work (even if I lay the foundation, or give impetus to it) is beyond my powers, and must remain for some bard in the future." This was not only for reasons of health but because "the physical and the sensuous, in themselves or in their immediate continuations, retain holds upon me which I think are never entirely released; and those holds I have not only not denied, but hardly wish'd to weaken" (*LG*, 746 : 40nff.).

Although in "Good-bye My Fancy" the physical self is merely the "I" standing at the threshold of dissolution, in the poet's prime the ease with which the physical and the spiritual aspects of the self could be totally integrated became one of Whitman's most impressive characteristics. Moreover, it was the perfect harmony of body and soul that made all the self's journeys possible. Significantly, the mystic union of body and soul in "Song of Myself" precedes all subsequent identifications; it is the initial condition for the self's growth through experience. For Whitman's self grows not only in time from sensuous to spiritual awareness; equally importantly it expands, so to say, outward, in contact with reality. In a helpful essay on Whitman, Denis Donoghue points out that unlike most Romantic poets, Whitman was not troubled by the question of the self's nature because he had "set up a covenant with nature, governed by the energy that makes all things equal." It seems hardly necessary to add that the energy was in fact that of his own faith.

For him, life is—in Yeats' phrase—the fire that makes all simple, simple because equal. Hence he begins by saying, Let x equal the self. Then x equals A plus B plus C plus D plus E and so on, where each letter stands for a new experience contained and possessed, and the self is the sum of its possessions. This is the law of Whitman's lists. If you say that the self—x—is the sum of its possessions A, B, C, D and so on, then the more you add to the right-hand side of the equation, the more you enrich the left, and you do this without bothering about the nature of the x. You assume, as most Romantic poets did, that the self is not at any moment fixed, complete, or predetermined, and you then are free to develop or enlarge it at any time by adding to its experience.[12]

The rationale of the self's journeys in Whitman is that they provide opportunities for its enlargement. The "me myself" can never be finally defined. The self must stay free to move on at any moment:

> Trippers and askers surround me,
> People I meet, the effect upon me of my early life or the ward and city I live in, or the nation,
> The latest dates, discoveries, inventions, societies, authors old and new,
> My dinner, dress, associates, looks, compliments, dues,
> The real or fancied indifference of some man or woman I love,
> The sickness of one of my folks or of myself, or ill-doing or loss or lack of money, or depressions or exaltations,
> Battles, the horrors of fratricidal war, the fever of doubtful news, the fitful events;
> These come to me days and nights and go from me again,
> But they are not the Me myself.
>
> ("Song of Myself," *LG*, 32:66–74)

The journey's goal—complete self-realization—is forever to be reached round the next bend of the road. The self's potential is as inexhaustible as its realization is imperative:

> This day before dawn I ascended a hill and look'd at the crowded heaven,
> And I said to my spirit *When we become the enfolders of those orbs, and the pleasure and knowledge of every thing in them, shall we be fill'd and satisfied then?*
> And my spirit said *No, we but level that lift to pass and continue beyond.*
>
> ("Song of Myself," *LG*, 83–84:1220–22)[13]

To arrive at the end of the road would mean that the self could not grow any more. But this must never happen as capability for growth, nothing else, is the self's essence for Whitman. The self is a promise and its lot is cast with the future. Thus no encounter on the way is ever final. A part of consciousness has to be withheld in every engagement, for the potential can never be finally exhausted.

The growth of the self through expansion in space, through endless incorporations of experiences met with on the road, postulates a boundless power of empathy. In fact, in "Song of Myself" the "I" is closer to a cosmic force than to a definable, therefore limited, individual.[14] Yet the energy of empathy by which the self (and the poem) moves and grows contains a destructive urge. Adhesiveness betrays the self into shame (in Calamus) or into insufferable agonies of pain (in the crucifixion section of "Song of Myself" or in "The Wound Dresser"). It is significant and perhaps inevitable that, as Whitman grew older, his persona became less vigorously protean, often single, and observing rather than powering transformations (see "Song of the Red-Wood Tree" or "The Prayer of Columbus"). The sense of weariness creeps in even before 1860 (in "Out of the Cradle" and "As I Ebb'd with the Ocean of Life") and becomes intensified as the poet's youthful bravado gives way to the humility of invalidism and old age. In short, Whitman's development, says Lawrence Buell, epitomizes the climax and demise of American Romanticism as the Transcendentalist vision of the heroic possibilities of self becomes progressively undercut in his poems.[15]

Not only does the energy of the expanding self reconcile body and soul, me and the world outside, it resolves as well the dichotomy between active and passive stances toward reality. The voyager is both active and passive. He chooses his road and moves along it, but he also passively absorbs what he meets during the journey. The ambiguities involved in such a position can perhaps be illuminated by the closing fragment of Section Thirty-Two in "Song of Myself," in which the traveler stopped to enjoy "a gigantic beauty of a stallion, fresh and responsive to my caresses" but soon feels that he has no use for the animal:

> I but use you a minute, then I resign you, stallion,
> Why do I need your paces when I myself out-gallop them?
> Even as I stand or sit passing faster than you.
>
> (*LG*, 61 : 707–9)

Unable to commit himself to any single experience without endangering the fluency of his journey, the traveler risks appearing (or rather becoming) callous. Paradoxically, the more energy that goes into keeping himself in motion, the more passive, emotionally and intellectually, he becomes. At the end of a long list of scenes he has witnessed, the voyager of "Song of Myself" catches himself in some such predicament:

> Enough! enough! enough!
> Somehow I have been stunn'd. Stand back!
> Give me a little time beyond my cuff'd head, slumbers, dreams,
> gaping,
> I discover myself on the verge of a usual mistake.
> . . . .
> That I could look with a separate look on my own crucifixion and
> bloody crowning.
>
> (*LG*, 72 : 959–62, 965)

In all his identifications Whitman's persona strives to resolve the opposition between active and passive stances. As lover, he assumes with facility male and female roles. As poet-sayer, he wants to be both the commanding leader: "Allons! whoever you are come travel with me! / Travelling with me you find what never tires" ("Song of the Open Road," *LG*, 154 : 114–15) and the instrumental voice of the masses: "Through me many long dumb voices, / Voices of the interminable generations of prisoners and slaves" ("Song of Myself," *LG*, 52 : 508–9). As prophet, he himself starts a new race of men: "I am the teacher of athletes / He that by me spreads a wider breast than my own proves the width of my own" ("Song of Myself," *LG*, 84 : 1233–34) or becomes the medium through which the divine principle speaks: "Through me the afflatus surging and surging, through me the current and index. / I speak the password primeval" ("Song of Myself," *LG*, 52 : 505–6).

The identity of Whitman's self eludes definitions because it is so cumulative. It is both infinitely active and wisely passive, commanding as well as yielding. It comprises equally body and soul. It is rational in so far as it appreciates and makes use of the achievement of science, but always pushes on from there to intuitive insights and spiritual illumination (see "Song of Myself," Section Twenty-Three or "Passage to India," Section Two). As a living organism it is equal to, and exchangeable with, any other such organism. If anything can be designated as the supreme characteristic of this self, it is its constant mobility. The joyful relish of the self's dynamism is made possible by an act of faith establishing strict correspondence between the fluidity of the "I" and the plastic nature of reality.[16] Just as in its social role the self is supported by the grandeur of the cause with which it identifies, in its metaphysical dimension it shares the inexhaustible variety and potential of nature. Emerson's conclusion to "Worship" best sums up the theory of Whitman's self: "Man is made of the same atoms as the world is, he shares the same impressions, predispositions and destiny. When his mind is illuminated, when his heart is kind he throws himself joyfully into the sublime order, and does, with knowledge, what the stones do by structure" (6:240). Whitman's "I" is therefore always ready for ever new divisions along most unexpected lines while the act of faith removes the threat of losing identity in endless fluctuations. For nature cannot stop being what it is in all its particular manifestations, even though "what it is" may never be finally pinpointed.

This is not to say that Whitman's identity is devoid of uncertainties. Fred Carlisle has extensively and convincingly shown, as has John Snyder,[17] that uncertain, pessimistic, even tragic moods were very much a part of the Whitman persona throughout *Leaves of Grass*, just as they must have been a part of the man, though this aspect need not concern us here. According to Carlisle, "the major tensions contributing to the problematic of identity in Whitman" are present in the poems from the beginning of Whitman's career. Although "I Sit and Look Out" ("A Hand Mirror") was not published until 1860, it was originally written in the exuberant period of 1856–57. And, if we want further confirmation of Carlisle's thesis, we can turn to large sections of "The Sleepers" published in the first *Leaves of Grass*. Then come the great poems of the depression of 1859–60 and the distressed Civil War poems. Finally, the disenchanted "Prayer of Columbus" follows the prophecies of "Passage to India." The most important fact, however, is that Whitman's concept of identity involves centrally the need to accommodate a state of mind into a holistic design. Thus faith in the reality of an ultimately harmonious plan motivates the self in its growth. The progress toward the ideal, however remote, constitutes the self's essence and resolves its uncertainties. Carlisle recognizes this indirectly when he chooses to discuss "Song of Myself" as the conclusion to his book; it is "Song of Myself," that offers the fullest realization of the inclusive, cosmic self of which other poems present but aspects to be fitted into the total design.

In an article on the originality of the concept of self in Emerson and his followers (from Hawthorne to Dickinson), James McIntosh says that the self as envisioned by Emerson becomes first of all "a fluid consciousness."[18] Emerson tends to blur distinctions between various faculties of consciousness; he frequently uses terms like "reason," "heart," "soul," "genius," or "consciousness" almost interchangeably, insisting on the unity of human psychic powers in their action. Though he suggests no hierarchy of faculties in the sense that his discriminations between understanding and reason, between thinker and Man Thinking, between talent and genius, are really discriminations between the outer and the inner, true, self, Emerson tends to put spiritual powers above man's "instinctive" or "sensual" ones. Except for the last distinction, Emerson's model of self may with equal accuracy refer to Whitman's. Whitman too insists on the wholeness of human powers in action. The term "soul," which he most often uses to suggest consciousness, comprises psychic and spiritual faculties, but we are kept sharply aware of how they are activated by sensuous impressions. And Whitman rigorously asserts bodily health as a *sine qua non* of spiritual poise. In this emphasis, he differs from Emerson, but Whitman's consciousness, as Emerson's, works outward by the fluid energy of its identifications which help to blur distinctions between the inner and the outer world, between the poet and the reader, between art and life.[19] When the poet of "Song of Myself" is ready to depart in the last section, eternal mobility, which is also mutability, has been established as the law of both nature and mind.

Something rather different happens with Emily Dickinson. She tends to focus her poems on single moments, and the isolation of an individual event in her poem corresponds to her sense of the self's ultimate loneliness. In the following poem Dickinson picks up, perhaps unintentionally, Emerson's stone. For him it served as a perfect illustration of unselfconscious accommodation into nature's grand design; Dickinson is clearly amused with the Romantic fallacy:

How happy is the little Stone
That rambles in the Road alone,
And does'nt care about Careers

And Exigencies never fears—
Whose Coat of elemental Brown
A passing Universe put on,
And independent as the Sun
Associates or glows alone,
Fulfilling absolute Decree
In casual simplicity—

(1510)

It is difficult to think the poem altogether unrelated to the passage from "Worship," but, even if no relationship was intended, the two utterances show well the divergence in philosophical position between Emerson and Whitman on the one hand, and Dickinson on the other. The Amherst poet stresses the gap dividing her speaker from the world of "the little Stone." The human speaker feels perhaps jealous because, by implication, her world can never be as simple: she is not free to associate, or not as she pleases; she must worry "about careers" and be ridden with other anxieties. This is the burden and privilege of a conscious creature. But certainly the world of a human individual is more complex than the "elemental brown" of the stone, even if brown is the color of universe. Moreover, the stone's contentment seems purely accidental, as the nicely ironic[20] use of "casual" indicates.

In another well-known poem, "I taste a liquor never brewed—" (214), the ecstasy of mystic communion with nature is deceptive and short lived. The human intruder insists on participating in nature's mood but only succeeds in becoming nature's clown—"the little Tippler / Leaning against the Sun," as a variant reading puts it, a comic figure very much like the village drunkard leaning against the lamppost. The amused and presumably contemptuous laughter of seraphs swinging "their snowy hats" and saints running to windows is well justified since neither intoxication nor ecstatic rapture seems "dignified" in a sensible human being. Charles Anderson thinks the poem may well be an intentional parody of Emerson's "Bacchus." As evidence he points to the close echoes in the language and to the contrastive conclusion.[21] Whether an intended parody or not, this poem too establishes the self as essentially alien to nature, though subject to moods of longing for the mystic communion.

The conflict between the psychic need to participate trustfully in nature's divine mystery and the intellectual compulsion to examine and question "nature's show" constitutes the center of "These are the days when birds come back," quoted in the previous chapter. In yet another early poem, the speaker lets the general mood of nature prevail upon her:

> The morns are meeker than they were—
> The nuts are getting brown—
> The berry's cheek is plumper—
> The Rose is out of town.
>
> The Maple wears a gayer scarf—
> The field a scarlet gown—
> Lest I sh'd be old fashioned
> I'll put a trinket on.
>
> (12)

If she does not want to be left out, the persona feels that she should "put a trinket on" in obedience to nature's gaudy fall fashion. The word "trinket," however, suggests cheapness and implicitly condemns her for her undiscriminating taste.

Similarly, no matter how much Dickinson yearns for a safe parent-child relationship with God, her poems repeatedly turn into denunciations charging him with arbitrary decisions and with insensibility to individual suffering. The very idea of basing God's relation to man on the principle of payment for service rendered seems objectionable since the human heart seeks first of all love, not gain:

> "Crowns of Life" are servile Prizes
> To the stately Heart,
> Given for the Giving, solely,
> No Emolument.
>
> (1357)[22]

The haughty, nearly sarcastic tone of the poem derives authority from the claim it makes for the dignity of human emotions.

After the death of her little nephew, the poet wrote bitterly:

> Apparently with no surprise
> To any happy Flower
> The Frost beheads it at it's play—
> In accidental power—
> The blonde Assassin passes on—
> The Sun proceeds unmoved

To measure off another Day
For an Approving God.

(1624)

The instance of lawless execution or treacherous murder suggested by the imagery calls for justice, at least in human understanding. Instead, it is met with the inscrutable indifference of nature and God. In fact, God's complicity in the crime is implied. Does God approve only of the Sun's indifference or does he approve of the killing of the flower as well? In either case, the conduct of both baffles the mind, violates sensibility, and contradicts human mores.

From the human point of view, the fact that eternal life has to be entered by way of death looks very much like an unfair business transaction: the exchange of existence whose value we know for one we know very little about at a rate we do not know at all:

For Death—or rather
For the Things 'twould buy—
This—put away
Life's Opportunity—

The Things that Death will buy
Are Room—
Escape from Circumstances—
And a Name—

With Gifts of Life
How Death's Gifts may compare—
We know not—
For the Rates—lie Here—

(382; see also 1461, 1732)

It is interesting to notice that what Dickinson singles out as life's essential quality is "opportunity," that is, possibility and expectation. In this she is rather like Whitman, though without Whitman's insistence on the fertile abundance. Compared with Whitman, Dickinson seems Spartan. But she has to have the essence; she does not need the outer crust, however gorgeous. "Opportunity" will do, and each reader must decide what it means for him rather than contemplate an all-comprising list. Significantly, "the things that death will buy" are earthly things, known from experience this side of the grave: a private plot in the cemetery, freedom from life's painful circumstances, and "a Name"—a name on the gravestone or a name in the hall of fame? The two sets of values are neatly juxtaposed as the human mind attempts to work out how one converts into the other. But the rates of exchange are buried in the grave. Mystery prevents man from consciously evaluating his position and making his own decisions.

Emily Dickinson's special regard for Christ is largely a result of the fact that she sees Christ as co-victim of his father's arbitrary plans:

> God is a distant—stately Lover—
> Woos, as He states us—by His Son—
> Verily, a Vicarious Courtship—
> "Miles," and "Priscilla," were such an One—
>
> But, lest the Soul—like fair "Priscilla"
> Choose the Envoy—and spurn the Groom—
> Vouches, with hyperbolic archness—
> "Miles," and "John Alden" were Synonym—
>
> (357; see also 1433)

Both Christ and the human soul have been deprived of the right of choosing or being chosen. The possibility of choice has been excluded by arrangements which cannot be argued and refuted because they are beyond comprehension. Emily Dickinson finds that God's arbitrary ways, constantly baffling human understanding, are as impossible to accept as the fallacy of perfect communion with nature. Her sense of separation from nature and God comes from two sources. In the first place, the indifference of both violates human sensibility:

> The Morning after Wo—
> 'Tis frequently the Way
> Surpasses all that rose before—
> For utter Jubilee—
>
> As Nature did not care—
> And piled her Blossoms on—
>
> (364; see also, e.g., 348)

And:

> My Business, with the Cloud,
> If any Power behind it, be,
> Not Subject to Despair—
> It care, in some remoter way,

For so minute affair
As Misery—
Itself, too great, for interrupting—more—

(293; see also 1624)

Second, both nature and divinity confront men with a mystery which defies the mind. Even as the poet recognizes how exposed the self is because of the vulnerability of emotions and the powerlessness of the mind, she refuses to adopt criteria for evaluating experience other than those of individual sensibility and understanding. In consequence, human interpretations of divine and natural mysteries are constantly juxtaposed with their impenetrable essences. The result is continuous doubt, while the tone varies from that of rebellious denunciation seen in, for example, 1624, 293, or 364, to gentle amusement at man's presumptuous self-delusion:

But God be with the Clown—
Who ponders this tremendous scene—
This whole Experiment of Green—
As if it were his own!

(1333)

Self-deception, however, may be something more serious than just a clown's phantasy; it may become a necessary strategy for survival, a consciously adopted defense:

We dream—it is good we are dreaming—
It would hurt us—were we awake—
. . . .
Cautious—We jar each other—
And either—open the eyes—
Lest the Phantasm—prove the Mistake—
And the livid Surprise

Cool us to Shafts of Granite—
With just an Age—and Name—
And perhaps a phrase in Egyptian—
It's prudenter—to dream—

(531)

Dickinson's position in this poem echoes Emerson's journal entry: "If the world is not a dualism, is not a bipolar Unity, but is two, is Me and It, then is there the Alien, the Unknown, and all we have believed and chanted out of our deep instinctive hope is a pretty dream" (*J*, 7:200). But Dickinson recognizes unambiguously a necessary strategy in what in Emerson's Journal is merely a suspicion, what in "Experience" seems a reluctance to face facts, and what in Melville's Captain Amasa Delano is clearly an intellectual deficiency.[23] Acceptance on trust is for Dickinson the easier way. When mere conformity, it may be cheap, as in the "trinket" poem (12), but it becomes deadly serious when turned into a prudent survival technique. In no. 761, where the speaker's mental powers left her as a result of extreme pain, she says resignedly: "'Twas lighter to be Blind—."

Despite her recognition that the privilege of independent thought often becomes a burden too heavy to carry, Dickinson courageously persists in questioning even her own hopeful visions. Her persona's greatest problem, however, lies in the fact that just as God and nature demand that man accept their terms on trust or be left out, so man's own irrational impulses threaten to overthrow the mind's tenuous grasp of experience. Intense emotions or sensations such as joy, pain, or fear repeatedly threaten to deprive her persona of initiative by submerging consciousness in an incomprehensible, therefore uncontrollable, element (see, for example, 252, 281, 315, 378, 615, 618). The poem beginning "'Tis so appalling—it exhilarates—" furnishes a particularly interesting example of this process:

> To Scan a Ghost, is faint—
> But grappling, conquers it—
> How easy, Torment, now—
> Suspense kept sawing so—
>
> The Truth, is Bald, and Cold—
> But it will hold—
> If any are not sure—
> We show them—prayer—
> But we, who know,
> Stop hoping, now—
>
> . . . .
>
> Others, Can wrestle—
> Yours, is done—
> And so of Wo, bleak dreaded—come,
> It sets the Fright at liberty—
> And Terror's free—
> Gay, Ghastly, Holiday!
>
> (281)

There are, it seems, two stages of fear. The initial fear of death can be controlled by "grappling" with the "Ghost." Recognizing death as a fact helps to master the fear of it without supplicating God for assistance: "But we, who know, / Stop hoping, now—." Ironically, though, the assertion of the power of reason in this life removes the possibility of any kind of certainty about the afterlife. Freeing the speaker from one kind of fear, the act of intellectual recognition only releases another kind of terror for which the mind has no remedy: "And Terror's free— / Gay, Ghastly, Holiday!" Terror's ghastly freedom comes not so much from its objective strength as from the fact that the speaker's intellectual initiative stops: the mind can seize no fact "to grapple" with and is overcome.

The self's unconscious depth can appear equally ominous because, like the incomprehensible powers external to man, it works according to laws which defy the human mind:[24]

> Ourself behind ourself, concealed—
> Should startle most—
> Assassin hid in our Apartment
> Be Horror's least.
>
> The Body—borrows a Revolver—
> He bolts the Door—
> O'erlooking a superior spectre—
> Or More—
>
> (670)

"The Body" in this confrontation with itself resorts to rational action in preparing a defense against the intruder. The "reasonable" precautions of bolting the door and having a pistol ready appear ridiculously inappropriate since "the Assassin" is already inside, having, in fact, never left the apartment (the body). Even though the conflict remains unresolved, the self's helplessness in confrontation with itself is made sufficiently clear. This is the only kind of confrontation Dickinson's speaker thinks it wise to avoid:

> What Terror would enthrall the Street
> Could Countenance disclose
>
> The Subterranean Fright
> The Cellars of the Soul—

Thank God the loudest Place he made
Is licensed to be still.

(1225)

While her persona can afford refusing to rely on prayer in dealings with death, the poet feels compelled to invoke God's help against her own unconscious nature:

The Loneliness whose worst alarm
Is lest itself should see—
And perish from before itself
For just a scrutiny—
. . . .
I fear me this—is Loneliness—
The Maker of the soul
It's Caverns and it's Corridors
Illuminate—or seal—

(777, see also 683)

The challenge of the confrontations within the self is exhilarating, but destruction hangs in the air. Robert Weisbuch sums up the problem succinctly: "An electric reality lives within us and abroad. Survival depends on its denial, but a life of power depends on its actualization."[25] When faced with the impossible dilemma, Dickinson's persona admits to helplessness:

Me from Myself—to banish—
Had I Art—
Impregnable my Fortress
Unto All Heart—

But since Myself—assault Me—
How have I peace
Except by subjugating
Consciousness?

And since We're mutual Monarch
How this be
Except by Abdication—
Me—of Me?

(642)

Like Whitman's divisions of the self this poem presents us with the awareness of two inner principles. With Whitman, however, the different aspects of self fuse ideally into identity; in Dickinson they are contending forces, forever locked in an unresolvable conflict. Her self is a compound of emotions or, better, of irrational impulses including subconscious and instinctive urges as well as affections which in this poem are specified as "Heart"—the "me" of the first stanza, and intellect—"Consciousness"—the "myself" of the second stanza.

In poem 47 the self is divided in a similar way into "Heart" and "I," where "I" is the self's thinking part associated with light of knowledge and of memory. Yet, even as Dickinson calls the intellectual faculty "I" and singles it out for the identifying feature, she makes it absolutely clear that the life of the heart and the life of the mind are as inseparable as warmth and light. What is more, emotional, nonrational life seems to feed and define the life of the mind: if the heart will not forget the lover, the mind cannot either. Dickinson makes the dependence even more explicit in poem 1355: "The Mind lives on the Heart / Like any Parasite—."

Emotions uncontrolled, on the other hand, are mortally dangerous. One of the images used to convey the power of primal impulses is that of a leopard (see, e.g., 492), the choice of the animal implying both attraction and fear. Another one is that of a volcano:

On my volcano grows the Grass
A meditative spot—
An acre for a Bird to choose
Would be the General thought—

How red the Fire rocks below
How insecure the sod
Did I disclose
Would populate with awe my solitude.

(1677)

In this poem, the self's condition is a state of precarious balance in which the rational "meditative" consciousness barely keeps confined the eruptive energy of potentially destructive inner life.

The poet seemingly lets her heart's desires play in the poignant "Wild Nights—Wild Nights!" (249), but the situation there is posited as a false condition: "Were I with thee / Wild Nights should be / Our luxury!" and "Might I but moor—Tonight— / In Thee!" and is fully controllable because it is unreal. Even so, the sense of danger in the poem is nearly as strong as that of desire. The power of unleashed elements can only partly account for the feeling of insecurity pervading the poem. By giving up the guidance of the mind, "Done with the Compass— / Done with the Chart!", the speaker has deprived herself of the possibility of at least struggling to influence her position, and the situation fills her with apprehension. Leaving oneself open to the play of uncontrolled emotions results in passiveness, in numbness, an attitude both tempting and destructive.

Dickinson's fascination with the power of self measured in duels with the circumstances of experience can be seen in the frequency with which she poses the self in situations where it must resist attacks of prevalent, if not overwhelming, forces. From "I'm Nobody! Who are you?" (288) through "I took my Power in my Hand—" (540) to the undated "No man saw awe" (1733),[26] we could multiply examples of poems built on the same situational pattern, with the self confronting and resisting more powerful forces:

> On a Columnar Self—
> How ample to rely
> In Tumult—or Extremity—
>
> (789)

The duel situation is the poet's image for the human condition. Heroic dimensions of the self can be confirmed only by performance in reaction to the overwhelming assault:

> There is a strength in proving that it can be bourne
> Although it tear—
> What are the sinews of such cordage for
> Except to bear
> The ship might be of satin had it not to fight—
> To walk on seas requires cedar Feet.
>
> (1113)[27]

The power of faith may have enabled Peter to "walk on seas,"[28] but Dickinson's persona feels better sustained by the power of lonely endurance.

The shaping and therefore identifying component of the self is for Dickinson consciousness—the faculty of being aware of what is happening to oneself, the questioning and judging faculty. Sometimes she divides the soul into Soul and Consciousness, "her awful Mate" (894), or Soul and "a single Hound / It's own Identity"

(822). The distinction seems to be between Soul as spiritual existence and its "identity" or "Consciousness" as detached awareness of that existence. At other times the poet treats soul as equivalent to consciousness and imagines immortality as "Costumeless Consciousness" (1454). Invariably, however, consciousness remains the supreme human faculty responsible for both human misery and heroic freedom (see 384, 383). Thus, while consciousness in Whitman equals perception or even being itself, the life principle, for Dickinson consciousness is far closer to awareness and knowledge; it is, in fact, intellectual power.

Dickinson never singles out as the identifying feature anything in her persona that is passive, yielding, and soft. Neither the body nor the heart alone is allowed to represent the whole self. That distinction is reserved for the struggling consciousness. When Robert Weisbuch says that she fears defeat of the self through "simply the battering of the nerves unto death,"[29] he tells only the first part of the truth. The final horror is not the damage done to the physiological self, but rather the extinction of consciousness. While one can control even the emotionally "numb" stages by reporting how they "felt," the final disaster occurs when the mind is vanquished. Dickinson's most powerful poems take us to the very brink of the catastrophe:

> And then a Plank in Reason, broke,
> And I dropped down, and down—
> And hit a World, at every plunge,
> And Finished knowing—then—
>
> (280)
>
> As Freezing persons, recollect the Snow—
> First—Chill—then Stupor—then the letting go—
>
> (341)
>
> And then the Windows failed—and then
> I could not see to see—
>
> (465)

Inarticulateness is inevitably the greatest danger the poet courts because her concern is with measuring the extent of the self's power in mastering overwhelming forces of experience through art.

The self of Whitman is perfectly symmetrical, its symmetry based on complementarity. For every single aspect there must exist a matching counterpart, equally valid, equally representative of the self: the body is matched by soul, active creativity by passive receptivity, sensuous perception by spiritual insight, and so on. The list of correspondences can be extended indefinitely as the self expands in contact with experience. Whitman's chief concern is providing opportunities for the self's unfolding. Possibilities of conflict have been practically excluded as Whitman's consciousness strives to abolish "the other." Since there is nothing that cannot be incorporated within the self, Whitman's persona does not fear losing identity in the primal flux, just as it is seldom threatened by betrayal from within. Ideally, the self, like atmosphere, should become without a taste of "the distillation," "odorless" (see "Song of Myself," Section Two), that is, all encompassing and wholly universal. Consciousness, for Whitman, is stimulated from only one source: the vision of ultimate oneness underlying the inexhaustible variety of life.

Dickinson's model of the self, on the other hand, is based on balancing the two carefully delimited principles of heart and mind, on balancing nonrational experience, which is dynamic but lawless and potentially destructive, and intellectual discipline, which wrests shape and meaning from sheer energy. Dickinson preserves "the other" respecting the mystery not only of nature and God but of the self's unconscious depths as well. Thus the grace of the unifying vision is possible for her but conflict is inevitable, and consciousness may be stimulated by either impulse. The balance within the self is founded not on complementarity but on opposition. Consequently, precise adjustment of the contending principles becomes a matter of life and death: "The Brain, within its Groove / Runs evenly—and true— / But let a Splinter swerve— . . ." (556), "Let an instant push / Or an Atom press . . . It—may jolt the Hand / That adjusts the Hair" (889). The balance is felt as infinitely delicate (see the already quoted 1677), and its fragility creates a constant sense of danger, another challenge for consciousness.

The respective visions of self in Whitman and Dickinson may be further illustrated by juxtaposing the following fragment of "Song of Myself" with poem 384:

> I know I have the best of time and space, and was never
> measured and never will be measured.

I tramp a perpetual journey, (come listen all!)
My signs are a rain-proof coat, good shoes, and a staff cut from the woods,
No friend of mine takes his ease in my chair,
I have no chair, no church, no philosophy,
I lead no man to a dinner-table, library, exchange,
But each man and each woman of you I lead upon a knoll,
My left hand hooking you round the waist,
My right hand pointing to landscapes of continents and the public road.

Not I, not any one else can travel that road for you,
You must travel it for yourself.

(*LG*, 83: 1201–11)

For Whitman here, as almost anywhere else, liberation of consciousness is identical with the opening up of time and space. Freedom of the mind is translatable into freedom of the body. Unlimited possibilities have been opened for complete man, that is, body and mind. The essence of the new vision is its power to do away with enclosures and constraints, with contradictions and necessities. As traditions, institutions, creeds are left behind, no sense of loss arises. The prospects of the journey more than compensate for the initial rejection. The whole glory of the new man, "the friendly and flowing savage," lies ahead. He is to be celebrated as possibility.

The liberated consciousness means a very different kind of freedom to Dickinson:

No Rack can torture me—
My Soul—at Liberty—
Behind this mortal Bone
There knits a bolder One—

You Cannot prick with saw—
Nor pierce with Cimitar—
Two Bodies—therefore be—
Bind One—The Other fly—

The Eagle of his Nest
No easier divest—
And gain the Sky
Than mayest Thou—

Except Thyself may be
Thine Enemy—

Captivity is Consciousness,
So's Liberty.

(384)

Her persona achieves not so much freedom "from" necessity as freedom "in spite of" necessity. The "mortal Bone" remains always exposed, so suffering, pain, and limitation have terrible immediacy. Possibilities for freedom are exclusively psychic or, rather, imaginative; Dickinson's acute awareness of the vulnerability of body and heart make her admire not the yet unrealized potential but the actual achievement: endurance and persistent effort. Emily Dickinson, as a matter of course, envisions the self as assaulted by external forces (in this poem signaled through the imagery of torture; in, e.g., "I'm Nobody" pointed to as "them" or "bog"). To such a siege, the eaglelike ability of consciousness to take to regions higher than its bodily habitat can be successfully opposed. But things are never easy for Dickinson; the greatest danger resides within. Surrendering to circumstances, consciousness can make captivity as real as liberty. It is, therefore, Dickinson's constant quest to find out how invincible consciousness is, to test it for power and endurance. Supporting her in the quest may have been Emerson's admonition:

Then first shalt thou know,
That in the wild turmoil,
Horsed on the Proteus,
Thou ridest to power,
And to endurance.

(6,308)[30]

For Emily Dickinson, "power and endurance" won in confrontations with experience could be made actual only in her art.

Notes

1. The letter is dated April 25, 1862. In *Emily Dickinson's Reading* (Cambridge, Mass.: Harvard University Press, 1966), 139, Jack L. Capps mentions Dr. Holland's editorial in the *Springfield Republican*—"Leaves of Grass—Smut in Them," which may have encouraged the poet to think Whitman "disgraceful."

2. Harold Bloom, ed., *Romanticism and Consciousness* (New York: W. W. Norton, 1970), 1.

3. See also, for example, poems 303 and 664, where a similarly exclusive stance is adopted. Dickinson's "aristocratic" attitude has been noticed and commented on by several critics. Charles Anderson contrasts her use of grass as a royal symbol (in 1333) with that of Whitman (*Emily Dickinson's Poetry: A Stairway of Surprise* [New York: Holt, Rinehart and Winston, 1960], 101–2). In the conclusion to his *Circumference and Circumstance: Stages in the Mind and Art of Emily Dickinson* (New York: Columbia University Press, 1968), William R. Sherwood calls her attitudes aristocratic (233).

4. Gay Wilson Allen, *The Solitary Singer: A Critical Biography of Walt Whitman*, rev. ed. (New York: New York University Press, 1967), 138. Whitman's reflection is quoted from Emory Holloway, ed., *Uncollected Poetry and Prose of Walt Whitman* (1921; reprint Gloucester, Mass.: Peter Smith, 1972), 2:66.

5. Allen in *The Solitary Singer* makes a comparison with Heine (560 n.140).

6. Roger Asselineau, *The Evolution of Walt Whitman* (Cambridge, Mass.: Harvard University Press, Belknap Press, 1962), 2:4.

7. *PW*, 2:415 (1669–70), quoted by Asselineau.

8. A letter to O'Connor, April 18, 1888, Berg Collection, New York Public Library, quoted by Asselineau.

9. Floyd Stovall, ed., *Walt Whitman: Representative Selections* (New York: Hill and Wang, 1961), LII.

10. Placed as the closing poem of the last annex to the 1891–92 edition of *Leaves of Grass*.

11. E. Fred Carlisle, *The Uncertain Self: Whitman's Drama of Identity*: "This initial distinction between the Soul and I is based on the degree of awareness or consciousness evident in the two aspects of identity. The awareness of the soul perceives unity where division previously existed. The I, of course, does not share this expanded consciousness; rather it is limited by time and space—in short by conventional human perceptions" (53).

12. Denis Donoghue, *Connoisseurs of Chaos* (London: Faber and Faber, 1965), 25. The chapter on Whitman is reprinted in Francis Murphy, ed., *Walt Whitman* (Harmondsworth: Penguin Critical Anthologies, 1969).

13. Compare also the fragment from the 1847 Notebook: "I think the soul will never stop, or attain to any growth beyond which it shall not go.—When I walked at night by the sea shore and looked up at the countless stars, I asked of my soul whether it would be filled and satisfied when it should become god enfolding all these, and open to the life and delight and knowledge of everything in them or of them; and the answer was plain to me at the breaking water on the sands at my feet: and the answer was, No, when I reach there I shall want to go further still" (Holloway, *Uncollected Poetry and Prose*, 2:66).

14. For observations in this paragraph I am indebted to Lawrence Buell, *Literary Transcendentalism: Style and Vision in the American Renaissance*

(Ithaca: Cornell University Press, 1973), 324ff. On Whitman's persona, see also Philip Y. Coleman, "Walt Whitman's Ambiguities of 'I,'" in *Studies in American Literature in Honor of Robert Dunn Faner*, ed. Robert Partlow (Carbondale, Ill.: Southern Illinois University Press, 1969); Donna L. Hensler, "The Voice of the Grass Poem 'I': Whitman's 'Song of Myself,'" *Walt Whitman Review* 15 (March 1969): 26–32; Bruce R. McElderry, Jr., "Personae in Whitman (1855–1860)," *American Transcendental Quarterly* 12 (1971): 25–32.

15. It should be noted that Emerson developed along similar lines (see Chapter 1).

16. It is interesting to observe that when Allen Ginsberg, a poet whose direct relationship to Whitman has been recognized by himself and others, denounces in "Howl" the deadly antagonism between the self and the modern world, he retains the image of self as fluid and mobile, opposing it to a reality congealed into an apocalyptic enclosure.

17. Carlisle, *The Uncertain Self*; John Snyder, *The Dear Love of Man: Tragic and Lyric Communion in Walt Whitman* (The Hague: Mouton, 1975).

18. James McIntosh, "Emerson's Unmoored Self," *The Yale Review* 65, no. 2 (1975): 232.

19. See Chapter 3.

20. Allen observes that there is "perceptibly little" irony in Whitman and comments: "Irony results from self-pity or loss of faith. The poet of this poem [i.e., "To Think of Time"] has complete faith that underlying birth and death is a process grander than life itself" (*The Solitary Singer*, 166). It is precisely "complete faith" that is absent in Dickinson's poems.

21. Anderson, *Emily Dickinson's Poetry*, 73–75.

22. The second version sounds even more rebellious: "'I will give' the base Proviso— / Spare your 'Crown of Life'— / Those it fits, too fair to wear it— / Try it on Yourself—" (Variorum ed., 3:938).

23. The fact remains that in "Benito Cereno," Delano survives precisely through his failure to inquire what lay beneath orderly appearances.

24. On Emily Dickinson's awareness of "the other" in external reality as well as within the self, see Glauco Cambon's excellent essay "Emily Dickinson and the Crisis of Self-Reliance," in *Transcendentalism and Its Legacy*, ed. Myron Simon and Thornton H. Parsons (Ann Arbor: University of Michigan Press, 1966), 123–32.

25. Robert Weisbuch, *Emily Dickinson's Poetry* (Chicago: University of Chicago Press, 1975), 134.

26. This poem was not included in either "fascicles" or "sets," so Ralph Franklin's dating in *The Manuscript Books of Emily Dickinson* (Cambridge, Mass.: Harvard University Press, 1981) offers no help in establishing the date of this poem.

27. Compare the following passage in Emerson's "Montaigne" (published 1850): "We want a ship in these billows we inhabit. An angular, dogmatic house would be rent to chips and splinters in this storm of many elements" (4:160).

28. Compare Matt. 14:25–33.

29. Weisbuch, *Emily Dickinson's Poetry*, 141.

30. This is a fragment of the poem used as epigraph to "Illusions." The coincidental similarity of my own phrasing with that of Emerson was kindly pointed out to me by James McIntosh.

3 / The Central Consciousness: Mediation versus Command

IN the essay already referred to, Geoffrey Hartman points out that in Romantic art "the traditional triad of Eden, Fall, and Redemption merges with the new triad of Nature, Self-Consciousness, and Imagination,"[1] where imagination must remedy the alienating effects of self-consciousness. Whitman and Dickinson both fall within Hartman's pattern, for both recognize that poetry functions analogously to religion. Yet while the poets view art as capable of rescuing man from chaos, each devises a different practical strategy. This chapter will, therefore, examine the relations which the redeeming poetic consciousness[2] develops with experiential reality in the work of both poets.

There have been many attempts at defining the structure of "Song of Myself,"[3] certainly Whitman's most famous poem, but as Malcolm Cowley observes: "In spite of revealing analyses made by a few Whitman scholars, notably Carl F. Strauch and James E. Miller, a feeling still seems to prevail that it has no structure properly speaking; that it is inspired but uneven, repetitive, and especially weak in its transitions from one theme to another."[4] Basically, two lines can be distinguished among the interpretations offered: one insists on the progressing pattern of thought (as Carl Strauch does) or a narrative sequence (as do James Miller and Cowley himself); the other, more wary of stressing the "forward" thrust of the poem, treats it as a "mosaic" (Roger Asselineau) or a symphony (Gay Wilson Allen), pointing to the repetitive, "circular" or "spiral" pattern of the poem (Allen and Davis). V. K. Chari puts even more emphasis on the static character of "Song of Myself," treating the whole poem as an expanded illustration of what he calls "the paradox of identity."[5] Thus the difficulty in interpreting the structure of the poem seems to lie in reconciling its static, repetitive element with its equally strongly felt dynamism. The controversy, one might add, hits the very core of Whitman's own problems with structure.

My suggestion for overcoming the difficulty is to refer to the pattern drawn by Emerson in "Circles": "The eye is the first circle; the horizon which it forms is the second; and throughout nature this primary figure is repeated without end. It is the highest emblem in the cipher of the world. St. Augustine described the nature of God as a circle whose centre was everywhere and its circumference nowhere" (2:301). "Every ultimate fact is only the first of a new series. Every general law only a particular fact of some more general law presently to disclose itself. There is no outside, no inclosing wall, no circumference to us" (2:304). The pattern of concentric circles rushing outward until they dissolve seems an appropriate analogy for the structure of "Song of Myself," more appropriate, in fact, than the widely accepted Emersonian spiral.[6] The circular figure recognizes the repetitive element in the poem as effectively as the spiral and, more effectively than the spiral, joins it to the energy of expansion. Moreover, it helps us avoid the implications of hierarchic arrangement, which undoubtedly were very real for Emerson when he proceeded from nature as "commodity" to nature as "spirit." Whitman does not stress the movement upward. At the end of the poem he still asks to be sought "under your boot-soles." His is "the long journey"[7] outward in space and forward in time, with the thrust ahead strongly emphasized and with equally strong insistence on the perfect democracy of God, all men and women, "brown ants," "mossy scabs of the worm fence, heap'd stones, elder, mullein and poke-weed" ("Song of Myself," *LG*, 33:98). Moreover, the circular pattern elicits the difficulties of transitions which the spiral conceals in its smooth coils.

The primary impulse, the stone dropped in water to start "the circles," is the self's desire to merge. The urge to union, mystical at the base, repeats itself throughout the poem in larger and larger contexts. Thus, somewhat like Malcolm Cowley, I see "Song of Myself" as "punctuated with chants of ecstasy."[8] The ecstasies of contact, of being in communion, power the progressions in time, onward to the realm of spirit and in space, outward to incorporate the cosmos. Both progressions are orderly. The advance in time is contained within the span of the speaker's life, from the birth of self-awareness to death. The journey in space is "graded" in stages from "the bank by the river" through "the populous city," the whole country, earth, and outer space. Comparing the beginning and the end of the poem clearly demonstrates its radial expansion:

> I celebrate myself, and sing myself,
> . . . .
> I loafe and invite my soul,
> I lean and loafe at my ease observing a spear of summer grass.
> (*LG*, 28:4–5)

and

> I depart as air, I shake my white locks at the runaway sun,
> I effuse my flesh in eddies, and drift it in lacy jags.
>
> I bequeath myself to the dirt to grow from the grass I love,
> If you want me again look for me under your boot-soles.
>
> You will hardly know who I am or what I mean,
> But I shall be good health to you nevertheless,
> And filter and fibre your blood.
>
> Failing to fetch me at first keep encouraged,
> Missing me one place search another,
> I stop somewhere waiting for you.
> (*LG*, 89:1341ff)

While Section One is preoccupied only with the single "I" observing an isolated fact of life, in the closing section the "I" merges bodily into the eternity of organic life and spiritually into the continuous presence of all those who read the poem. At the beginning is Emerson's first circle of the eye; at the end, a boundless circumference of an immanent God suggested through sacramental imagery.

Within this open-ended but clearly structured pattern, "Song of Myself" consists of a sequence of "movements" toward an ecstatic union. Each ecstasy enlarges the protagonist's consciousness and so the scope of the poem. Each ecstasy pushes consciousness outward to encompass a circle larger than the one just completed. The first ecstatic union occurs in Section Five and is prepared by Sections One to Four, in which the speaker introduces himself.[9] An individual, consisting of body and soul, he must extricate himself from the past and society to reach his essential, "naked" self. The ecstasy in Section Five is conveyed, appropriately, through autoerotic imagery, for its outcome is the perfect fusion of the so far disjoined aspects of the self. Full acceptance of the complete "me"—body and soul alike—endows the speaker with the gift of sympathetic observation.[10]

After the poem's central symbol has been established and explained in Section Six, the gift is put to use in the wanderings of Sections Seven to Sixteen. Toward the end of this sequence, the observing protagonist begins to feel that he has grown into a powerful personality: an athletic body and an all-embracing soul. The culminating ecstasy of this realization comes in Section Twenty-Four, in which the speaker is virtually blinded with the sense of joy and power of living. Section Twenty-Five poses the famous question: "Walt you contain enough, why don't you let it out then?" (*LG*, 55 : 568). The answer is negative, for the speaker must proceed beyond observation to actual involvement, sensual as well as emotional. In the subsequent sections other senses participate in experiencing to show that "mine is no callous shell" (*LG*, 57 : 614). The climax of this sequence comes in an actual sexual union (Sections Twenty-Eight and Twenty-Nine). The love relationship, even if expressed primarily in sensuous terms and with a good deal of ambiguous autoeroticism, demands identification with others, destroys self-defenses, and makes the speaker vulnerable to pain:

> Treacherous tip of me reaching and crowding to help them,
> My flesh and blood playing out lightning
> to strike what is hardly different from myself,
> . . . .
> The sentries desert every other part of me,
> They have left me helpless to a red marauder,

They all come to the headland to witness and
assist against me.
I am given up by traitors,

(*LG*, 57 : 621–22; 633–36)

It allows the cosmic vision of Section Thirty-Three and makes of him a Christ figure, suffering for all humanity in Section Thirty-Eight. Yet in the agony of pain a new man is born with power to teach and prophesy before he finally loses himself in the eternity of organic and spiritual life.

Fragments of the poem dividing the ecstatic experiences record the progress of consciousness toward moments of transport. Consciousness actively seeks experience until, in a culminating moment, it becomes wholly receptive when a new perspective reveals itself and the journey "to the horizon" can continue. Each moment of communion and each ecstatic contact endows consciousness with a new power, with new energy. The journey continues as long as consciousness expands while establishing contacts.

The alternating movements of reaching out toward a point of contact and then undergoing the revelation of the moment of communion are crucial for the whole poetry of Whitman. His two "shore odes,"[11] like "Song of Myself," gather momentum from the progress of consciousness toward illumination. In "Out of the Cradle Endlessly Rocking,"[12] the protagonist, now a mature man, relives the central experience of his youth.[13] The first twenty-two lines of the poem, called "Pre-Verse" in the first version, form syntactically one giant sentence. Within it the narrative present of the poem is established and the three principal actors, the sea, the bird, and the boy, are introduced. The main part of the poem re-creates a past experience: the young boy's nightly visits to the seashore, where throughout the summer he listened to the mockingbird's song of love and loss. In the reflection beginning with the line "Demon or bird!" (*LG*, 251 : 144ff.), it becomes clear that the boy identifies with the bird. The bird speaks for the pained and bewildered man-child who, however, unlike the bird, is finally able to transcend his sense of loss and frustration, given the clue by the sea.

Until the boy identifies exclusively with the bird's solitary song, nothing is clear to him; only vague, disordered emotions are stirred:

"The messenger there arous'd, the fire, the sweet hell within, / The unknown want, the destiny of me" (*LG*, 252 : 156–57). It is when he is ready to disengage himself from the plight of the bird, to turn away from private suffering, that knowledge may come to him. In his bewilderment he addresses the sea:

> O give me the clew! (it lurks in the night here somewhere,)
> O if I am to have so much, let me have more!
> . . . .
> Are you whispering it, and have been all the time, you
> sea-waves?
>
> (*LG*, 252 : 158–59, 163)

To someone actively seeking wisdom in her, the sea changes her aspect; no longer "the fierce old mother incessantly moaning with angry moans," she becomes the contact edge of "liquid rims and wet sands," the measured movement "Delaying not, hurrying not," her voice friendly and seductive: "[the sea] Whisper'd me through the night, and very plainly before daybreak, / Lisp'd to me low and delicious . . ." (*LG*, 252 : 167–68), "Hissing melodious, neither like the bird nor like my arous'd child's heart" (*LG*, 253 : 169). The revelation occurs when the boy, with passive acceptance, lets the sea act upon him: "But edging near as privately for me rustling at my feet, / Creeping thence steadily up to my ears and lovingly laving me softly all over . . ." (*LG*, 253 : 171–72). At this point, with Armin Frank, I see the boy lying on the beach with his feet to the water rather than wading into it, which is the more customary interpretation. The quiet conclusion asserts the importance of the illuminating moment transforming the pained and puzzled youth into the poet. "A word out of the sea"[14] makes him capable of fusing the isolated experiences into the coherence of "songs."

"Out of the Cradle" is a "learning" poem; it tells how the boy-protagonist learned to transform emotion into art. Structurally the progress is rendered in five parts. The first is the Prologue (Pre-Verse), in which a man revisits the scene and experience of his youth. Second comes the actual experience recollected and relived. Now the narrator occasionally ignores the distance between the boy-persona and his older self,[15] expressing his mature knowledge rather than adolescent intuitions. For example, when the boy addresses the bird directly, "Yes my brother I know, / The rest might not, but I have treasur'd every note" (60–61), his sympathy with the bird seems to derive much more from the older man's experience than from the youth's innocence of heart. Third is a reflection on how the beach experience affected the boy. Again, although it is the youth who reflects, the distance between the mature narrator and his youthful double is often crossed so that what the boy says reveals the man's insights:

> Never more shall I escape, never more the reverberations,
> Never more the cries of unsatisfied love be absent from me,
> Never again leave me to be the peaceful child I was before . . .
> (*LG*, 252 : 152–54)

Fourth is the revelation, and last comes the concluding assessment of the revelation's importance.

The third and reflective section with its climactic moment of receiving the sea's message is the central, though not the longest, part of the poem's structure; there are other structure-content correspondences. For example, only the entire text offers the realization that the poem acts out what it says and thus identifies its reader with its speaker. From the midnight seashore and the bird's song through the "yearning and love there in the mist," through the recognition of death—"the word stronger and more delicious than any"—to the final making of the poet and this poem in particular—"I, chanter of pains and joys, uniter of here and hereafter, / Taking all hints to use them, but swiftly leaping beyond them, / A reminiscence sing." (*LG*, 247 : 20–23)—the poem's total movement is contained in its prologue. Yet this knowledge remains inaccessible to the reader until he has read the poem through:

> . . . all data, all bits of information, all impressions are there, right from the beginning, but not yet understood: only when looking back from the end and, perhaps, rereading, are we able to gather the full meaning. We realize in retrospect, that it was impossible to understand everything at first reading. . . . The very structure and texture incorporates the learning process of the speaker in a way which forces the reader to undergo a similar experience.[16]

The assertions in the text of the importance of the youthful experience for the whole life of the poet-narrator are reinforced because the man who revisits the scene of his youth is distressed and bewildered, while the man who has relived the revelation sounds quiet and accepting:[17]

> Which I do not forget,
> But fuse the song of my dusky demon and brother,
> That he sang to me in the moonlight on Paumanok's gray beach,
> With the thousand responsive songs at random,
> My own songs awaked from that hour,
> And with them the key, the word up from the waves,
> (*LG*, 253: 174–79)

The poem vindicates not so much "emotion recollected in tranquility" as the permanent healing power or the continuous inspiration of a moment of vision.

On both time levels, the narrative present and the time of the recollected experience, the poem is a progress from ignorance and frustration to the realization of order. To achieve reconciliation the speaker must not center on personal loss but turn to look for a vaster, more primary law. The wisdom of acceptance has to be sought, the sea reached and implored, but the moment of revelation is granted only when the speaker yields himself completely to the sea's influence. The actual creative power, the inspiration, is contained in the "word out of the sea." Knowledge of it is imperative for the realization of order incorporated in the poem. Although inherently there all the time, the order can only be made actual when the poet has been granted the illuminating vision. The poem is a "discovery" of order and makes the reader undergo a similar "exploring" experience.

"As I Ebb'd with the Ocean of Life" is a structurally simpler lyric. It operates on one time level as the speaker progresses from despair to a sense of at least partial reconciliation. The movement from disorder to order, even if incomplete and tentative, constitutes the underlying pattern the two poems share.[18] "As I Ebb'd" is perhaps Whitman's most disconsolate poem, his "Dejection: An Ode." Certainly, the poet's personal situation at the time it was written[19] influenced its tone, but the poem's dominant note is not strictly one of personal desolation. Rather, the poem recognizes self-doubt and frustration, "the ebb of the ocean of life," as an integral part of the human condition and seeks to accommodate them within the universal design.

The entire text is divided into four sections of fairly uniform length (16 to 21 lines). In the first one the scene is set for the shore ode with the poet-persona walking on a Long Island beach on an autumn afternoon by "the ocean of life," its inspiring power often acknowledged by Whitman.[20] In the poems stemming from the major crisis of his life, the poet instinctively relied upon the beaches of Long Island to provide appropriately charged imagery.

The opening section establishes the mood with images of late afternoon, of unquiet, "hoarse and sibilant sea," of the beach strewn with "chaff, straw, splinters of wood, weeds, and the sea-gluten."[21] As in "Out of the Cradle," the introductory part contains all data to be elucidated in the course of the poem. The speaker wandering along the shore "thought the old thought of likenesses" while his eyes, "fascinated," followed "those slender windrows, / Chaff, straw, splinters of wood, weeds, and the sea-gluten, / Scum, scales from shining rocks, leaves of salt-lettuce, left by the tide" (*LG*, 254:10–12). Thus the reader becomes prepared for the concluding identification made in a more loving and more hopeful mood. The "electric self," "seeking types," sounds depressed because it is "seized by the spirit that trails in the lines underfoot"; in the final section the same identification anticipates the inevitable rise of the tide:

> Me and mine, loose windrows, little corpses,
> Froth, snowy white, and bubbles,
> (See, from my dead lips the ooze exuding at last,
> See, the prismatic colors glistening and rolling,)
> ("As I Ebb'd with the Ocean of Life," *LG*, 256:57–60)

To acquire a sense of the range of moods from which Whitman's consciousness reaches out to embrace "the other," one should read this poem with "Song of Myself" in mind. The most vital assumptions of the earlier poem are being questioned here. In fact, "As I Ebb'd" can be viewed as a sort of anti-"Song of Myself" in which the "barbaric yawp over the roofs of the world" turns into "all that blab whose echoes recoil upon me."[22] In place of unshaken faith in the resources of the self, frustration and self-doubt prevail. These moods result from a radical division within the self in contrast to "Song of Myself" which postulated harmony as the primary condition of creativity. The noninvolved, observing "I" not only stands detached but assumes mocking postures. Consequently, nature too becomes a jeering stranger while the crippling sense of disunion undercuts the very basis of creativity:

> I perceive I have not really understood any thing, not a single object, and that no man ever can,
> Nature here in sight of the sea taking advantage of me to dart upon me and sting me,
> Because I have dared to open my mouth to sing at all.
>
> (*LG*, 254:32–34)

The urgency of this "night of the soul" is reflected in the switch from the narrative use of the past tense in the first section to the immediacy of the present tense cancelling the distance between the speaker and the narrated experience. From a reported "action" the poem turns into dramatic enactment.

In Section Three the protagonist, aware that the evil consists in separation, attempts to recover the sense of contact with the world around him. As in "Out of the Cradle," he turns from contemplating a private misery to the primary reality—this time of the land, the father—Paumanok:

> I throw myself upon your breast my father,
> I cling to you so that you cannot unloose me,
> I hold you so firm till you answer me something.
>
> Kiss me my father,
> Touch me with your lips as I touch those I love,
> Breathe to me while I hold you close the secret of the murmuring I envy.
>
> (*LG*, 255:45–50)

This passage is analogous to the fragment of "Out of the Cradle" in which the boy implores the sea, hoping that the secret key word may be revealed to him and harmony restored in his world:

> O give me the clew! (it lurks in the night here somewhere,)
> O if I am to have so much, let me have more!
>
> A word then, (for I will conquer it,)
> The word final, superior to all,
> Subtle, sent up—what is it?—I listen;

Are you whispering it, and have been all the time, you sea-waves?
Is that it from your liquid rims and wet sands?
(*LG*, 252 : 158–64)

In both fragments the imploring figure lies prostrate on the beach, attempting to bridge the division of sea and land with his body and, correspondingly, to embrace imaginatively "the other," to leap across the gulf opened by the sense of separation from nature. In such a passive and receptive position, both protagonists await revelation. The sea obliges in "Out of the Cradle." No secret, however, is revealed to the frustrated man in "As I Ebb'd," so he is left with the sense of the self's irremediable alienation. Yet the loving, sympathetic part of the self continues its search for a point of contact while the disengaged observer, the "phantom," is "looking down where we lead, and following me and mine." The phrase "me and mine" eventually establishes a love relationship with the humblest facts of nature: "loose windrows, little corpses / Froth, snowy white and bubbles." The act of humble but loving union signals the simultaneous change of tide and the return of inspiration. There is no total restoration of harmony in this poem. Whatever hope there is, is based on trust in the inevitability of natural laws by which ebb must be followed by flow. We do not, however, witness the restoration of order, the return of fertility and plenitude. Though the poem ends on an accepting note, it is one of resignation rather than affirmation:

Just as much for us that sobbing dirge of Nature,
Just as much whence we come that blare of the cloud-trumpets,
We, capricious, brought hither we know not whence, spread out before you,
You up there walking or sitting,
Whoever you are, we too lie in drifts at your feet.
(*LG*, 256 : 67–71)

If the "you" of the penultimate line refers to God, the protagonist's ability to merge with nature depends in this poem on the introduction of a transcendent Deity, a concept not usual in the earlier Whitman.[23] If it refers to the reader, as at least one critic thinks,[24] it is even more unusual, because nowhere else does Whitman assume such a self-deprecatory tone when addressing his reader. If the "you" still refers to the observing, mocking part of the self, as I believe it does, that self has become endowed with frightening superiority and remoteness. Regardless of the reading, the sense of estrangement stays. It has only been juxtaposed with the loving contact achieved with the humble "sea-drift." No sense of power or exhilaration accompanies this success of consciousness in incorporating a wholly passive, impotent world. Rather, the love relationship functions as a defense mechanism against the destructive feeling of isolation. Thus the poem's essential two-part pattern moves from the *de profundis* of self-doubt through the rising tide as the "I" attempts to transcend personal misery and to embrace if only the lowest aspects of reality. The poem incorporates in its structure the law of the tide of which it speaks. Like "Out of the Cradle," it too acts out what it says.

"Song of Myself," "Out of the Cradle," and "As I Ebb'd" are all organized by the movement of the speaker's consciousness outward to absorb "the other," whatever concrete form "the other" may for the moment take. It is important to realize that the direction of the movement remains the same while the mood in which the journey is undertaken may range from the near-arrogance of "Song of Myself," a parade of the self's prowess, to the defensive urgency of "Of the Terrible Doubt of Appearances" or "As I Ebb'd." In these two poems establishing the love contact, reaching the moment of identification with an aspect of "the other," becomes imperative for security or even for self-preservation. Thus, it is essentially a love impulse which lends shape to the central part of Whitman's poetry. For the essential Whitman, as Howard Waskow has extensively shown, is "above all a blender." "Standing at a position between removal from the past and involvement in it, between a stance as observer and a stance as experiencer,"[25] he mediates between consciousness and reality, mind and matter, spirit and body, past and future.

The best metaphorical rendition of that formula is offered by Whitman himself in a short poem first published in the *London Broadway Magazine*:[26]

> A noiseless patient spider,
> I mark'd where on a little promontory it stood isolated,
> Mark'd how to explore the vacant vast surrounding,
> It launch'd forth filament, filament, filament, out of itself,
> Ever unreeling them, ever tirelessly speeding them.

And you O my soul where you stand,
Surrounded, detached, in measureless oceans of space,
Ceaselessly musing, venturing, throwing, seeking the spheres to
connect them,
Till the bridge you will need be form'd, till the ductile anchor
hold,
Till the gossamer thread you fling catch somewhere, O my soul.
("A Noiseless Patient Spider," *LG*, 450)

The poem consists of but two stanzas, each describing a different creator, linked on the basis of analogy by the correlative "and." The relational correspondence is stressed by the equal number of lines in both stanzas, by the syntactic similarities in the extensive use of repetitions, and by the echoing present participles. In the second stanza the lines are longer, as if less assured, when the simple activity of the spider that "launch'd forth filament, filament, filament, out of itself" is juxtaposed with the more complex effort of the soul "ceaselessly musing, venturing, throwing, seeking the spheres to connect them," yet the analogy holds. The poem itself is a filament connecting the creating soul to the spinning spider, strong enough to make us accept analogy as equivalence.

The soul, "detached" in the "measureless oceans of space," makes bridges, throws anchors "till the thread catch somewhere," and in the process both grows in an orderly way and defends itself against immense, frightening loneliness. Whitman avoids insisting on the conquering, subsuming role of consciousness by treating the law of creativity as identical for the soul and the spider. For both, spinning the web of connections means growth in power as well as a means of survival. As the spider's activity is inseparable from his life and inherent in his nature, so is the soul's "seeking the spheres to connect them." Thus equating the biological creativity of the spider with the imaginative creativity of the "soul," the poem sees the mind as participating in the central natural process. And relations of equivalence are still possible for Whitman as the mind discovers its place within the life of nature.[27]

The active role of consciousness consists in traveling to the discovery of the mind's identity with "the other." When the needed bridge is built and the thread thrown, the vision of underlying unity comes as revelation. As consciousness embarks on its "connecting" mission, the poem incorporates the journey. The voyage can be made in different moods. In "Song of Myself" and "Passage to India" it is pervaded with the exultant sense of proselytizing for a new faith. In "Out of the Cradle" it becomes a healing pilgrimage at the end of which the lost balance is restored. It is a desperate dash for self-preservation in "As I Ebb'd" and a poignantly resigned journey in "Prayer of Columbus," in which the protagonist feels so absolutely estranged that he can no longer rely for contact on this world but must turn for sympathy to the traditional and transcendent God.

About a year after Whitman first published "A Noiseless Patient Spider," Emily Dickinson employed the same image in her own poem on the nature of creativity:[28]

> A Spider sewed at Night
> Without a Light
> Upon an Arc of White.
>
> If Ruff it was of Dame
> Or Shroud of Gnome
> Himself himself inform.
>
> Of Immortality
> His Strategy
> Was Physiognomy.
>
> (1138)

Like the poem by Whitman, this one is structured by analogy, but instead of there being a symmetrical relation between the referent and analogue, the poem's divisions are asymmetrical. Two stanzas are given to the activity of the spider and only one to the analogue—immortality. The two parts are not linked in any way, the sudden "leap" stressing the arbitrary character of the association. The analogy is further undercut by the fact that the speaker remains outside the poem; even as she makes the associative connection, she admits to ignorance. In Whitman's poem the speaker observes the spider and then relates directly to it, the crossing of the distance emphasized by the shift from the narrative past to the present tense. Here the speaker recollects having watched the spider and having related him to immortality. The preservation of the past tense in the third stanza, "Of Immortality / His Strategy / *Was* Physiognomy," carefully disclaims the validity of the analogy as a general law; rather, it gives it the status of a temporary proposition, valid only for the recollected moment. The analogy is also qualified by the speaker's bewildered preoccupation with mystery and by the explicit statement of her own ignorance of the nature of the spider's (and so of immortality's) work. The relationship of likeness established in the poem turns out to rely on mystery. Ultimately, nothing can be said about the essential nature of either of the creative agents. Only outward manifestations can be observed. Consistently, the poem devotes two of its three stanzas to describing the spider's work. In doing so the *creatio ex nihilo* situation is stressed: the spider works in darkness, without external light of any sort, upon the inscrutable whiteness of the "Arc" of reality, according to the design known only to himself. Thus what Dickinson sees in the spider's work is almost directly opposed to Whitman's vision of the soul forming bridges and throwing anchors to reach "somewhere" beyond itself. This poem emphasizes the absolute self-sufficiency of the creator, be he spider, God, or, by implication, the maker of the poem. It is his inscrutable autonomy that makes him divine.

No claim is made, however, that the spider and "Immortality" work by identical law. The use of the word "Physiognomy" effectively prevents analogy from becoming identity. Physiognomy is the art of reading the inner character from external features or, simply, a set of such features. A guaranteed reading depends on who the physiognomist is—the spider or the speaker of the poem. If it is the spider, only faith can assure that he knows the secret correctly (and faith is reserved by Dickinson for special occasions, as discussed in the previous chapter). If it is the speaker, which seems more likely, she herself puts emphasis on mystery and ultimately admits to ignorance. The mystery of the creative essence cannot be penetrated by even the most careful attention to its outward manifestations. The poem questions, in fact, its own method and undercuts its own major device. Its world consists of three hermetic realms: the realm of nature as it is represented by the spider; the realm of God, only to be inferred from its natural "Physiognomy"; and the realm of the human mind whose work the poem demonstrates. All three agents create, but the only process we come to know is the associative, ordering work of the human intellect.

In Dickinson's vision, the stress on the effort of consciousness to reach out and embrace "the other" is replaced by the insistence on the mind's self-sufficiency and its God-like power of *creatio ex nihilo.* The same fascination with the mind's autonomy can be illustrated by "This is a Blossom of the Brain" (945), "I Never Saw a Moor" (1052), "To make a prairie" (1755) and, perhaps best of all, by this poem:

I reckon—when I count at all—
First—Poets—Then the Sun—
Then Summer—Then the Heaven of God—
And then—the List is done—

But, looking back—the First so seems
To Comprehend the Whole—
The Others look a needless Show—
So I write—Poets—All—

Their Summer—lasts a Solid Year—
They can afford a Sun
The East—would deem extravagant—
And if the Further Heaven—

Be Beautiful as they prepare
For Those who worship Them—
It is too difficult a Grace—
To justify the Dream—

(569)

More directly than the spider poem, this one juxtaposes the three separate domains of nature, of God, and of poets. The speaker begins with the reservation that ordinarily she is reluctant to compare them at all. The remark, coming as it does before "the ranking," emphasizes the distinct character of the provinces brought together. In "the ranking" the poets come first because their creation can be the most satisfying in human terms, more permanent than the transitory perfections of nature, more accessible than "the Heaven of God" which seems "too difficult a Grace— / To justify the Dream—."[29]

The note of rivalry, detectable in this poem between the poet and the other two creators, nature and God, is more obvious in others. Competition with nature is the explicit subject of the lighthearted poem 308 and the theme of the more serious "Of Bronze—and Blaze—" (290),[30] and it can be inferred from a whole series of late poems on sunset (1609, 1622, 1642, 1650, 1676, 1693). Dickinson never believes that her province is identical with or an extension of the province of nature. On the contrary, the different grounds and terms in which nature and the artist work are always kept in view. The day's sunset was "ampler" but "Mine—is the more convenient / to Carry in the Hand" is her lighthearted distinction (308). In a more reflective mood, she juxtaposes the cosmic, inhuman splendors of an aurora borealis with the more limited but equally unique "competeless show" of her art.

Always insisting on her own terms, Dickinson emphasizes the active, commanding power of consciousness in its domain. Nowhere is this idea expressed more beautifully than in the lovely, balladic poem 520:

> I started Early—Took my Dog—
> And visited the Sea—
> The Mermaids in the Basement
> Came out to look at me—
>
> And Frigates—in the Upper Floor
> Extended Hempen Hands—
> Presuming Me to be a Mouse—
> Aground—upon the Sands—
>
> But no Man moved Me—till the Tide
> Went past my simple Shoe—
> And past my Apron—and my Belt
> And past my Bodice—too—
>
> And made as He would eat me up—
> As wholly as a Dew
> Upon a Dandelion's Sleeve—
> And then—I started—too—
>
> And He—He followed—close behind—
> I felt his Silver Heel
> Upon my Ancle—Then my Shoes
> Would overflow with Pearl—
>
> Until We met the Solid Town—
> No One He seemed to know—
> And bowing—with a Mighty look—
> At me—The Sea withdrew—

Whatever happened, and it is one of Dickinson's favorite techniques to blur the details of "the story" and deal only with what really matters to her—its psychic significance,[31] the experience started as something menacing. The narrator casually, perhaps ignorantly, challenged a vast elemental force. The sea is Dickinson's usual image for the unknown, exhilarating but dangerous. As early as 1850 she wrote to Abiah Root: "The shore is safer, Abiah, but I love to buffet the sea—I can count the bitter wrecks in these pleasant waters, and hear the murmuring winds, but oh, I love the danger!" (*L*, 1:104).[32] The effectiveness of the symbol, whether the force challenged was love, death, or some other power, lies largely in its resistance to any close-ended interpretation.[33]

Encroaching upon "the Sea's" territory, the speaker is reduced to "a Dew upon a Dandelion's Sleeve," the image conveying not only the disproportion between the forces of the opponents but also the fact that "the Sea" recognizes its own element, its own "wildness" in the speaker, and threatens self-destruction by appealing to it. She, however, rejects the confrontation on the sea's territory. Retiring to her own ground of "Solid Town" where the sea appears a complete stranger, she manages to reverse the situation. As soon as the initiative belongs to her, the experience loses its menacing aspect and the sea becomes a docile companion, finally withdrawing with a courteous, "civilized" gesture. "Shifting grounds," insisting on meeting experience on the artist's terms is, I find, Dickinson's key strategy (see Chapter 4). As the "Mighty look" sent by the sea at parting indicates, the speaker's triumph in this poem is by no means final. It is an achievement in a single confrontation (i.e., a single poem) and more encounters must be expected.

A somewhat similar mechanism of surviving in a critical confrontation is suggested in poem 1733, where the speaker is saved from giving in to "awe" by intellectually grasping her predicament:

> No man saw awe, nor to his house
> Admitted he a man
> Though by his awful residence
> Has human nature been.
>
> Not deeming of his dread abode
> Till laboring to flee
> A grasp on comprehension laid
> Detained vitality.

It is a narrow escape and mere survival must count as success. That Dickinson can treat such a hairbreadth escape as next to victory is only possible through her clear realization of how insufficient are the powers of the human mind and what formidable opponents they have to deal with. Her reverence for "awe" only increases her loyalty to the mind coping as best it can with forces vastly surpassing its compass.

Dickinson remains acutely aware of the limited possibilities of cognition. She frequently asks what can be known, and the answers are usually not very encouraging. Yet she recognizes the psychic need for holistic knowledge. The paradoxical plight of the mind yearning for comprehensiveness and certainty, but equipped with tools glaringly inadequate to the ambition, is the theme of poem 1602:

> Pursuing you in your transitions,
> In other Motes—
> Of other Myths
> Your requisition be.
> The Prism never held the Hues,
> It only heard them play—

At the urge of some imperative specified only as "you" (God perhaps, or the inner need, or some unifying principle, unidentified but intuited),[34] man keeps following what he presumes is a whole, as opposed to "mote," and solid fact, as opposed to myth, in the evidence which is both fragmentary and esoteric. Not only are the data insufficient; the urge to pursue "other Motes—of other Myths" may very likely be a false clue, for the phrase involves the gospel reproach of "And why beholdest thou the mote that is in thy brother's eye but considerest not the beam that is in thine own eye?" (Matt. 7 : 3) with its implication that the most substantial material for investigation can be found within the self. The more so since "the prism" of consciousness, incapable of synthesis, can only break experience into components. To concatenate the image, in the process of perception the perceived material becomes transposed into altogether different categories: "the prism" cannot actually "see" the light it analyzes; it "hears" it instead.[35]

Other related puzzles of cognition are the subject of the grimly humorous "Split the Lark—and you'll find the Music—" (861). The sceptic in the poem sets out to find the source of the bird's song but succeeds only in turning the live creature into "gushes of blood." The mystery of life and creativity escapes him; it cannot be located through the "scarlet experiment" of dissection and cannot be comprehended through a scientifically rational approach. In both poems the whole appears not only greater than the sum of its parts but also as different in kind as light is from sound, or the lark's song from its bleeding flesh.

In the world of Emily Dickinson it is impossible to claim that "He ahold of my hand has completely satisfied me" ("Of the Terrible Doubt of Appearances," *LG*, 120 : 16) because "he" can neither be reached nor fully admitted into the mysteries of the self:

> I had not minded—Walls—
> Were Universe—one Rock—
> And far I heard his silver Call
> The other side the Block—
>
> I'd tunnel—till my Groove
> Pushed sudden thro' to his—
> Then my face take her Recompense—
> The looking in his Eyes—
>
> But 'tis a single Hair—
> A filament—a law—
> A Cobweb—wove in Adamant—
> A Battlement—of Straw—
>
> A limit like the Vail
> Unto the Lady's face—
> But every Mesh—a Citadel—
> And Dragons—in the Crease—
>
> (398)

The poem is organized by syllogism. All the images in the major premise point to monolithic structures (one rock), corresponding desires (her tunneling answered by his silver call), and definite directions in which to act (tunnel, pushed thro'). In such reality a happy ending comes as a natural reward of persistent effort. When the partners come together, their physical closeness is accompanied by spiritual communion, eyes being "windows of the soul." In the kind of reality presented in the minor premise, however, the solid qualities of universe are altogether absent. Instead, reality appears infinitely elusive—a hair, a filament, a cobweb—but also infinitely forbidding—a law, a battlement, a citadel. Its nature is incongruity and paradox—"A Cobweb—wove in Adamant," "A Battlement—of Straw," "every Mesh—a Citadel." In this reality no action can be effective, no silver call heard while all sense of direction is lost. Tunneling a straight groove was a course of action adequate when dealing with the solidity of the rock, but there seems to be no efficient way of getting past the uncountable mesh-citadels. The speaker's confidence and resourcefulness are gone. She hides behind the conventional feminine role of a "beauty in distress" relying on her "knight" for deliverance. Yet while in the solid universe of the rock he cooperated with the "silver Call," in the complex reality of cobwebs wove in adamant no signal comes from him, no meeting of the eyes is possible.

Emily Dickinson knows about the elusive nature of reality and about the insufficiency of methods and tools of perception; she knows too that there is practically no possibility of breaking out of the magic enclosure of the self. However, giving up the claim that reality can be directly apprehended, she manages to convert the severe limitation into the chief asset of consciousness. She sets out to find out about life in her own "slant" way, through investigation of the inner world. The "properties" of consciousness and its "adequacy" must do as the basis of whatever certain knowledge is accessible to man:

This Consciousness that is aware
Of Neighbors and the Sun
Will be the one aware of Death
And that itself alone

Is traversing the interval
Experience between
And most profound experiment
Appointed unto Men—

How adequate unto itself
It's properties shall be
Itself unto itself and none
Shall make discovery.

Adventure most unto itself
The Soul condemned to be—

Attended by a single Hound
It's own identity.

(822)

This poem, dated by Thomas Johnson as c. 1864, was written by the mature artist at the height of her creative powers with an already confirmed view of her vocation and as clear an idea of what she was trying to do as she would ever have. The proposition that "Adventure most unto itself / The Soul condemned to be" comes, on the one hand, as a conclusion to her recognition of the limited scope and illusory certainty of all knowledge directed outward. On the other hand, it results from the conviction that the way consciousness deals with the overwhelming forces of chaos and the unknown is the only measure of the heroic stature of the self.

In his excellent essay on Emily Dickinson, Denis Donoghue penetratingly observes that "it might be almost said that Emily Dickinson did not suffer loneliness; she commanded it. She commanded everything she needed. When she needed a relationship she commanded it."[36] Donoghue's observation offers a key to Dickinson's poetry. Her starting point is the refusal to take life, nature, even God, on their own terms, so that poems become a continuous struggle to make experience meet the poet on her grounds. The opponent is always powerful:

I took my Power in my Hand—
And went against the World—
'Twas not so much as David—had—
But I—was twice as bold—

I aimed my Pebble—but Myself
Was all the one that fell—
Was it Goliah—was too large—
Or was myself—too small?

(540)

Not recognized as one of her best, this poem is nevertheless an explanation of the core of her poetry: poems are battles between the poet and those larger powers against which creativity measures itself in order to make an experience meaningful. Humanly speaking, in so many instances the battle has been lost: love remains unfulfilled; God and nature, inaccessible; pain and death, unvanquished. However, it is not the human failure which counts, nor even the heroic willingness to fight and risk defeat, though the constant endeavor is the basic principle of life. The most important result is the poem which has crystallized in the struggle to testify to a larger triumph founded on the mind's ability to endure the experience and order it.

While Dickinson celebrates the imaginative possibilities of the mind, she also insists on the necessity of an intense emotional life as the condition for the mind's activity. The emphasis on the mastering function of consciousness in its confrontation with the intensity of experience incurs something which I call psychological violence. Consciousness needs to be tested constantly for power and endurance in situations of extreme tension. It is in the moments of trial that poetry is made, when consciousness has to rise up to the challenge of the intense moment and cope with it:

> The Frosts were her condition—
> The Tyrian would not come—
> Until the North—invoke it—
>
> (442)

The purple beauty of the poem will not blossom until forced by the severity of circumstances. Quite suitably too, the exotic "Tyrian" is also the color of martyrdom. The authority of the poem is the authority of heroic consciousness resisting overwhelming experience.

The triumph of shaping consciousness over chaotic experience requires that always new violent moments (real or imaginary) be mastered in new poems; yet in a different order, no less logically and truly, a poem becomes an act of psychic salvation in crisis (see 755). It is unnecessary and impossible to decide which aspect of Dickinson's art is primary. The circle closes. A poem is both salvation and an act of defiance of all those forces that threaten to subdue awareness, to render it inactive or inarticulate, that is, to render it nonexistent. Art is treated as order—aesthetic, psychological, and moral:

> The Martyr Poets—did not tell—
> But wrought their Pang in syllable—
> That when their mortal name be numb—
> Their mortal fate—encourage Some—
> The Martyr Painters—never spoke—

Bequeathing—rather—to their Work—
That when their conscious fingers cease—
Some seek in Art—the Art of Peace—

(544)

By rejecting more immediate reliefs and by dedication to their art, "the poets" and "painters" turn ordinary human suffering into purposeful "martyrdom." This is their personal "designing" achievement. But beyond the "biographical" level, their art has a further moral dimension when the reader can be "encouraged" or can find "peace." Characteristically, no didactic "message" is mentioned. The message, one suspects, is unimportant; what really matters is the work of "conscious fingers," the triumph of skill and order.[37] Thus, one could almost say, technique replaces revelation.

Dickinson's poems about the creative process are full of images of effort and conscious craft: a gymnast wrestles with an angel until he proves stronger than God (59), essential oils of poetry are wrung from the raw material of emotions symbolized by the rose (675), the poet distills amazing sense from ordinary meanings (448), or he becomes a blacksmith beating the "vivid ore" of language and experience into the "designated light" of the poem:

Dare you see a Soul *at the White Heat*?
Then crouch within the door—
Red—is the Fire's common tint—
But when the vivid Ore
Has vanquished Flame's conditions,
It quivers from the Forge
Without a color, but the light
Of unanointed Blaze.
Least Village has it's Blacksmith
Whose Anvil's even ring
Stands symbol for the finer Forge
That soundless tugs—within—
Refining these impatient Ores
With Hammer, and with Blaze
Until the Designated Light
Repudiate the Forge—

(365)

The introductory question, invitation, takes the reader to the doorstep of a village forge to watch the making of the "Designated

Light." The poem ends when the product, ready to "Repudiate the Forge," acquires an autonomous existence. The poem clearly falls into two parts, each presenting a distinct stage in the making of the final product. The first part contrasts the ordinary "red tint" of the flames with the "White Heat" prevailing at the moment in the soul (forge). It is important to observe that the "White Heat" is not a given or accidental condition; it has been striven for, as the word "vanquished" suggests. In the striking phrase "when the vivid Ore / Has vanquished Flame's conditions," the causality of "White Heat" is reversed. Instead of appearing a passive outcome of the "Flame's conditions," the "White Heat" is presented as a triumph of the "vivid Ore"—sensibility subsuming and intensifying common circumstances. Action and effort have been put into achieving the state of "unanointed Blaze." Only at that point does the blacksmith appear. His delayed entrée moves what happened earlier into the background as but a preliminary process. The blacksmith applies his skill: he works "with Hammer" and "with Blaze" and the two combine to produce the "Designated Light."

The poem depends for its central meaning upon the juxtaposition of the two products of the two stages in the process: the "unanointed Blaze" and the "Designated Light." Both are imaged as light, but "Blaze" suggests elemental qualities of energy: violent outburst, bright display, glow of color. "Light," in turn, suggests clarity and vision. Light makes sight possible; it implies the state of being visible or revealed (as in the expression "bring to light"). Finally, light is illumination, also divine illumination or revelation. "Unanointed" means first of all unsanctified, but also not chosen, unmarked, not even distinct (as it is still confined to the forge). "Designated," on the other hand, suggests in the first place that it is specified, but also appointed (for a purpose), marked, distinct, and defined. The stage of "unanointed Blaze" requires effort but no craftsmanship; the "Designated Light" needs the skill of the blacksmith. The one belongs within "the Forge"; the other, finally, becomes independent of it.

The essential difference between "unanointed Blaze" and "Designated Light" seems to be one between sensibility and art. The first transforms common circumstances, intensifying their ordinary qualities; the second comes into being when craft is applied to the raw energy of the first. Interestingly enough, both demand active effort. Throughout the poem the pattern of exertion obtains: first, the strain to "vanquish" the common condition, then the labor "with Hammer" to give heightened emotions the "Designated" quality.

The poem makes it clear that in the final count, art, for Dickinson, consists in conscious craft. It is through technique that experience can be shaped and put at a distance so that, eventually, it "repudiates the forge." It is also technique that makes vision possible. More explicitly than in poem 544, art here equals making one's own light, as it were, constructing revelations.

Even when, like Emerson, Dickinson associates creativity with a visionary moment, her revelation comes in terms of the release of energy through intellectual ordering:

> The Thought is quiet as a Flake—
> A Crash without a Sound,
> How Life's reverberation
> It's Explanation found—
>
> (1581)

"Life's reverberation," the response to experience, must be "explained," must be ordered through understanding; this is revelation. The stress is not on the message in the vision but on the vision's shaping effect.

Dickinson emphasizes the active role of consciousness in enforcing patterns of order. Her artist is not a man who "has seen the light" or moves toward it and, therefore, relies through faith on some external gift of knowledge which makes order possible. Her poet is, first of all, a skilled craftsman who can release through aesthetic discipline the accumulated emotional energy, at whatever personal cost. The question of personal cost is never lost sight of. The poet well realizes that the inner force, when activated, is mortally dangerous, while its orderly discharge is imperative for sanity. This psychic risk undertaken willfully to provide the necessary energy potential invests Dickinson's poetry with an aura of violent intensity. Ruth Miller points out that Dickinson treats her poetry "as a means of release."[38] This seems to be the idea behind what she wrote Higginson: "I had a terror since September—I could tell to none—and so I sing, as the Boy does by the Burying Ground—because I am afraid—" (*L*, 2:404, April 25, 1862). And again, not quite two months later: "I felt a palsy, here—the Verses just relieve—" (*L*, 2:408, June 7, 1862).

However, lest Dickinson's poetry be erroneously viewed as the outcome of instinctive activation of defense mechanisms, attention must be paid to the amount of conscious strategy that went with her into ensuring the constant supply of emotional energy—"the ore" of art. In "Dare you see a Soul at the White Heat?" she presents the initial stage of achieving inner intensity as the result of an active effort. Similarly, the narrator of "I Years had been from Home" (609) seems to have fled from the doorstep not exclusively in fear of the anticipated confrontation but, first of all, in a strategic attempt to protect the emotional intensity inherent in yearning.[39] Some poems deal with situations in which desire, hunger, or craving has been satisfied but in which there is no exhilaration in consummation. Satiety removes emotional intensity needed to challenge intellectual powers (see, for example, 439, 579). Unfulfillment and failure, as Richard Wilbur has beautifully shown,[40] enlarge consciousness:

> Good, without alarm
> Is a too established Fortune—
> Danger—deepens Sum—
>
> (807)

Energy is equally crucial for Whitman, but with him there is no sense of separation between "the sheen" and "the disk" (1550), that is, between the energy principle and the shaping principle. Ideally, there is no division of consciousness into sensibility and intellect; when it occurs, as in "As I Ebb'd with the Ocean of Life," the speaker senses that he is in trouble. What is even more important, Whitman gives initiative not to the intellectual, critical "I" but to the emphatic self, denouncing the dispassionate observer. The emphatic consciousness provides in Whitman both energy and order because it is the energy of reaching out to "the other" with an inbuilt sense of direction. It constantly pushes outward to a moment when the self becomes united with the divine essence in any of its manifestations. To realize the fundamental unity of each and all—men, creatures, and objects—is the ultimate triumph of consciousness on its journey.

The essence and meaning of all life are telescoped into a single moment when such a vision has been obtained. The poet straddles, exultant, the Cartesian abyss. Emerson's entry in the journal for October 28, 1835, provides a theoretical statement of the nature of Whitman's quest: "Man stands on the point betwixt the inward spirit and the outward matter. He sees that one explains, translates the other: that the world is the mirror of the soul. He is the priest and interpreter of nature thereby" (*J*, 5:103). And Whitman echoes in the *1847 Notebook*:

> I am the poet of the body
> And I am the poet of the soul
> I go with the slaves of the earth equally with the masters
> And I will stand between the masters and the slaves,
> Entering into both, so that both shall understand me alike.
>
> (*UPP*, 2:69)

In the 1891 annex to *Leaves of Grass* ("Good-bye My Fancy"), Whitman restored to life a poem originally published in the Centennial Edition of 1876 but excluded from the 1881 *Leaves of Grass* which thus, at the end of his life, again expresses the conviction that the true poet is first of all a "blender" and "uniter":

> When the full-grown poet came,
> Out spake pleased Nature (the round impassive globe, with all its shows of day and night,) saying, *He is mine*;
> But out spake too the Soul of man, proud, jealous and unreconciled, *Nay, he is mine alone*;
> —Then the full-grown poet stood between the two, and took each by the hand;
> And to-day and ever so stands, as blender, uniter, tightly holding hands,
> Which he will never release until he reconciles the two,
> And wholly and joyously blends them.
>
> ("When the Full-grown Poet Came," *LG*, 550)

The journey which Whitman embarks upon is not to establish the dominion of mind over experience but to mediate between the two. When consciousness and nature operate by the same law, the question of whether the order man sees in the universe is of the mind or of nature can be left unanswered. As in "A Noiseless Patient Spider," the important thing is that the filament of the poem provides the needed bridge.

The nature of creativity and the character of the artist's work are ambivalent in Whitman. Whether what the poet does is transposition or only transcription of "natural" order is kept deliberately indistinct. Tracing Whitman's development from early mysticism to increasing awareness of form, Roger Asselineau finds that the poet could write within the same year, 1871, that is, quite late in his creative period: "In these *Leaves* everything is literally photographed. Nothing is poetized, no divergence, not a step, not an inch, nothing for beauty's sake, no euphemism, no rhyme." And, on the other hand: "(No useless attempt to repeat the material creation by daguerreotyping the exact likeness by mortal mental means."[41]

This contradictory view of the nature of poetic composition resulted in the posture of "spontaneity imitator," to use Paul Zweig's apt phrase.[42] Whitman himself told Traubel that "the style is to have no style" (Traubel, 1 : 105). Mistrusting art as artificiality, the poet constantly undercut the controlling, designing aspect of composition, striving for the effect of artless transcription:

> In spite of his growing respect for art, all discipline seemed to him a useless constraint and any convention a dangerous artifice which risked raising a barrier between his thought and the reader. To art he opposed what he called simplicity, that is to say, strict adherence to nature. . . . In fact, of course, he had to transpose, but he was not any less convinced that he had remained completely faithful to nature.[43]

The purpose of Whitman's poetic quest, then, is to make a discovery,[44] a phrase which conveys well the mediating, active-passive role that becomes assigned to poetic consciousness. By comparison, for Dickinson the effort of consciousness establishes an "ennobling" order where no inherent order can be discovered, only an energy potential:

> For Pattern is the Mind bestowed
> That imitating her

Our most ignoble Services
Exhibit worthier.

(1223)

Charles Feidelson, who has already called Ahab and Ishmael artist figures, has associated Whitman with Ahab;[45] I have compared Dickinson to Ishmael.[46] The relation between Ahab and Ishmael may serve as a further illustration of the attitudes underlying the work of both poets. Whitman is like Ahab in that his art is a pursuit of the cosmic unity of life. To touch "the other," name it, and declare it one with the idea in mind is his poem-journey's purpose. Notwithstanding the buoyant self-assurance of his early years, the attempt to reach with art beyond art presented considerable risks—for example, the necessity to reject the questioning self demonstrated in "As I Ebb'd with the Ocean of Life." It had some embarrassing consequences too. When Mrs. Gilchrist, encouraged perhaps by the poet's insistence that "Who touches this touches a man" (*LG*, 505 : 54),[47] decided that her love for the book really belonged to its author, Whitman responded: "Dear friend, let me warn you somewhat about myself—and yourself also. You must not construct such an unauthorized and imaginary ideal Figure, and call it W.W. and so devotedly invest your loving nature in it. The actual W.W. is a very plain personage, and entirely unworthy such devotion" (*C*, 2 : 170). Obviously, the man and the persona of the book did not stay one, even if they came close to perfect unity when the poems were being written.

Even more poignantly, in the long run, Whitman's insistence on using poetry as a sort of Brooklyn Ferry made art excessively dependent on circumstantial reality. Paradoxically, the more successful the poem was as a connective, the more limited was its autonomy as a work of art. In the poet's later years, when nature painfully curbed his pride in exuberant health, when he was beaten by critical opinion and largely ignored by the public, he must have felt bitterly that there was little use any more for his mediating art, that the connections he had established no longer held, and that reality was bypassing him as well as his poems. "Also it must be carefully remember'd," he wrote in "A Backward Glance O'er Travel'd Roads," "that first-class literature does not shine by any luminosity of its own; nor do its poems. They grow out of circumstances, and are evolutionary. The actual living light is always curiously from elsewhere—follows unaccountable sources, and is lunar and relative at the best" (*LG*, 565 : 126–29).[48] This indeed is the end of the Pequod's journey; this is the admission that art powered by a desire to reach beyond itself will finally lose autonomy and will depend upon accidental circumstances for its worth.

Dickinson is the poet—Ishmael, who has questioned all truths and found them but momentary and subjective. There are no certainties for Dickinson, as there are none for Ishmael. Instead, both proceed "to tell the tale" in order to survive. Art alone must become man's and its own salvation. For Dickinson, the artist's consciousness is neither fluctuating nor enveloping; it never yields passively to an external principle. Despite its limitations, it is central, radiating its own meanings:

> The Poets light but Lamps—
> Themselves—go out—
> The Wicks they stimulate—
> If vital Light
>
> Inhere as do the Suns—
> Each Age a Lens
> Disseminating their
> Circumference—
>
> (883)[49]

A poem is not a connecting filament, its existence instrumental and relative. As "Costumeless Consciousness" incorporating the victory of the poet's mind and skill over accidental circumstances of her life, it stays a central existence in its own right, far superior to the human life of its maker.

Notes

1. Geoffrey Hartman, "Romanticism and Anti-Self-Consciousness," in *Beyond Formalism: Literary Essays, 1958–1970* (New Haven: Yale University Press, 1970), 307.

2. I use the term "consciousness" rather than "imagination" first of all

because neither Whitman nor Dickinson speaks much of imagination. Whitman's word is most often "spirit" or "soul" (in the last annex to *Leaves of Grass*, it is "fancy"); Dickinson's words are "consciousness," "mind," or "soul." Whitman's terms bear strong religious connotations and seem closer to Emerson's "Oversoul" or even to Bergson's "l'élan vital" (see Gay Wilson Allen, *The Solitary Singer: A Critical Biography of Walt Whitman*, rev. ed. [New York: New York University Press, 1967], 359), while Dickinson's "Transcendent consciousness" (John F. Lynen's formulation in "Three Uses of the Present: The Historian's, the Critic's, and Emily Dickinson's," *College English* 28 [November 1966]: 126–36) is more clearly related to imagination. Both poets, however, associate creativity with their respective terms.

3. The poem was first published untitled and unsectioned in the 1855 *Leaves of Grass*. In 1856 it was given the title "Poem of Walt Whitman, an American." In the 1860 and succeeding editions of *Leaves of Grass*, it was simply called "Walt Whitman" and became "Song of Myself" in 1881. Revisions were made throughout until 1881 but they cannot be considered fundamental.

4. Malcolm Cowley, ed., Introduction to *Walt Whitman: Leaves of Grass* (1855; reprint, New York: Viking Press, 1959). Cowley's Introduction is also reprinted in Francis Murphy, ed., *Walt Whitman* (Harmondsworth: Penguin Critical Anthologies, 1969), 347–48.

5. V. K. Chari, *Whitman in the Light of Vedantic Mysticism* (Lincoln, Nebr.: University of Nebraska Press, 1964), 121–27.

6. For discussion of the spiral figure as "the heart of Emerson's aesthetics," see Vivian C. Hopkins, *Spires of Form: A Study of Emerson's Aesthetic Theory* (Cambridge, Mass.: Harvard University Press, 1951).

7. See Gay Wilson Allen, "The Long Journey Motif," in *Walt Whitman as Man, Poet, and Legend: With a Check List of Whitman Publications, 1945–1960* (Carbondale, Ill.: Southern Illinois University Press, 1961), 62–83.

8. Also, Roy Harvey Pearce maintains that "the argument of the poem centers on points of psychic intensity," *The Continuity of American Poetry* (Princeton: Princeton University Press, 1961), 74–75.

9. Moreover, Sections One through Four announce the main themes of the poem very much like the argument of the traditional epic, which the poem also evokes with the characteristic opening "I celebrate . . ." "I sing . . ."

10. See Carl Strauch, "The Structure of Walt Whitman's Song of Myself," *English Journal* 27 (September 1938): 597–607; reprinted in James E. Miller, Jr., ed., *Whitman's Song of Myself—Origin, Growth, Meaning* (New York: Dodd, Mead, 1964).

11. I use the term as defined by Paul Fussell in "Whitman's Curious Warble: Reminiscence and Reconciliation," in Richard Warrington Baldwin Lewis, ed., *The Presence of Walt Whitman* (New York: Columbia University Press, 1962), where the American Shore Ode "is a lyric of some length and philosophic density spoken (usually at a specific place) on an American

beach; its theme tends to encompass the relationship of the wholeness and flux of the sea to the discreteness and fixity of land objects" (31).

12. "Out of the Cradle" and "As I Ebb'd" were published within a few months of each other. "Out of the Cradle" appeared in the Christmas (December 24, 1859) edition of the *New York Saturday Press*. "As I Ebb'd" was printed in the *Atlantic Monthly* for April 1860. Both were finally revised for the 1881 edition of *Leaves of Grass* and were there given their present positions.

13. In my discussion of "Out of the Cradle" I am most indebted to Armin Paul Frank's excellent paper "The Long Withdrawing Roar: Eighty Years of the Ocean's Message in American Poetry," first read at a poetry symposium at the University of Wuppertal in November 1978 and published in Winfried Fluck, Jürgen Peper, and Willi Paul Adams, eds., *Forms and Functions of History in American Literature: Essays in Honor of Ursula Brumm* (Berlin: Erich Schmidt Verlag, 1981). Other notable discussions of the poem include Leo Spitzer's "Explication de Texte Applied to Walt Whitman's Poem 'Out of the Cradle Endlessly Rocking,'" *Journal of English Literary History* 16 (September 1949): 229–49; Richard Chase's "Out of the Cradle as a Romance" and Fussell's "Whitman's Curious Warble," both in Lewis, *The Presence of Walt Whitman*, 52–71 and 28–51, respectively. See also Robert D. Faner, *Walt Whitman and Opera* (Philadelphia: University of Pennsylvania Press, 1951).

14. This was the poem's title in the 1860 and 1867 editions of *Leaves of Grass*.

15. See also Howard Waskow, *Whitman: Explorations in Form* (Chicago: University of Chicago Press, 1966), chap. 5.

16. Frank, "The Long Withdrawing Roar," 80.

17. This is also Armin Frank's observation.

18. The poems, of course, share more than just the overall pattern. They are usually regarded as resulting from the emotional crisis which the poet experienced around 1859. But, as Howard Waskow points out in *Whitman: Explorations in Form*, note on p. 124, the vision in "The Sleepers" published in 1855 is equally "crowded with fear and death" (124n).

19. In 1859, when the poem was most likely written, Whitman was out of a job, uncertain about either his poetic or his journalistic career, and, most probably, going through a personal crisis whose exact nature remains a mystery (see Allen, *Solitary Singer*, 216, 246).

20. See, e.g., "Specimen Days," "Paumanok, My Life on It as a Child and Young Man": "Here, and all along the island and its shores, I spent intervals many years, all seasons, sometimes riding, sometimes boating, but generally afoot (I was always a good walker) absorbing fields, shores, marine incidents, characters, the bay-men, farmers, pilots . . . went every summer on sailing trips—always liked the bare sea-beach, south side, and have some of my happiest hours on it to this day" (*PW*, 1:12).

21. I find Howard Waskow's reading of this section as reporting no seizure by "a sense of his [Whitman's] own pettiness" (*Whitman: Explorations in Form*, 204) unconvincing. The tone of desolation sounds clearly from the very beginning of the poem. It deepens rather than "shifts" in the first part.

22. Harold Blodgett and Sculley Bradley, editors of the Comprehensive Reader's Edition of *Leaves of Grass* (New York: New York University Press, 1965), point to this particular contrast (255n).

23. However, the last two great poems, "Passage to India" (1871) and "Prayer of Columbus" (1874), are both marked by the speaker's desire for the sanction of divine authority for his work. The God invoked there is clearly a transcendent God.

24. See Waskow, *Whitman: Explorations in Form*, 209.

25. Ibid., 128.

26. October 1868. The poem appeared there as the third of a cluster of five lyrics, all under the single title "Whispers of Heavenly Death." Composed around 1862–63, its earliest version can be found in a Washington notebook for that period. It was considerably different from the one above, as the spider's filament originally expressed the "Calamus" sentiment. The history of the poem's revisions, however, supports the thesis that the drive of Whitman's creativity was a love impulse, possibly first of an erotic nature, then sublimated into an aesthetic principle (see Allen, *The Solitary Singer*, 341–42).

27. Roland Hagenbüchle makes a similar observation in footnote 13 to his article "Precision and Indeterminacy in the Poetry of Emily Dickinson," *Emerson Society Quarterly* 20, no. 1(1974): "In Whitman's work, by contrast, relations of equivalence seem still to be possible. The poet, not unlike the spider, tries to 'connect' the world through his comparisons 'till the ductile anchor . . . hold somewhere.' . . . However, the adverb 'somewhere' points at the element of growing indeterminacy" (53).

28. I am not indicating echoes of Whitman in Dickinson's poems; however, as one reads both poets one becomes aware of coinciding images used with a different symbolic intention (see Dickinson's "grass" poem 333). These images are best treated, it seems, as evidence of "the spirit of the times."

29. Compare a brief discussion of the poem by Charles Anderson in *Emily Dickinson's Poetry: Stairway of Surprise* (New York: Holt, Rinehart and Winston, 1960), 93–94, and a different interpretation by Robert Weisbuch in *Emily Dickinson's Poetry* (Chicago: University of Chicago Press, 1975), 174–75.

30. For an excellent discussion of this poem see Anderson, *Emily Dickinson's Poetry*, 47–54.

31. Weisbuch comments extensively on the scenelessness of Dickinson's poems in *Emily Dickinson's Poetry*, Chaps. 2 and 3.

32. See also poem 249 discussed in Chapter 2.

33. This is also Weisbuch's position: "If we wish to take account of all

the meanings of 'sea' the symbol's definition must become less precise. It is simply the opposite of 'home', the place of risk, or query, of changes of all kinds. It entices the wildness of the spirit to quest" (*Emily Dickinson's Poetry*, 53).

34. The poem was enclosed in a letter to Helen Hunt Jackson written in late September or early October 1884 and, in this context, the "you" referred specifically to Mrs. Jackson. But, as always with Dickinson, the particular situation became so abstracted in the poem that the text virtually demands a generalizing reading.

35. For another comment on the complexities of perception, see poem 1071.

36. Denis Donoghue, *Emily Dickinson*, Pamphlets on American Writers, no. 81 (Minneapolis: University of Minnesota Press, 1969), p. 10.

37. See the introduction to David Higgins's *Portrait of Emily Dickinson: The Poet and Her Prose* (New Brunswick, N.J.: Rutgers University Press, 1967), 113–24, where Higgins convincingly argues that Dickinson's letters, let alone her poems, were conscious compositions often executed over a period of years since she kept "the scrap basket" of choice phrases to be used later according to her need. The argument shows Dickinson as a very conscious craftsman indeed, observing the rigors of composition even in the informal art of letter writing.

38. Ruth Miller, *The Poetry of Emily Dickinson* (Middletown, Conn.: Wesleyan University Press, 1968), 7.

39. See also, e.g., poems 421 and 1413.

40. Richard Wilbur, "Sumptuous Destitution," in *Emily Dickinson: Three Views*, reprinted in Richard Sewall, ed., *Emily Dickinson: A Collection of Critical Essays* (Englewood Cliffs, N.J.: Prentice-Hall, 1963).

41. Roger Asselineau, *The Evolution of Walt Whitman* (Cambridge, Mass.: Harvard University Press, Belknap Press, 1962), 2:220–21. The first quotation is a manuscript fragment, the second comes from "Democratic Vistas" (*PW*, 2:419; 1770–71).

42. Paul Zweig, "Spontaneity Imitator," review of William White, ed., *Walt Whitman: Daybooks and Notebooks*, in the *New York Times Book Review*, April 16, 1978.

43. Asselineau, *The Evolution of Walt Whitman*, 2:220–21.

44. Frank in "The Long Withdrawing Roar" makes the following observation: "Insofar as Whitman, in this poem [i.e., "Out of the Cradle"], gives full due to the physical and material, he is a modern poet. Yet to the extent that for him, wisdom, meaning, order are provided, dispensed by a Natural agent, he is still a Romantic" (83). This view puts Dickinson close to the modernists, an opinion shared, for example, by Denis Donoghue, who brings together Dickinson and Wallace Stevens in his *Connoisseurs of Chaos* (London: Faber, 1965), 60.

45. Charles Feidelson, *Symbolism and American Literature* (Chicago: University of Chicago Press, 1953), 27, 184–86.

46. Agnieszka Salska, "Emily Dickinson's Commanding Consciousness," *Zeszyty Naukowe UL*, 1st ser., no. 20 (1977), 47–55.

47. "So long!" The poem was placed as epilogue to the 1860 edition of *Leaves of Grass*.

48. "A Backward Glance O'er Travell'd Roads" helps one realize how much Dickinson's attitude of consistently uncompromised power was helped or even made possible by her choice not to compete in the public scene. Uninvolved in the general concerns of her times, she could stay independent. Aspiring to be at the center of the major issues of his age, Whitman ended by doubting his art.

49. This poem is dated by Johnson as c. 1864 and by Ralph William Franklin, ed., *The Manuscript Books of Emily Dickinson* (Cambridge, Mass.: Harvard University Press, 1981) as about 1864–65; see also poem 365 discussed earlier in this chapter.

4 / *The Design of Mediation*

In the preceding chapter, I argued that the purpose of Whitman's poetic quest is to discover the mind's identity with "the other." The poem is thus an incorporation of the journey of consciousness toward the unifying vision. I would like now to examine some of the stylistic and structural consequences of such a conception of the poem.

The impulse toward "the expression of future promise, an articulation of imminent fulfilment,"[1] connects the writings of the artists within the orbit of Transcendentalism to the Puritan legacy of "the language of Canaan." The Puritan commitment to the future harmonies of the millennium was, however, articulated within the scriptural frame of reference while the Transcendentalists related man's spiritual regeneration to nature. To demonstrate the mechanism of the transfer in the final chapter of his book, Mason Lowance chose the example of Thoreau, but Whitman is different only in his stress on the city and people rather than on virginal nature. For Whitman, as for Thoreau, the immediate American surroundings provide language and images as well as the frame of reference in which to celebrate the promise of the heroic, self-reliant man in harmony with his world.

In the course of the journey toward revelation, the processes of psychic growth are correlated with the processes observed in nature. Thus, it does not seem appropriate to look in Emerson, and even less in Whitman, for such static use of analogy and symbol as would weld a single image with a single idea into an inseparable complex. In the Transcendental vision isolated images, like isolated moments, are simply not natural equivalents of thought units. They are a necessity caused by the fragmentary nature of human experience and perception. They are but metonymic substitutions for the pursued whole. The essence of the vision being promise, the core of self-reliance being growth to self-fulfillment, the directly correlative aspects of organic (and for Whitman also of social) life are evolution, progress, and metamorphosis. The preference for the catalogue technique must, I believe, be viewed in this context. It allows the stringing and multiplying of images while the unity of the underlying principle is kept intact by an act of faith.

Lawrence Buell sees the catalogue technique as a stylistic device inseparable from the correspondential vision at the roots of the philosophy of Transcendentalism: "The habit of conveying ideas by means of a barrage of linked analogies is distinctly transcendental. It is the end product of transcendentalism's cardinal tenet: that the Oversoul is immanent in all persons and things, which are thereby symbols of spirit and conjoined by analogy in an organic universe."[2] "All thinking is analogizing, and it is the use of life to learn metonymy," says Emerson, or as Buell adds, "the intersubstitution of images for the same principle. Emerson grounds this judgement in the nature of the universe, 'the endless passing of one element into new forms, the incessant metamorphosis. . .'" (8:15).[3] Asserted here is not only the inseparability of the metonymic technique from the correspondential vision but also the necessary correlation between the dynamics of nature, dynamics of the mind, and the flow of images in the poem.

The uneasy response of critics like Vivian Hopkins and Charles Feidelson[4] to this theory and practice of dynamic symbolism may very well originate, as Buell suggests, in the philosophical difficulty we experience in accepting the universe as a catalogue. No longer able to participate in the act of faith which both artists made the cornerstone of their vision, we tend to forget that the universe (and so the literary universe too) remained for them a catalogue with an inbuilt sense of direction. For coupled with Whitman's vision of nature as a seething principle is his sense of orderly unfolding and progression of the divine plenitude. Whitman, as Emerson, wants "to overwhelm us with the multiplicity of instances but at the same time impress us with the design inherent in these."[5]

Tying Whitman's catalogues only to the vision of democratic equality of all life forms leads to focusing on the particular items, the images, which, for whatever reason, seem striking to the reader.[6] But the catalogue's adaptability to Whitman's purposes lies, more centrally, in its fitness for demonstrating patterns of progression and growth inherent in life's abundance. Mattie Swayne suggests that structures of growth underlying Whitman's catalogues can be inferred even from their syntactic characteristics. The lists range from enumerations of bare words through sequences of items elaborated by descriptive words and phrases, catalogues of larger grammatical units, to catalogues consisting of whole stanzas: "There seems, indeed, no limit to the possible methods of expansion or diminution of catalogue items. The enumerative form is found in the phrases, sentences, and cadences of lyrics, in the lists of episodes or movements of narratives, and in the adjectives or separate items of descriptions."[7]

And, of course, the catalogue expansion is not lawless. It is "directed" by being envisioned as a progression in time and space. In fact, the concept of unfolding in time and space is as crucial for Whitman's sense of form as is his notion of "cosmic consciousness." Denis Donoghue's observation (quoted in Chapter 2) that Whitman's self grows in time by adding experience to experience ad infinitum implies that poems grow by adding image to image with corresponding open-endedness. When Charles Feidelson says that Whitman's greatest discovery is the view of the self as a traveler and explorer, not as a static observer, he adds immediately that "the shift of image from the contemplative eye of 'establish'd poems' to the voyaging ego of Whitman's poetry records a large-scale theoretical shift from categories of 'substance' to those of 'process.'"[8] In other words, the road along which the voyaging self moves is not only a symbol, however central; it becomes the poem's most fundamental structural principle.

An illuminating fragment found among Whitman's papers shows how the poet systematically cultivated his natural "cosmic" sense of space:

First of all prepare for study by the following self-teaching exercises. Abstract yourself from this book; realize where you are at present located, the point you stand that is now to you the centre of all. Look up overhead, think of space stretching out, think of all the unnumbered orbs wheeling safely there, invisible to us by day, some visible by night. . . . Spend some minutes faithfully in this exercise. Then again realize yourself upon the earth, at the particular point you now occupy. Which way stretches the north, and what countries, seas, etc.? Which way the south? Which way the east? Which way the west? Seize these firmly in your mind, pass freely over immense distances. Turn your face a moment thither. Fix the direction and the idea of the distances of separate sections of your own country, also of England, the Mediterranean Sea, Cape Horn, the North Pole, and such like distant places.[9]

Long inventories of things, place names, and occupations which Whitman drew up in his poems show how such spiritual exercises, prompted by the poet's mystical predispositions, were methodically turned into aesthetic rules and how efforts to attain a state of grace defined the structural principles.

"My right hand is time, and my left hand is space—both are ample—a few quintillions of cycles, a few sextillions of cubic leagues, are not of importance to me—what I shall attain to I can never tell, for there is something that underlies me, of whom I am a part and instrument" (*UPP*, 2:79–80).[10] According to Gay Wilson Allen, Whitman had made here not only a philosophical discovery but also a very important aesthetic one. "Let him now create a cosmic 'I' that can travel through time and space like a Greek god—or a soul freed of all finite limitations—and he will have found a new literary technique."[11] This seems a very accurate formula for Whitman's sense of poetic form. Indeed, analyzing even a simple catalogue poem like "There Was a Child Went Forth," it is easy to isolate two distinct progressions of imagery.[12] One is organized by seasonal advance, which also suggests a corresponding growth in the boy; the other, by expansion in space: from the child's conception, through family influences, outward to city scenes, and outward again to the "horizon's edge." The two progressions, one might add, serve to render poetically the same process—the natural course of the child's maturation. He grows in wisdom as he grows in years and as he becomes increasingly aware of the people and the land around him. The two progressions are developed by counterpoint to demonstrate their interchangeability. Both work upon the child to the same effect and so are reducible to identity.

Translating movement in time into movement in space to show their essential equivalence is Whitman's persistent practice. He uses the device brilliantly in the Section Eight of "Song of Myself." The section opens with three vignettes arranged within the frame of a life span:

> The little one sleeps in its cradle,
> I lift the gauze and look a long time, and silently brush away flies with my hand.
>
> The youngster and the red-faced girl turn aside up the bushy hill,
> I peeringly view them from the top.
>
> The suicide sprawls on the bloody floor of the bedroom,
> I witness the corpse with its dabbled hair, I note where the pistol has fallen.
>
> (*LG*, 35–36 : 147–53)

The three scenes offer close-ups of life's major events as they follow its course from the cradle to the grave. The slow advance of time can be felt in the unhurried diction, in the extending length of lines (the third scene consists of two long lines instead of the one short and one longer one of the two earlier vignettes; also, the last line is the longest in this part of the section), even in the way each vignette is separately spaced.[13] The temporal, single-life perspective is emphasized by the repetition of the first person pronoun each time the observer moves to a new scene.

The second part of the section changes both the tempo and the perspective. Time becomes compressed in a single glance as the observer takes in a busy street scene:

> The blab of the pave, tires of carts, sluff of boot-soles, talk of the promenaders,
> The heavy omnibus, the driver with his interrogating thumb, the clank of the shod horses on the granite floor,
> The snow-sleighs, clinking, shouted jokes, pelts of snow-balls,
> The hurrahs for popular favorites, the fury of rous'd mobs,
> The flap of the curtain'd litter, a sick man inside borne to the hospital,
> The meeting of enemies, the sudden oath, the blows and fall,
> The excited crowd, the policeman with his star quickly working his passage to the centre of the crowd,
> The impassive stones that receive and return so many echoes,
>
> (*LG*, 36 : 153–60)

In such an instant of simultaneous perception the speaker-observer is bombarded with the events of life and overwhelmed by life's teeming energy:

> What groans of over-fed or half-starv'd who fall sunstruck or in fits,
> What exclamations of women taken suddenly who hurry home and give birth to babes,
> What living and buried speech is always vibrating here, what howls restrain'd by decorum,
> Arrests of criminals, slights, adulterous offers made, acceptances, rejections with convex lips,
>
> (*LG*, 36 : 162–65)

In the last line, however, the speaker regains his composure:

> I mind them or the show or resonance of them—I come and I depart.
>
> (*LG*, 36 : 166)

He recognizes that the plenitude he is witnessing can contain neither more nor less than the fullness of human experience, whose skeletal pattern has been drawn in the first part of the section. Appropriately, it is redrawn in essence in the final simple sentences "I come and I depart."

As in "There Was a Child Went Forth," progress in time and expansion in space are interchangeable because they are reducible to the same basic principle. In the complete poem as well as in the fragment, the two movements combine to reveal the progress of consciousness. For growth of consciousness coincides for Whitman with the "natural" advance of biological and social life. The psychic, or spiritual, content can only be talked about in terms of the biological and social patterns in which it manifests itself. These patterns are seen as cyclic and repetitive, and Whitman insists on exposing their "representative," archetypal dimensions. Thus, though the poems contain enough details for the reader to realize that they are firmly anchored in personal experience,[14] neither can properly be called a private utterance.

Of the two, "There Was a Child" seems more personal, even though, technically speaking, its narrator is only a voice telling the story of the child "who went forth every day, and who now goes, and will always go forth every day." Not only do we feel that the child persona objectifies the speaker's private experience but, as readers, we recognize that the child projects our own progress within the poem. Through this "double facing," as it were, back to the author and forward to the reader, the poem generalizes personal experience into a "representative" pattern. In fact, by the end of the poem the reader is made aware that through his reading experience he has reenacted the child's progress and so himself has completed the educative cycle of which the poem speaks.

From its very beginning the poem insists on turning private experience into a timeless reality:

> There was a child went forth every day,
> And the first object he look'd upon, that object he became,
> And that object became part of him for the day or a certain part of the day,
> Or for many years or stretching cycles of years.
>
> (*LG*, 364 : 1–4)

The open-ended conclusion asserts the archetypal nature of the child's journey:

> These became part of that child who went forth every day, and who now goes, and will always go forth every day.
>
> (*LG*, 366 : 39)

Finally, and most subtly, the reader confirms by autopsy the general validity of the poem's law.

The fragment of "Song of Myself" seems more public in tone, although its speaker is the "I" persona, mostly because the reader is not asked to identify directly with the experiences narrated. Instead, he participates in the detached narrator's "learning" process. What is being observed functions as scientific material with which the narrator's consciousness works. Except for rather perfunctory sympathy, the speaker, and the reader with him, keeps his distance. The scope of the observed material as it enters the field of vision, either through progression in time or through a godlike act of simultaneous perception, ensures cosmic applicability of the discovered pattern. Moreover, as in "There Was a Child," the reader confirms the law in his reading experience as he participates in the speaker's progress to knowledge. The same ordered movement reveals itself in the succession of images from birth to death, in the coming and departing of the poet-speaker, and in the reader's progress to the poem's meaning: a cyclic development from beginning to fulfillment.

The patterns of movement from conception to maturity, from birth to death, from ignorance to knowledge, serve a twofold purpose. On the level of "message," the cyclic progressions are shown to inhere in every manifestation, every sphere of life. They organize eruptive life forces into orderly processes. They are instrumental, and even more, decisive in discovering unity in variety, the one—in all. For the poems themselves, they act as structuring devices allowing the radical, "open road" procession of items to be organized into coherent units so that a poem or its section can be recognized as a completed whole. On the other hand, however, they keep the form open since we are always encouraged to expect a renewal of the cycle, and, in the act of reading, we ourselves accomplish such a renewal. The patterns of cyclic unfolding are perhaps best seen as structural analogies bringing together the living world of organic reality and the artefact world of the poem. They become the vital common ground which both worlds share. In addition, since these "regularities" can be observed at work in organic life and confirmed in individual reading experience, they persistently impress the reader as having been "incorporated" into, rather than "made" for, the poem, "discovered" in the course of the poem's composition just as they are discovered in the course of its reading. Thus they work to hide technique, to blur the distinction between the "artificial" nature of the poem and the organic nature of reality. They emphasize, instead, the poem's participation in the spontaneity of life.

For reasons of economy I have used a short poem and a fragment in a detailed analysis, but it is not difficult to recognize similar structures in the longer poems as well. "As I Ebb'd with the Ocean of Life" is organized by the undulating movement of the tide. In the course of the poem its central structuring principle acquires symbolic extensions of meaning. The law of the turn of the tide becomes analogous to the law of life and death, to the changing psychic moods, and the inscrutable ebb and flow of poetic inspiration. Even as we recognize that the poem completes a cycle from the last of the ebb to the beginning of the rise, its overall frame is kept open by the insistence on the regularity of the sea's undulations incessantly repeating the same unit of movement.

"Song of Myself" begins with the awakening of the poet-persona's self-awareness and ends with his physical and spiritual dissolution in the universe. And while the time progression follows the span of the speaker's conscious life, Whitman takes every opportunity to turn this individual progress into an archetype: the persona's "representative" character is firmly established; religious imagery suggests further that the "poem of Walt Whitman, an American"[15] should be read as a kind of exemplum; and the central grass symbol, especially when it becomes "the beautiful hair of graves," points to cyclic renewal, as does the final stanza which projects another cycle.

The outward movement in space is equally pronounced. The protagonist starts "undisguised and naked" in the seclusion of "the bank by the wood," but in Section Forty-Six the endless vistas beyond the horizon become perpetually available to all who dare live on the road. By the final lines, the whole earth and its atmosphere are turned into the self's natural abode. Progressions in time and space combine to unfold the limitless prospects of self-realization.

Just as Whitman's temporal progressions tend to follow biological cycles of human life, in dealing with America or humanity in general the course of the poem may evoke the course of history from remote, perhaps legendary beginnings (as in "Passage to India" or "Starting from Paumanok") far ahead into the glorious future. The "organic," "evolutionary" nature of such progressions may be stressed by a significant number of stanzaic units. For example, "Song of Myself," undivided in the 1855 version, in the final, 1881 arrangement consists of fifty-two sections corresponding to fifty-two weeks in the year. And both "Crossing Brooklyn Ferry" and "Passage to India," with their arrangement into nine stanzas, suggest the period of human gestation.

Progressions in space begin in a concrete "here" and move outward. Invariably, they start from "the point you stand that is now to you the centre of all." Beginning on the grassy "bank by the wood," in the parental home, on Paumanok, they proceed to include larger and larger "circles," often achieving an extraterrestrial point of view.

Direction is never a problem; it inheres in the movement. Thus, although the ultimate destination remains forever unattainable,[16] Whitman's progressions are clearly directed. They are shaped by the cyclic character of temporal processes and by "graded" expansion outward.

Even so, many critics have felt, as did Charles Feidelson, that "long poems generally lack [a] stabilizing factor" and "that whatever the nominal subject, it soon becomes lost in sheer process."[17] Those critics usually prefer one or more from the four poems "Crossing Brooklyn Ferry," "Out of the Cradle Endlessly Rocking," "When Lilacs Last in the Dooryard Bloom'd," and "Passage to India," though the latter poem's reputation has been somewhat marred because one tends to object to its insistently prophetic tone. The four poems come from different periods in Whitman's career: "Brooklyn Ferry" was the most outstanding of the new poems in the 1856 edition; "Out of the Cradle" first appeared in 1860, "When Lilacs Last"—in 1865, and "Passage to India"—in 1871. Yet, somehow, they seem close. What brings them together is perhaps first of all their thematic affinity. All four are poems about death, and they are about death in a similar way; each seeks to accept and transcend the fact of individual mortality. On the other hand, read in chronological order, the four poems outline their author's evolution from a more personal, even confessional stance to an increasingly prophetic and nationalistic stance. "Crossing Brooklyn Ferry" and "Out of the Cradle" are private in their concerns and intimate in tone; "When Lilacs Last" and especially "Passage to India" bring to the foreground national and universal considerations, and their tone is public.

Each of the four poems, however, is firmly anchored in a particular occurence; each is, in fact, occasional. In "Crossing Brooklyn Ferry" and "Out of the Cradle" the occasion is strictly private, and the immediacy of the poems' appeal derives from the sense of personal urgency of the occasion. The point in both poems is to achieve perfect reader-speaker identification, to make the reader accept the emotional intensity of the occasion. The scene for the central event in both poems can be found in Whitman's biography. In "Crossing Brooklyn Ferry" the detailed landscape, evoked with lingering affection, becomes itself a major character, a co-protagonist in the poem. In "Out of the Cradle" the sea takes its powerful, symbolic presence directly from Whitman's intimacy with the beaches of Long Island.

The occasions for "When Lilacs Last" and "Passage to India" are furnished by important public events whose historical significance alone provides the needed sense of weight. Even so, in the case of the Lincoln elegy the importance of the public event combines with an intensely personal note, made possible, no doubt, by Whitman's involvement in the Civil War.

In all four poems then, a significant moment is isolated from time's undifferentiating flow and held suspended for contemplation. On the other hand, the reader is never allowed to forget the law of mutability. As in the poems discussed earlier, however, the flow is not left formless. Its rhythm is carefully established through the familiar device of stressing its cyclic, repetitive nature. The shuttlelike course of the ferry between the banks of the East River provides a pattern of crossing into immortality and into the world of each future reader. The undulations of the sea in "Out of the Cradle" punctuate cycles of destruction and creativity, frustration and sublimation. The journey of the coffin through the country in spring affirms a similar cycle and the essential unity of death, love, and new life. Encircling the earth with facilities for communication fulfills and projects the direction of general, historical evolution.

Against those rhythmical but open-ended patterns of movement kept in the background, a set of interrelated images is arranged so that they acquire distinctly symbolic dimensions. The mechanism of converting such symbols into "stabilizing factors" has been perhaps best explained by John Lynen in his discussion of "When Lilacs Last":

> The most striking technique is that of giving the symbol an exaggeratedly "symbolic" character. This is mainly achieved through naming the symbol frequently and in more or less identical language. Thus lilac, star and bird not only function as symbols but seem to announce themselves as such, so that we are certain of their symbolic character long before we can discover what they symbolize. The effect is to make the symbol persist as something we are constantly perceiving. It becomes a static point of reference which conceals the poem's real progression by anchoring all its phases to the first phase of experience.[18]

And, while the individual symbols interact, often in a triadic configuration,[19] toward transcendence of oppositions, for the final resolution their static quality must be seen against the dynamic background. The ultimate unity can be effected only if we refer the symbols to the inclusive, dynamic frame.

The four poems are perhaps equally satisfying in the way they balance the foreground prominence of their symbolic images against the inclusive movement in the background. A closer look at "Crossing Brooklyn Ferry"[20] reveals yet another progression which is crucial for Whitman: the progression toward identification with the reader. Recognizing its importance in Whitman's poetry, Howard Waskow[21] speaks of poems of "reader engagement," but he tends to see the engagement Whitman requires from his reader as imaginative or intellectual rather than emotional. For this reason, I think Waskow would be hard pressed to explain what it is that distinguishes Whitman from any poet who succeeds in the imaginative and intellectual involvement of his reader. Whitman, however, is special in that he demands a vicarious love relationship with his reader.

The emotional progression in "Crossing Brooklyn Ferry" has been sensitively brought into focus by James E. Miller.[22] Clearly, the movement defines the poem's structure: the first three sections establish the physical basis for identification—the scene and experience of crossing the East River by ferry; the next three sections insist on sharing common humanity, vice and sin included; and, finally, the last three sections mount toward a mystical union through love. This construction is foreshadowed in the manipulation of tenses within the three opening sections. First, the present tense is the speaker's present in his time; in the second section the speaker looks forward to the future which is the reader's present; and in the third section he actually moves into what was the future in Section Two, so that the future becomes present—the reader's as well as the speaker's. Thus the approach of the speaker in time in the first part of the poem projects the whole's development.

Behind the poem's ostensibly philosophical theme, there hides an urgent personal need to face and transcend the fact of death.[23] The problem turns into a paradox because the speaker who confronts death loves the earthly, sensuous life almost too much. He loves it so unconditionally that he must find ways of accepting its inevitable termination.[24] The paradox in which he is caught is embodied in the image of the crowded ferry crossing the river at sunset. The ferry, subject to the river's currents yet pursuing its own course, constitutes a perfect vehicle for conveying the speaker's desire to linger and "loafe" among the glories of sensual life together with his realization that all the time he is being hurried "with the swift current." The full meaning of the scene unfolds in the course of the poem until the revelation of cosmic order comes in the final section. There everything falls into place. Material objects, details of landscape so lovingly dwelt upon, so much in the foreground from the beginning of the poem, are now regarded in relation to the "flood—tide," as "appearances," "dumb, beautiful ministers" deriving their significance from the flowing spirit they reveal. The speaker, elated, celebrates the beauty of the grand design, totally reconciled to personal transience. As always with Whitman, the progress is from matter to spirit, from here to hereafter, from now into the future, and from sensuous enjoyment to emotional and intellectual acceptance.

All data and all conditions needed for the illumination in Section Nine are present from the very beginning. Section Two makes this sufficiently clear:

> The impalpable sustenance of me from all things at all hours of the day,
> The simple, compact, well-join'd scheme, myself disintegrated, every one disintegrated yet part of the scheme,
> The similitudes of the past and those of the future,
> The glories strung like beads on my smallest sights and hearings, on the walk in the street and the passage over the river,
> The current rushing so swiftly and swimming with me far away,
> The others that are to follow me, the ties between me and them,
> The certainty of others, the life, love, sight, hearing of others.
> (*LG*, 160:6–12)

The poem must "discover" or "unfold" their full meaning and make it personal for both the speaker and the reader. The reader must not be told truths; he must discover them for himself. The poem's line of development toward illumination is thus strengthened.

All Whitman's progressions are calculated to include the reader. When he stretches his temporal progressions infinitely into the future and turns them into spatial arrangements, when he asserts the timelessness of the present moment at the cost of disregarding the possibility of Brooklyn Ferry being discontinued,[25] his ultimate goal is to draw the reader within the scope of envisioned continuities. Only then "time nor place—distance avails not" . . . and "I am with you, you men and women of . . . so many generations hence." In the same way Whitman's progressions of "emotional intensification"[26] strive to bring the reader and the speaker together. The notorious closing of "So Long" shows how miserably the strategy can fail:

> I spring from the pages into your arms—decease calls me forth.
> . . . .
> Dear friend whoever you are take this kiss,
> I give it especially to you, do not forget me,
>
> (*LG*, 505:57, 506:64–65)

But, when successful, the emotional identification will make the reader see "steamers steaming through poems" and exultantly "haste on" to the next vision.

Similarly, in "Crossing Brooklyn Ferry," when the reader has himself followed its emotional progression, the revelation in Section Nine becomes his own. The "crossing" is accomplished, proving Whitman's art resistant to time's changes and making complete Whitman's triumph over mortality:

> What is more subtle than this which ties me to the woman or man that looks in my face?
> Which fuses me into you now, and pours my meaning into you?
>
> We understand then do we not?
> What I promis'd without mentioning it, have you not accepted?
> What the study could not teach—what the preaching could not accomplish is accomplish'd, is it not?
>
> (*LG*, 164:96–100)

And the incantation which follows may celebrate the univeral flow of life on behalf of both the speaker and the reader. The reader's emotional engagement in the poem's progress is as indispensable for Whitman as the presence there of his own powerful personality. The two are co-makers of the poem. It is, therefore, of crucial importance that a Whitman poem should not be judged on the intellectual level alone. Denying the poem a chance to work upon him emotionally, the reader cancels its aesthetic impact. Vision and design simply cannot be separated in Whitman.

It has become sufficiently clear, I suppose, that in my view of Whitman's art I tend to agree with those critics[27] who emphasize the mystical qualities of his poetry. Seen as progressions toward a moment of contact, an illumination, or reconciliation, the poems resemble religious mediations as they strive to attain a state of grace; though grace may come in shockingly secular guises—as a sexual (even homosexual) union or as a political vision of perfect democracy. The visionary climax of a Whitman poem constitutes its structural climax as well, whether of the whole poem or of a distinct unit of the poem. Opposition and variety become resolved into unity both on the plane of vision and on the plane of compositional strategies. Not only do we perceive that particular catalogue items are interchangeable because they are fundamentally equivalent; we are also forced to recognize that all progressions, temporal, spatial, and emotional, inevitably and inextricably come together as they do in, for example, the closing section of "Crossing Brooklyn Ferry."

Whitman's chief province is "the road," the striving for moments of perfect fusion. But at various points in his career, he also wrote poems which omit the meditative progression altogether. Such poems deal only with the lucid moment, with the vision itself, when the scene or object becomes alive with spirit. They are imagistic in the modern understanding of the term. They present "an intellectual and emotional complex in an instant of time"[28] and provide ground for speculations whether T. S. Eliot's famous "objective correlative" may not also have origin in Whitman.[29]

Many of the imagistic poems are to be found in "Children of Adam" and, first of all, in "Drum—Taps," "Cavalry Crossing a Ford" furnishing a justly celebrated example:

> A line in long array where they wind betwixt green islands,
> They take a serpentine course, their arms flash in the sun—hark
>   to the musical clank,
> Behold the silvery river, in it the splashing horses loitering stop
>   to drink,
> Behold the brown-faced men, each group each person a picture,
>   the negligent rest on the saddles,
> Some emerge on the opposite bank, others are just entering the
>   ford—while,
> Scarlet and blue and snowy white,
> The guidon flags flutter gayly in the wind.
>
> (*LG*, 300)[30]

An overview of the cavalry unit approaching a ford is subsequently decomposed into separate opposing and complementary elements ("each group, each person a picture") and the whole is reassembled in terms of blending colors of guidon flags. The flags, "scarlet and blue and snowy white," draw together the various components as they finally dominate the scene. The overall design is a familiar one: the main theme is stated at the beginning, then elaborated in detail and restated with new lucidity. But the effect of progression is absent here and is only vestigial in similar poems such as "A Sight in Camp at Daybreak" or "By the Bivouac's Fitful Flame." Obviously the scope of vision is lost. Less obvious, but perhaps more important, is the loss of the dynamic quality of the poem and of a good deal of the reader's engagement, for he now becomes a decoder rather than a fellow traveler on the road which is the poem.

For, if Whitman's poems are dramatic, as a number of critics maintain,[31] the drama resides totally in the oppositions and counterpoints of the progression while the final vision inevitably reconciles the various elements and resolves everything into harmony. The ultimate unity remains a certainty, a matter of faith and a constant for Whitman. He does not change in this respect. But he can travel to his destination by many different routes and see his ideal incorporated in many different forms. Eventually, the physical world seems valuable to Whitman because it reveals the living idea. He loves and uses objects as means of access to spiritual unity. His analogies are, in fact, equivalencies tending to identity. Identity is precisely the effect of the imagistic poems, perfect fusions of object and idea. Paradoxically, however, even as Whitman attains his philosophical and aesthetic goal, he loses much of his poetic power. His forte is striving and progression with the road always stretching ahead and the journey's end forever receding. Possibility, not achievement, is Whitman's domain.

Although it is tempting to view the sweep of "Song of Myself" as the tour de force opening of Whitman's career and the delicate vignette of "Sparkles from the Wheel"[32] as its graceful but subdued closing, one cannot claim without too many qualifications that such was the consistent line of Whitman's poetic development. "Children of Adam"[33] contains a number of imagistic poems while "Prayer of Columbus"[34] is still a poem of progression though its protagonist, no longer capable of powering transformations, remains a reviewer of experience. On the other hand, grouping Whitman's poems into those structured mainly by progressions, then into poems balancing patterns of progression against "stabilizing factors" (such as insistent symbols or a distinct sense of the poem's occasion), and finally into basically static, imagistic poems, helps to elucidate problems of design with which the artist struggled throughout his creative years. Further light may be cast upon his experiments by paying attention to perhaps less accomplished poems, such as "Song of the Open Road" or "Song of the Broad-Axe," which still reveal a lot about the poet's search for his own form: a form, that is, which would combine the flexibility and dynamism of life with the shapeliness of an artefact, a form which, in Ezra Pound's later phrase, would be "as water poured into a vase."[35]

"Song of the Open Road,"[36] as the title suggests, centers on the image of life as journey. Its pattern is thus radically open, for Whitman's journey, unlike *Pilgrim's Progress*, has no specific destination. The symbol of the open road intertwines two themes: one, of life as "the long journey"; the other, of comradeship on the road. The urge to push forward is balanced, even in Section One, with the necessity to carry "my old burdens" of emotional rapport with other human beings:

> Afoot and light-hearted I take to the open road,
> Healthy, free, the world before me,
> The long brown path before me leading wherever I choose,
>
> . . . .
>
> (Still here I carry my old delicious burdens,
> I carry them, men and women, I carry them with me wherever I go,
> I swear it is impossible for me to get rid of them,
> I am fill'd with them, and I will fill them in return.)
>
> (*LG*, 149:1–3, 12–15)

As in other of Whitman's characteristic openings, all the main themes, all data, are present from the outset, and their full implications will be developed in the course of the poem. Consequently, Sections Two through Five celebrate the open road as the site of freedom and limitless vistas, as the principle of creative life:

O public road, I say back I am not afraid to leave you, yet I love
you,
You express me better than I can express myself,
You shall be more to me than my poem.

I think heroic deeds were all conceiv'd in the open air, and all free
poems also,

(*LG*, 151:46–49)

Sections Six to Eight, on the other hand, elaborate "the gospel of adhesiveness." The turning point comes in Section Five, in which free life on the road has endowed the speaker with the authority to lead and teach:

I am larger, better than I thought,
I did not know I held so much goodness.

All seems beautiful to me,
I can repeat over to men and women You have done such good to
me I would do the same to you,
I will recruit for myself and you as I go,

(*LG*, 151:60–64)

It is important to notice that the "you" in this section refers generally to "men and women" who "have done such good to me." In the course of the next section, however, the "you" becomes progressively more specific. It may still be generic or, perhaps, ambiguous in the line "The past, the future, majesty, love—if they are vacant of you, you are vacant of them" (*LG*, 153:87), but it sounds direct and specific in the closing questions of Section Six: "Do you know what it is as you pass to be loved by strangers? / Do you know the talk of those turning eye-balls?" (*LG*, 153:92–93). When, after further exposition of the doctrine of "adhesiveness," the speaker exclaims with growing urgency: "Allons! whoever you are come travel with me! / Traveling with me you find what never tires" (*LG*, 154:114–15), the "you" refers individually to each reader, "whoever he is," reading the poem at the moment. Through the manipulation of the second person pronoun, the speaker, as it were, approaches in comradship the reader traveling from the remoteness of his abstract reflections to the active, concrete realization of human solidarity. The strategy works only if the reader cooperates, if he is able and willing to respond emotionally. For neither rational argumentation nor aesthetic impressions can serve as adequate common ground between the reader and the speaker. The appeal is made to the emotional recognition of the human bond stemming from the simple fact of being: "I and mine do not convince by arguments, similes, rhymes, / We convince by our presence" (*LG*, 155 : 138–39). The sense of community experienced through traveling the same road of life is enlarged in Sections Twelve and Thirteen to include the sharing in common of human guilt, however secret the knowledge and recognition of it may be.

After the *confiteor* of Section Thirteen the last two sections sound again the double call to endless journeying and striving and to faithful comradeship on the road. By the time the reader reaches the final invocation, the distance between him and the speaker has been canceled:

> Camerado, I give you my hand!
> I give you my love more precious than money,
> I give you myself before preaching or law;
> Will you give me yourself? will you come travel with me?
> Shall we stick by each other as long as we live?
> (*LG*, 159 : 220–24)

Preceded by the exclamatory "camerado," the "you" is made both more direct and more affectionate while the following lines postulate a ritual of blood brotherhood, a thoroughly human Holy Communion.

The theme of "adhesiveness," stated in general terms in the introductory section of the poem, is thus developed toward a climax of communion with each particular reader. While the theme of "the long journey" remains open, the movement toward identification with the reader constitutes the poem's closed principle. The progressive anchoring of the poem's action in the reader functions as the main structuring device, indispensable for the poem's success. The poem fails if the reader refuses to supply the "stabilizing factor" of his emotional involvement, if he rejects the part of the "camerado."

Whitman resorted to a similar device in many poems, most successfully, perhaps, in "Starting from Paumanok"[37] and, as we have seen, in "Crossing Brooklyn Ferry." In both poems, however, the progressive intensification of emotions became enriched by patterns of temporal progression and, in the case of "Starting from Paumanok," by a more specified progression in space.[38]

In "Song of the Broad-Axe"[39] the background pattern is formed by evolutionary progression of civilization from the natural fertility of the wilderness (in "a sterile landscape" that "covers the ore, there is as good as the best for all the forbidding appearance") to the spiritual energy of "a great city" / "that which has the greatest men and women." The pattern is evoked, reflected, and epitomized in the progress of America from "the log at the wood-pile," "the sylvan hut," "the space clear'd for a garden" to "the constructor of wharves, bridges, piers" and "stays against the sea." Both, universal progress of mankind and historical development of America, are to be crowned in "shapes of Democracy total, result of centuries." Interwoven, the two progressions establish the background rhythm of an ordered, if turbulent, march ahead while the "stabilizing factor" is provided by the returning image of the broad-axe.

The poem falls into two parts, each consisting of an equal number of sections. The first part—Sections One through Six—is dominated by the motif of individual deeds and by progression in space. The second—Sections Seven through Twelve—concerns itself chiefly with progress "en masse" in time. The division is marked by the return of the initial image of land covering the ore—the beginning of the axe. The axe, then, provides a symbolic center from which associations and meanings expand, and yet always return to the basic solidity of the tool. In the course of the poem the broad-axe becomes a material realization of the law of evolution. Its various uses—peaceful, military, constructive, and destructive—reflect multiple aspects of the "law of Nature" whose essence—progress—remains sharply in focus. The axe stands as the embodiment of the evolutionary law itself, and, at the same time, it anchors the overall process to its "thingness."

I hope that enough has been said to allow the conclusion that central to Whitman's concept of poetry as mediation, as "the liquid rim" between the living sea of natural forms and the firm land of the artifact, is the problem of striking balance between the principle of spontaneity, capable of transmitting life in its seething energy, and the demands of art for definite, and therefore, petrifying forms. Just as Whitman's conception of the self singles out growth as the property which consciousness and nature share, so his poetic designs incorporate patterns of temporal, spatial, and emotional progressions that hide technique beneath the ostensible spontaneity of their movement. Late in his life, Whitman still admired the structural simplicity of the Bible and held it for his ideal: "Compared with the famed epics of Greece, and lesser ones since, the spinal supports of the Bible are simple and meagre. All its history, biography, narratives, etc., are as beads, strung on and indicating the eternal thread of the Deific purpose and power" (*PW*, 2:546). Believing in the purposeful evolution of the universe, he wanted to make the sense of its procession "the spinal support" of his poems. Yet all through his career Whitman felt the need to search for ways in which evolutionary "flows" could be stabilized into art forms without losing their spontaneity. And he was more aware of his problem than he is usually given credit for: "The play of Imagination, with the sensuous objects of Nature for symbols, and Faith—with Love and Pride as the unseen impetus and moving-power of all, make up the curious chess game of a poem" (*PW*, 1:292).

The reader's preferences within the Whitman canon will ultimately depend upon the individual sense of balance between the dynamic and the static elements of a poem. There are those who prefer Whitman the imagist, although they are relatively few; those, perhaps most numerous at the moment, who delight in "Crossing Brooklyn Ferry," "Out of the Cradle," and "When Lilacs Last in the Dooryard Bloom'd"; and those who, like Richard Chase, let themselves be carried away by the energy and sweep of "Song of Myself," feeling that they have been given enough guidance not to drown in its swift current.

Notes

1. Mason I. Lowance, *The Language of Canaan* (Cambridge, Mass.: Harvard University Press, 1980), 295.

2. Lawrence Buell, "Transcendentalist Catalogue Rhetoric: Vision versus Form," *American Literature* 40 (1968): 334.

3. Lawrence Buell, *Literary Transcendentalism: Style and Vision in the*

American Renaissance (Ithaca: Cornell University Press, 1973), 175. Quotations from Emerson are from the same work.

4. Vivian C. Hopkins, *Spires of Form: A Study of Emerson's Aesthetic Theory* (Cambridge, Mass.: Harvard University Press, 1951), see especially the comments on pp. 130–31. Charles Feidelson, *Symbolism and American Literature* (Chicago: University of Chicago Press, 1953), see especially the discussion of the Lincoln elegy and the comments on p. 25. It might be apropos to remember at this point that when Ezra Pound, impatient with the static quality of imagism, opted for the dynamism of the "vortex," he was able to make "a pact" with Walt Whitman.

5. Buell, "Transcendentalist Catalogue Rhetoric," 332.

6. Randall Jarrell's justly celebrated essay "Some Lines from Whitman" provides an example of a sensitive reading in this vein (in *Poetry and the Age* [New York: Alfred A. Knopf, 1953]).

7. Mattie Swayne, "Whitman's Catalogue Rhetoric," *University of Texas Studies in English*, no. 21 (1941), p. 178.

8. Feidelson, *Symbolism and American Literature*, 17.

9. Richard M. Bucke, ed., *Notes and Fragments* (London: privately printed, 1899). Quoted in Roger Asselineau, *The Evolution of Walt Whitman* (Cambridge, Mass.: Harvard University Press, Belknap Press), 2 : 101–2.

10. Quoted in Gay Wilson Allen, *The Solitary Singer: A Critical Biography of Walt Whitman*, rev. ed. (New York: New York University Press, 1967), 142.

11. Ibid.

12. Compare discussions of the poem in Buell, *Literary Transcendentalism*, 172–73; and in Howard Waskow, *Whitman: Explorations in Form* (Chicago: University of Chicago Press, 1966), 130–35.

13. They were so spaced already in the 1855 edition of *Leaves of Grass*.

14. The pictures of mother and father in "There Was a Child Went Forth" seem to correspond to the images Whitman had of his own parents. Moreover, both poems follow the way from quiet, rural surroundings to the scenes of "populous city"—Whitman's own progress as a child and young man.

15. The poem's title in the 1856 edition of *Leaves of Grass*.

16. And, correspondingly, Whitman's poems, properly speaking, "do not end." See John Lynen, "Three Uses of the Present: The Historian's, the Critic's and Emily Dickinson's," *College English* 28, no. 2 (November 1966): 126–36.

17. Feidelson, *Symbolism and American Literature*, 25.

18. John F. Lynen, *The Design of the Present: Essays on Time and Form in American Literature* (New Haven: Yale University Press, 1969), 322–23.

19. See Alfred H. Marks, "Whitman's Triadic Imagery," *American Literature* 23 (March 1951): 99–126.

20. The poem first appeared in the 1856 edition of *Leaves of Grass* as "Sun-Down Poem," but it is possible that Whitman began it even before the

first edition went to press (see Harold W. Blodgett, ed., *An 1855–56 Notebook toward the Second Edition of Leaves of Grass* [Carbondale: Southern Illinois University Press, 1951]).

21. Waskow, *Whitman: Explorations in Form*, chap. 7.

22. James E. Miller, Jr., *A Critical Guide to Leaves of Grass* (Chicago: University of Chicago Press, 1957), 80–89.

23. The poem's first title, "Sun-Down Poem," indicates that death was indeed Whitman's main preoccupation here, and that he was not, perhaps, quite clear as to what he was doing. The final title shifts emphasis from death as termination to death as transcendence and focuses on the poem's proper intention.

24. See also Gay Wilson Allen and Charles T. Davis, eds., *Walt Whitman's Poems: Selections with Critical Aids* (New York: New York University Press, 1955), 27.

25. Hart Crane's "Bridge" (where Brooklyn Bridge replaces the Ferry as symbol) and Allan Ginsberg's delightful "A Supermarket in California" (where the disappearance of Brooklyn Ferry measures the gulf between Whitman's vision of America's future and Ginsberg's perception of its reality) stand as evidence of the continuing reality of Whitman's Ferry.

26. Allen and Davis, *Walt Whitman's Poems*, 9.

27. Compare, for example, Asselineau, *The Evolution of Walt Whitman*, vol. 2, chap. 10: "Style: From Mysticism to Art"; James E. Miller, Jr., "Song of Myself as Inverted Mystical Experience," in *Whitman's Song of Myself—Origin, Growth, Meaning*, ed. James E. Miller, Jr. (New York: Dodd, Mead, 1964), 134–56; John Lynen, *The Design of the Present*, chap. 5 (esp. pp. 308–33).

28. Ezra Pound's definition of image "A Few Don'ts" in "A Retrospect," in *Literary Essays of Ezra Pound*, ed. with an introduction by T. S. Eliot (New York: New Directions, 1968), 4.

29. Sydney Musgrove, *T. S. Eliot and Walt Whitman* (New York: Columbia University Press, 1953), 79 n.2. The author writes: "Eliot's conception of the 'objective correlative' is that of a situation 'such that when the external facts, which must terminate in sensory experience, are given, the emotion is immediately evoked.' The whole passage (in Hamlet, T. S. Eliot, *Selected Essays*, p. 145), with its discussion of adolescent 'bafflement,' 'disgust . . . occasioned by his mother,' 'the buffoonery of an emotion . . . which can find no outlet in action,' should be read in conjunction with Whitman's 'From Pent-up Aching Rivers,' which has these lines: '. . . O resistless yearning! / O for any and each the body correlative attracting! / O for you whoever you are your correlative body! . . .'"

30. It is perhaps of some interest that while the whole poem was first published in 1865 and remained unchanged in all subsequent versions, line six, with its blending of national colors, was only added in 1871.

31. Some critics regard Whitman's poems as "monodramas"; see, for example, Allen and Davis, Introduction to *Walt Whitman's Poems* or Waskow,

Whitman: Explorations in Form, chap. 6. John Lynen, however ("Three Uses of the Present," *College English* 28, no. 2 [November 1966]), maintains that, in contrast to Dickinson's talent, Whitman's gifts are "lyric and bardic": "Whitman's poetic plot is essentially the enactment of the discovery of this fact [i.e., that the substance of ego is universal spirit] through spiritual merging. We are shown how the poet, by observing the way objects of his experience become part of him, moves toward the realization that he is at one with God" (133).

32. This poem first appeared in 1871 (in *Passage to India*).

33. First published as "Enfants d'Adam" in the 1860 edition of *Leaves of Grass*.

34. First printed in *Harper's Magazine* for March 1874, included in *Two Rivulets* (1876), and finally placed in the 1881 *Leaves of Grass*.

35. Eliot, *Literary Essays of Ezra Pound*, 9.

36. First published in the 1856 edition of *Leaves of Grass*.

37. The poem was apparently begun immediately after the publication of the 1855 edition of *Leaves of Grass*. A notebook of 1856 contains many first draft lines. The first manuscript title (Clifton Waller Barrett Collection, University of Virginia, Charlottesville) was "Premonition." When published, in the 1860 *Leaves of Grass*, the poem was titled "Proto-Leaf." The present title appeared in the 1867 *Leaves of Grass* and the poem was finally placed following "Inscriptions" in the 1871 edition.

38. In "Crossing Brooklyn Ferry" the particular landscape acts as the main stabilizing element.

39. First published in the 1856 edition of *Leaves of Grass*.

5 / *The Design of Command*

The world of difference between Emily Dickinson's art and Whitman's is the result of their having made alternative responses to the same problem, of their having organized the same sort of time in exactly opposite ways. The goal of the Whitman poem is to bring a timeless process into view, to comprehend the import of such a statement as "I mourn'd, and yet shall mourn with ever-returning spring." The cyclic return of sorrow is seen as the cyclic movement of seasons, and time is opened up by projecting this process into indefinitely remote past and future. But Emily Dickinson undertakes to crystallize event into circumstance . . . , the distinction between now and always becomes irrelevant, because the "time" proves to be an experience which is interchangeably that perceived by the self in its narrow moment or that of the transcendent spectator.[1]

ACCOUNTING as John Lynen does for the difference between Whitman's and Dickinson's poetry exclusively in terms of their opposite response to time may seem an oversimplification. However, it is essential to recognize that whereas Whitman insists on revealing an unbroken continuity, Dickinson shatters it by juxtaposing "now" with "always" without offering a discernible route from one to the other.

Thus Robert Weisbuch perhaps misses the point when he claims that "when the images which organize the world become dire, when the grass of Whitman's 'Song of Myself' is replaced by the 'chaff, straw, splinters of wood, weeds and the sea-gluten,' 'the few sands and dead leaves' of his 'As I Ebb'd with the Ocean of Life,' we are fully prepared for Dickinson's second world."[2] For, ultimately, the difference lies not in the quality of vision, pessimistic or optimistic, but in its deep structure, so to say.[3] Whether in a celebrating or despairing mood, Whitman seeks to incorporate his vision within a unifying law. Hence the ebb and flow of the ocean lends the authority of a natural cycle to fluctuations of mood. At no point does Dickinson feel a comparable need to "legitimize" experiential and psychic vicissitudes by referring to an inclusive, external principle as her structural analogy. The conflicting views, the tensions and contradictory moods are there in her poetry as aspects of consciousness, not as diverse manifestations of cosmic continuity. The unity is gone or, rather, it remains beyond comprehension—the challenging unknown, "the largest need of the intellect" (*L*, 2:559).

Neither time nor space is patterned into cycles or "graded" for Emily Dickinson. Unlike the road which, "starting from Paumanok," leads, seductively familiar, to everywhere and forever, Dickinson's images of "degreeless" (287) or "perpetual" (1056) noon, of "the Ocean too silver for a seam" (328) or "Seamless Grass" (409) emphasize the absence of cognizable markers in the expanse of time and space. Dickinson's characteristic method, in Ruth Miller's words, is "a leap or a swirl up and out beyond the real world to some realm of infinity."[4] This "realm of infinity," however, is not a direct extension of "home." Instead, it is the vast region of "supposition" where, amid "acres of perhaps" (696), one is distinctly not "at home" or where access is bluntly denied.

When Dickinson contemplates a bird which "came down the Walk" in her garden, her poem (328) naturally divides into two contrasting scenes. In the first one, the speaker observes the bird on her own territory. The scene is full of movement and humor. In a characteristic Dickinsonian manner, the bird becomes "domesticated" and has to behave like a polite guest:

> And then he drank a Dew
> From a convenient Grass—
> And then hopped sidewise to the Wall
> To let a Beetle pass—

Although the bird's "strange" habits are noticed, at first they are treated as only eccentricities which add to the quaintness of his presence:

> He did not know I saw—
> He bit an Angleworm in halves
> And ate the fellow, raw,

But as her guest is leaving the garden and the speaker's eyes follow his flight, infinity of space opens in sharp contrast to the playful domesticity of the previous scene:

> And he unrolled his feathers
> And rowed him softer home—
>
> Then Oars divide the Ocean,
> Too silver for a seam—
> Or Butterflies, off Banks of Noon
> Leap, plashless as they swim.

More ominously, in poem 287, the contrast between life and death is conveyed by juxtaposing sound, movement, and transience, all implied in the image of the working clock, with the grotesque unfamiliarity of absolute stasis:[5]

> A Clock stopped—
> Not the Mantel's—
> Geneva's farthest skill
> Cant put the puppet bowing—
> That just now dangled still—
>
> An awe came on the Trinket!
> The Figures hunched, with pain—
> Then quivered out of Decimals—
> Into Degreeless Noon—

There seems to be no perceptible connection between motion and its absence; the distance is not quantitatively "graded" but is seen as a radical, qualitative change:

> Decades of Arrogance between
> The Dial life—
> And Him—

In the celebrated poem "I heard a Fly buzz—when I died—" (465), the ebb of life is rendered in terms of progressive failure of senses. The contrast between "the Stillness in the Room" and the sound of the fly thrusts itself upon the speaker's ear when the poem opens. But as it moves on, the buzzing becomes "uncertain" and "stumbling," and ebbs into silence. Similarly, the speaker at first is able to look around the room where people gathered "for that last Onset." Then her vision grows narrower and narrower until the eyes fix on the fly alone:

> And then the Windows failed—and then
> I could not see to see—

Thus the poem equals life with perception as well as with motion. As long as the waning motion continues, whether of the eyes or of the fly, life is there. When it ceases, the change cannot be accommodated in the continuity of decline. The quality has altered and its nature remains a mystery. "I could not see to see" is all that can be said.

The strategy of exploring the moment when the known is abruptly brought into the presence of the unknown may be further illustrated by a poem employing the Whitmanesque image of life as journey:

> Our journey had advanced—
> Our feet were almost come
> To that odd Fork in Being's Road—
> Eternity—by Term—
>
> Our pace took sudden awe—
> Our feet—reluctant—led
> Before—were Cities—but Between—
> The Forest of the Dead—
>
> Retreat—was out of Hope—
> Behind—a Sealed Route—
> Eternity's White Flag—Before—
> And God—at every Gate—
>
> (615)

Unlike Whitman, Dickinson concentrates not on the journey's course but on its termination, on the moment when change is bound to occur. As in "A Bird came down the Walk" or "A Clock stopped" or "I heard a Fly buzz," nothing can be said about the reality beyond the turning point. Despite the assurance that "Before—were Cities," the view is blocked by "the Forest of the Dead." This poem, too, ends in the sudden confrontation with the unknown: "Eternity's White Flag—Before— / And God—at every Gate—."

As a rule, the balance of a Dickinson poem is "tipped" (see the discussion of the poem on the spider in Chapter 3). The poem progresses by intense, meticulous exploration of the known, then "leaps" into the infinity of the unknown. The change occurring at this point can no longer be accommodated in any continuity. It is qualitative and absolute. While we employed the figure of concentric circles whose perimeters expanded gradually in order to visualize the structure of "Song of Myself," a Dickinson poem may be imagined as consisting of "center" and "circumference" with the rings in between missing. The "center" provides a springboard for "the leap," and, consequently, receives more attention. It anchors eternity to "here and now" and mystery to the familiar. Nevertheless, it is the freedom of "the leap" that counts most. One suspects that the ability or inability to "leap out and beyond" the limiting center of immediate reality was precisely what the poet had in mind when she insisted that "Captivity is Consciousness— / So's Liberty" (384). The way consciousness operates for Dickinson brings to mind Emerson's meditation in "Circles" on St. Augustine's definition of God as "a circle whose center was everywhere and its circumference nowhere" (2: 301). Except, Dickinson's center could not easily be everywhere. It was necessarily limited by the accidental circumstances of the poet's experience, by the "nows" out of which "forever" could be composed (624). The haunting image offered in poem 378 visualizes the appalling predicament of the mind rent between the alternatives of claustrophobic enclosure within the center and absolute alienation upon circumference:

> I saw no Way—The Heavens were stitched—
> I felt the Columns close—
> The Earth reversed her Hemispheres—
> I touched the Universe—
>
> And back it slid—and I alone—
> A Speck upon a Ball—
> Went out upon Circumference—
> Beyond the Dip of Bell—

Dickinson's vision is in itself dramatic. Its essence is conflict and confrontation. Not only does she pose the self against the world and experience but she thinks in oppositions all the time: home to measureless space and faraway places; the present, fleeting moment to the forever of eternity; the motion of ordinary life against the stasis of any overwhelming emotion, but, most of all, against the final stillness of death. Just as there seems to be no property or attribute which the self could unquestionably share with nature, the polarities of Dickinson's oppositions do not gradually blend into each other. Instead, they are locked in an unresolvable confrontation.

The conflict is echoed, as Brita Lindberg-Seyersted has shown, by lexical and semantic contrasts: "the colloquial diction is constantly set off against another vocabulary: literary, technical, or exotic; or against a solemn subject-matter, such as suffering, death and immortality; *or* the non-colloquial vocabulary is played off against a simple subject-matter, an everyday theme, a consciously low-keyed statement."[6] And "concrete elements are very strikingly set off against abstract ones; native words are counterbalanced by learned words of Latin origin; and, in close connection with these two sets of contrasting items, there is evident in the verse a marked counterpoint of monosyllables and polysyllables."[7]

The discontinuous character of Dickinson's vision is reflected even in the brevity of individual poems. Although this particular feature of her art has sometimes been ascribed to the fact that Dickinson "was personally incapable of logical, not to say theological, thought," that "system and argument . . . were too hard and frigid for her,"[8] it seems more rewarding to view it with Roland Hagenbüchle as integrally related to the nature of her vision:

> The concentration on the "critical" moment is a crucial element in Emily Dickinson's poetry and is closely connected with the shift from analogue to digital thinking—itself responsible for the experience of life as a discontinuous or "angled Road" [*J*, 910]. It finds expression, first, iconically, in the epigrammatic shortness of her poems, second thematically, in the numerous descriptions of unstable phenomena in nature such as the rising and setting of the sun or its precarious poise at the meridian hour of noon, the changing of the seasons at the solstices, and certain fleeting effects of light in general. It can further be observed in the elliptical and often ambiguous syntax (including the hyphen), and finally in the use of polysemantic and therefore unstable words and expressions.[9]

Aspects of structure and style in Dickinson's poems must be seen as functions of the discontinuous vision. For where Whitman insists on placing each event within a continuum, Dickinson excludes and isolates for analysis. She does not share Whitman's gift for familiarizing time by exposing its recurrent patterns. Instead, she looks hard at a single moment for whatever meaning it may yield unsupported by its location within an archetypal cycle. "The myth is reduced to an act of pure consciousness," to use again Roland Hagenbüchle's apt formulation. The way the mind crystallizes moments into aspects of eternity is what her poetry is about. The "critical moment" of Roland Hagenbüchle's observation or "a conflict compressed into a transient moment" (which is Ruth Miller's expression[10] and as good a definition of crisis as any) constitutes a metaphor as well as a structural analogy for such vision.

The poet's own definitions of crisis focus on two aspects: on crisis as a turning point and as a moment of infinitely precarious balance. Crisis as a turning point provides a metaphor for her "Compound Vision" (906), and, in most general terms, interests her as the meeting point between what has been and therefore appears dear and familiar, like life, and what is yet to be, which looms large and terrifying because it cannot be known, like death, or better, like the impenetrable mystery on the other side of dying.

> Crisis is sweet and yet the Heart
> Upon the hither side
> Has Dowers of Perspective
> To Denizens denied
>
> Inquire of the closing Rose
> Which rapture she preferred
> And she will point you sighing
> To her rescinded Bud.

(1416; quoted from the 1960 edition of *The Complete Poems of Emily Dickinson*)

Crisis as a turning point provides a perspective upon "the hither side," upon what has been, which invariably involves an acute sense of loss. As each moment is unique, each is irrevocably lost when it recedes into the past. Present only to the mind, it becomes "memory and desire," "the landscape of absence" as opposed to Whitman's timeless reality in the collective human experience. Its participation in or contribution to the design of "the whole" is negligible compared to the psychic impact it effects.

For Dickinson, the unknown remains "the largest need of the intellect," not in the sense of providing space for imperialistic expansion of the self but because it demands confrontations in which creativity is released. No matter how fascinated with the beckoning "other," Dickinson never hopes for its smooth incorporation. There remain points everywhere beyond which the mind, deprived of the certainty of faith, cannot progress. "Nature's show" can only be watched, not penetrated in essence. The other side of the grave invariably proves the ultimate in mystery. There are mysteries, too, which like the soul's subconscious "caverns" are better left "sealed." If Dickinson constantly courts self-destruction in critical encounters with the unknown, it is because failure enlarges awareness[11] but also, and perhaps first of all, because the commanding power of aesthetic consciousness must be tested. Aesthetic—not in the sense of frivolously cultivating art for art's sake but redemptive, capable of imposing its own order, of "making revelations." The unknown is "the largest need of the intellect" because it provides a constant challenge to the mind. Converging upon the known, the unknown teaches the value of security in the familiar. On the other hand, however, exposing the provisional character of any order, it forces the mind to struggle to maintain poise:

Crisis is a Hair
Toward which forces creep
Past which forces retrograde
If it come in sleep

To suspend the Breath
Is the most we can
Ignorant is it Life or Death
Nicely balancing.

(889)

Significantly, if crisis occurs when the mental faculties are at rest, one is left helpless at the mercy of unspecified but powerful "creeping" forces. Yet, when the faculties of consciousness are awake, the crisis situation stimulates the aesthetic achievement of exquisitely poignant balance.

Confrontation, crisis, is thus the central figure in the carpet of Dickinson's poetry. It is an encounter between the disorderly, eruptive forces of the unknown which come in experience in the various guises of nature, love, Deity, death, or one's own irrational psychic powers on the one hand, and the assaulted consciousness which must react so as not to be submerged and annihilated. The confrontation of the critical moment furnishes Dickinson's poems with a thematic and structural design analogous in its role to the progression image in Whitman. Concentration on the drama of the critical moment, as opposed to Whitman's focus on the progress of the journey, gives Dickinson's poetry its discontinuous character. Her confrontations are unresolvable, for the contending principles are, in fact, mutually supportive. Neither can win. The point is to keep the contenders tautly poised. Dickinson explains the relationship casually, with the sort of grim humor that often characterizes her most striking utterances:

A Bomb upon the Ceiling
Is an improving thing—
It keeps the nerves progressive
Conjecture flourishing—

(1128)

The moment of suspense becomes "a capsule" of energy demanding release, and is therefore conducive to creativity.

The poet's most extensive comment on the way conditions of extreme stress stimulate to performance comes in this early poem:

A *Wounded* Deer—leaps highest—
I've heard the Hunter tell—
'Tis but the Ecstasy of *death*—
And then the Brake is still!

The *Smitten* Rock that gushes!
The *trampled* Steel that springs!
A Cheek is always redder
Just where the Hectic stings!

Mirth is the Mail of Anguish—
In which it Cautions Arm,
Lest anybody spy the blood
And "you're hurt" exclaim!

(165)[12]

As the opening line makes clear, the speaker of the poem is chiefly interested in the action-reaction relationship of wound and leap. "The Hunter" is introduced to draw attention to the cost of the impressive performance. He seems expert in the symptoms of death and points to the imperfect, because momentary, quality of the achievement. The hunter can think the leap insignificant when compared with its brevity and cost. His interest focuses on the existential or the "biographical" sequence of wound—death. The first speaker, however, is obviously fascinated with the way the inevitable ebb of life has been arrested, if only momentarily, by the energy of the leap. It is on this aesthetic sequence of stimulus and performance that the remaining part of the poem concentrates. The second stanza piles up instances of achievement under stress as if to discredit the hunter's slighting remark. On the other hand, the hunter's observation has made the reader aware that as the deer must die, the rock will be crushed, the spring will burst, and fever will eventually consume life. All sense of heroic power displayed in the reaction to assault derives from that knowledge. As long as the "Mail of Mirth" can cover "Anguish," consciousness remains unvanquished and in control of the predicament. The triumph of sheer performance over the most acute existential pain testifies to the commanding power of consciousness.[13]

It may be of some interest to remember at this point that Emerson, in the emotional crisis following the death of his first wife, felt a similar need to balance the pain of his bereavement with the discipline of his art. The overwhelming intensity of emotions defied formal control. His poem breaks down in the middle with the direct, painful cry "dearest Ellen, dearest Ellen":

> O pleasant pleasant in my eye
> The grave is become
> And with all this green majesty
> 'Twill be a sweeter home
> The hours of . . . her [?]
> may not [?] dearest Ellen dearest
> Ellen can we not yet meet on
> the midnight [dr] wing of dreams.
>
> (*J*, 3:230)[14]

General reflection of the philosophical-sentimental kind is used in the first part of the fragment as a means of distancing experience.

When the poem breaks down, it is because the unique character of personal emotion refuses to be relieved through generalizations. Emerson, however, as the inclusion of the poem in *Journals* implies, was not interested in pursuing the aesthetic problems underlying the poem's failure. The poem was not intended as anything more than emotional therapy.

There is much evidence that a similar emotional need lay at the roots of Dickinson's poetry, and that she had to resolve for herself precisely the aesthetic questions which Emerson left unanswered. That concentration on the way pain is borne became her method of distancing personal misery is indicated by another poem:

> . . .—yet to me
> A piercing Comfort it affords
> In passing Calvary—
>
> To note the fashions—of the Cross—
> And how they're mostly worn—
>
> (561)

Paying attention to the aesthetics of suffering, to the "how" rather than the "what" of experience, is the core of her strategy of "shifting grounds." Particular poems are resolutions of particular critical encounters with experience not on the biographical or, generally, existential but only on the aesthetic plane. The characteristic "scenelessness" of Dickinson's poems, observed by Jay Leyda, Ruth Miller, and Robert Weisbuch,[15] is, I believe, chiefly the outcome of this strategy.

On the "biographical" level, confrontations remain mostly unresolved (especially confrontations within the self; see, e.g., 642, 640, 777) or even failure is openly invited (see, e.g., 540, 609, 791) in order, one suspects, to maintain the condition of extreme stress which, in turn, necessitates release in a poem. The "piercing Virtue" of renunciation (745) ensures power, becomes almost a device (if it is not too insensitive a word) for staying in command. The drama of the critical moment becomes a metaphor for the way consciousness operates, while the poem records the moment in which the mind succeeds in drawing a design "upon the arc of white." If Dickinson's poetry can be called the poetry of release,[16] it is a "slant" release, deliberately transferred onto the aesthetic plane. Emersonian in identifying creativity or inspiration with intense moments of consciousness, Emily Dickinson deliberately uses crisis situations, at whatever personal cost, to will the recurrence of the heightened moments of consciousness, an achievement which Emerson always felt was beyond his power.[17]

The intensity of a critical moment, however, cannot be continuously sustained. Dickinson knows that truth as well as Emerson. The deathlike, "numb" stages following crisis are the necessary intervals between the heightened moments. These "hours of lead remembered if outlived" keep the threat of annihilation real to the mind and measure the human cost of the violent confrontation. Time, then, consists of isolated moments of achievement incorporated in individual poems. Whatever sense of continuity can be rescued derives not from any continuous principle to be "discovered" in organic reality; rather it comes, emphatically, from the untiring effort of consciousness to control and organize experience:

> Each Life Converges to some Centre—
> Expressed—or still—
> Exists in every Human Nature
> A Goal—
> . . . .
> Ungained—it may be—by a Life's low Venture—
> But then—
> Eternity enable the endeavoring
> Again.
>
> (680, see also, e.g., 108)

Immortality in this poem is not given; it must be earned through "the Saints' slow diligence." Persistent effort, even if assessed a failure in life's temporal dimension, will survive into eternity. It seems, therefore, only logical that the poet should conceive of immortality as "Costumeless Consciousness" (1454) and, at times, practically identify it with the life of the poem as consciousness encapsulated (as in, for example, "The Poets Light but Lamps" [883] or "He ate and drank the precious Words" [1587]).

Just how the crisis situation serves as "the spinal support" of Dickinson's poems can be clearly seen in her love lyrics. Let me state at the outset that I do not think it plausible to argue that the experience behind them is purely imaginary. And yet the lover in the poems, as many critics have noticed, is a curiously abstracted figure.[18] Rather than a particular man, he is a version of, a metaphor for "the other"; a power principle which must be confronted, and at least counterbalanced, if not unambiguously mastered.

What makes a poem like "Wild Nights" (249) disquieting is the way in which it gives us the essence of passion without passion's personal context. It is a "capsule" of emotion (998), its perfume distilled beyond recognizable connections with the raw material of its origins (448, 675). The personally or factually identifiable setting is replaced by a broad sketch of tempestuous sea—an objective correlative of the heart's yearning. The sea's wildness brings into focus the double edge of desire: its overwhelming power and its potential destructiveness. The lover present only as "thee" and identified with the stormy expanse of water fails to materialize as a person, fails even to assume a distinctly masculine identity. He is present only as the object of yearning and source of the sense of danger. His elemental presence serves to analyze the contradictory impulses within the self.

In an earlier, less complex poem a similar practice can be observed:

> With thee, in the Desert—
> With thee in the thirst—
> With thee in the Tamarind woods—
> Leopard breathes—at last!
>
> (209, c. 1860)

Again the lover present only as the other, the completing "thee," not even specifically identified as a male, is endowed with the ability to release the instinctive, "wild" aspects of the self, the leopard within whom "Civilization—spurns" (492). In the impressive yet perplexing "My Life had stood—a Loaded Gun—" (754, c. 1863), the necessary release of the power within depends upon the union with the masculine hunter-owner, who alone can discharge the otherwise inert energy of the gun. But the imagery throughout the poem points in two directions: to the exultation in the exercise of power and to the deadly danger involved in its violent release.[19]

The ambivalent images, not so much of the lover as of how he affects the self,[20] are complemented by more conventionally "feminine" poems in which the overwhelming yearning for fulfillment removes all sense of danger to the self (see, for example, 162, 212, 284). Love, the need for completing the self with "the other," is, as Dickinson recognizes, as natural as wind and sun, as instinctive as the shutting of eyes against the blaze of lightning (480). It is, like faith, a primary human need. But more often than not Dickinson's poems examine the two sides of this basic urge. Characteristically, even in what seems at first glance a very conventional though also a very sensuous allegory of the sexual act, there occurs a confusion of roles which effectively subverts the orthodox ecstasy of the intensely erotic

> Come slowly—Eden!
> Lips unused to Thee—
> Bashful—sip thy Jessamines—
> As the fainting Bee—
>
> Reaching late his flower,
> Round her chamber hums—
> Counts his nectars—
> Enters—and is lost in Balms.
>
> (211, c. 1860)

The poem opens with the speaker casting herself in the receiving feminine role, but the fourth line shifts the focus to the masculine bee as he enters the chosen flower. An optimistic reading of this seemingly slight poem would focus on the perfect fusion of lovers in union and on the resulting irrelevance of gender. Fulfillment is one and makes them one beyond problems of sexual roles. But a different reading seems equally valid: the intensity of the she-flower's (or his own) ecstasy annihilates the bee. The fact that he is "lost in Balms" seems more destructive than creative, more like a murder or suicide than like conception. The edge of the deceptively smooth surface of the poem remains painfully cutting.[21]

For, to put it in a straightforward way, whenever Emily Dickinson's lovers come together the intensity of their emotions shows its destructive underside; the balance of the relationship is upset. The threat of the loss of self for either of the partners is never out of sight; destruction hangs in the air. It is significant that the union of the lovers in "Wild Nights—Wild Nights!" is made controllable by being posited as a false condition. Integration threatens with loss of distinct identity, that is, with loss of consciousness.[22] Ultimately, the erotic encounter becomes a version of the critical moment of confrontation when survival depends on counterbalancing the partner by holding one's own:

> He was weak, and I was strong—then—
> So He let me lead him in—
> I was weak, and He was strong—then—
> So I let him lead me—Home.
>
> 'Twas'nt far—the door was near—
> 'Twas'nt dark—for He went—too—
> 'Twas'nt loud, for He said nought—
> That was all I cared to know.
>
> Day knocked—and we must part—
> Neither—was strongest—now—
> He strove—and I strove—too—
> We did'nt do it—tho'!
>
> (190, c. 1860)

The poem dismisses all the external context, focusing instead on the struggle for balance. It is not important what it was they "didn't do." It is important how they arrived at the point when they could afford not doing it. We are presented with a feat of psychological as well as aesthetic tightroping. The balance tips this way and that. Through their wavering adjustments the lovers finally come to a standstill which in ordinary life must mean separation. The poem, however, does not dwell on the human price of this exercise in balance. The final simultaneous striving of both partners and their resulting poise are unmistakably presented as achievement. The moment is left frozen for contemplation with a triumphant exclamation. Perhaps the victory is moral. It strikes me, though, as primarily psychological and aesthetic.

When the lovers come too close too intensely, the meeting often becomes menacing, envisioned in terms of rape, violation of the self, or sweeping trance (see 315, 470, 712, 1053). Just as it is impossible to narrow the symbolic content of the sea image to any single interpretation, it is frequently impossible to tell if the "He" in some ominous encounters is man, God, death, or perhaps some other superior natural or supernatural power.

A Wife—at Daybreak I shall be—
Sunrise—Hast thou a Flag for me?
At Midnight, I am but a Maid,
How short it takes to make it Bride—
Then—Midnight, I have passed from Thee
Unto the East, and Victory—

Midnight—Good Night! I hear them call,
The Angels bustle in the Hall—
Softly my Future climbs the Stair,
I fumble at my Childhood's prayer
So soon to be a Child no more—
Eternity, I'm coming—Sir,
Savior—I've seen the face—before!

(461, c. 1862)

The Variorum edition lists variant readings of this poem in two other extant copies. The important lexical change in both (presumably earlier) versions is "Master" for "Savior" in the last line.[23] Also line twelve was first written as "The Vision flutters in the door" then crossed out and the present line substituted. Thus it seems that in revisions the lover became progressively more remote from any concrete man, developing instead into the compound bridegroom-death-Christ-Eternity figure.[24] However, the organizing first night image remains to give immediacy and concreteness[25] to the ambivalent reaction of the speaker as the second stanza largely takes back in fear ("I fumble at my Childhood's prayer / So soon to be a Child no more—") what the first stanza strives to assert as triumph. In the last analysis the lover in this poem is a presence typifying all the major mysteries of existence while the framing first night situation serves to concretize the psychic content of the encounter with the unknown. The lover is a principle of power and necessity whose call cannot be resisted, though it is accompanied by terrors of apprehension.

Consequently, in poem after poem erotic encounters develop into contests for control. The widely anthologized poem 712, "Because I could not stop for Death—," imposes a courting image upon the speaker's final journey with death in order to wrest from him "Immortality," perhaps only immortality of poetic achievement. The beautiful poem 520 (c. 1862) is so rich in sexual imagery that one is tempted to read it as a straightforward allegory of a love affair; nevertheless, the poem resists such narrowing of its focus by the familiar device of identifying the lover with the elemental power of the sea. Direct confrontation within the realm of his wildness threatens the speaker with being eaten "up— / As wholly as a Dew" in a trance-like, irrational fascination. Awakened to the danger, she retreats to what she obviously considers her familiar territory. There not only does the sea appear a stranger, it also has to assume the civilized manners of the "Solid Town" and act like a gentleman escorting his lady home and politely saying good-bye on her doorstep.

The image of the encounter with the erotic partner in these poems functions very much like images of confrontations with superior forces in such poems as "What mystery pervades a well!" (1400), in which the "lid of glass" opens into floorless abyss, or "No man saw awe" (1733), where venturing too near the mystery means annihilation and stunned retreat offers the only chance of surviving. In "I read my sentence—steadily—" (412), the actual confrontation is disarmed of its destructiveness by intense anticipation. Because the meeting has been poised psychically, the "extremity" befriended before it occurred, the soul "and Death, acquainted— / Meet tranquilly, as friends— / Salute, and pass, without a Hint— / And there, the Matter ends—." Like the poem on the lovers' wavering (190) this one too focuses on counterbalancing the partner into inaction. The "angle of vision" is different since neutralizing the ominous power is not a shared achievement but a lonely victory of the exerting consciousness. Essentially, the poems discussed above are reports on how consciousness manages to resist inarticulate surrender to "floorless abyss." Moods vary from confident to desperate, from frivolous to tragic; metaphors change from bees and flowers to star-crossed lovers, to soul and death, to abstractions such as the generalizing voice reporting the visit to "awe" in 1733. Yet the central issue remains stable: to re-create the route by which confrontations turn into poised moments, to freeze for contemplation the moment's dramatically unresolved but psychologically and aesthetically exquisite achievement.

Radical detachment from the fascinating partner removes the creative stimulus. Thus danger lies in numbing consciousness to indifference, and satiety is as lethal as psychic coma from extreme pain. Love poems, therefore, cover much of the territory explored in poems of suffering and poems on thirst and hunger. The piercing virtue of renunciation (745) comes dangerously close to "the letting go" (341), and the question of the effectiveness of "that White Sustenance— / Despair" (640) must never be asked. On the other side of the emotional spectrum, gratification of desire is equally killing. Poem 1772 which, as Johnson suggests, may have been sent to Judge Lord, considers again in images of drink and riches the possibility-creating power of desire. In a poem dated about 1862 the overpowering yearning for fulfillment dominating "Wild Nights—Wild Nights!" yields to a deliberate choice of "the tossing—wild though the sea— / Rather than a Mooring—unshared by thee" (368). Rejected are the "*spicy isles*" of sensuous pleasure and emotional security; protected is the wild energy of "the tossing." The lover's absence is thus remade from an external circumstance into a willed psychic condition.

The lovers' separation constitutes the recurring theme of some of Dickinson's most poignant love poems. Reasons for the piercing parting are never given. It is presented instead as an impalpable but absolute necessity, and one feels justified in suspecting that its nature is primarily psychological.[26] In poem 322 (c. 1861), the suffering of parting is offset by the proximity of the lovers' holy moment of communion. The brevity of ecstasy prevents danger through integration while its intensity provides poise for the "Calvaries of Love" ahead. What was "Clutched tight, by greedy hands—" in their one moment together is endowed with meaning by the extent of bleak pain before them. The difficult balance offsetting communion with the long perspective of loss neutralizes the destructive potential and becomes itself a triumph. "I cannot live with You" (640, c. 1862) goes even further toward the explicit use of distance as basis for a balanced relationship between the lovers. Every conceivable possibility of being together here or hereafter is considered and rejected precisely because it would upset the equilibrium of belief, of custom or personal values. "I cannot live with You— / It would be Life— / And Life is over there— / Behind the Shelf / The Sexton keeps the Key to—"; "I could not die—with You— / For One must wait / to shut the Other's Gaze down—"; we cannot be judged together "Because You saturated Sight— / And I had no more Eyes / For sordid excellence / As Paradise." The only way of remaining together in an acceptable relation is by staying apart:

So We must meet apart—
You there—I—here—
With just the Door ajar
That Oceans are—and Prayer—
And that White Sustenance—
Despair—

Distance alone permits a safe connection with the superior powers whom the lover typifies while the void felt within keeps the link vital. Despair of ever being united is this union's one immaculate sustenance.

The shifting of the lover's presence in space and time to adjust the emotional tension within the speaker-persona again brings to mind poems of thirst and starvation or the willful distancing of home in "I Years had been from Home" (609). Love poems, thirst and starvation poems, and away-from-home poems share the basic structuring pattern in which distance to consummation is controlled to protect the energy of desire and the resulting heightened consciousness. One may argue that Emily Dickinson "loved no one except herself"[27] or that she was confused about her sexual identity,[28] that her lover was Death or God or Immortality,[29] or that he personified the creative principle within, which it was difficult for her to accept and accommodate because she was a woman in a patriarchal society.[30] All these points have been made by different readers, critics, and scholars. The efforts to tie Dickinson's poems to particular interpretations, however, too often result in a narrowing down of the poems' scope and concerns, while the actual poems strive passionately to disengage themselves from stifling literariness in order to leap into openness, next only to infinity. Nowhere is this process revealed more clearly than in "If you were coming in the Fall" (511, 1862), which starts as a love poem but ends as an existential query:

If you were coming in the Fall,
I'd brush the Summer by
With half a smile, and half a spurn,
As Housewives do, a Fly.

If I could see you in a year,
I'd wind the months in balls—
And put them each in separate Drawers,
For fear the numbers fuse—

If only Centuries, delayed,
I'd count them on my Hand,
Subtracting, till my fingers dropped
Into Van Dieman's Land.

If certain, when this life was out—
That yours and mine, should be
I'd toss it yonder, like a Rind,
And take Eternity—

But, now, uncertain of the length
Of this, that is between,
It goads me, like the Goblin Bee—
That will not state—it's sting.

As the time of waiting for the lover's return lengthens, his figure evolves from human to perhaps divine until his place is completely taken by the overwhelming metaphysical doubt. The expansion of time in each successive stanza signals the development away from the specific toward increasingly abstract meaning. First the lover's meeting is expected in the fall; then postponed till the next year; then it becomes a matter of "centuries," and, finally, of eternity, so that "he," whom at first we take for a human lover, may well be God. What is more, we also come to recognize that it is not the separation from the lover which is the main problem but suspense and lack of certainty. Appropriately, the conclusion drops "him" altogether and focuses exclusively on the haunting doubt. In retrospect, the succession of provisional situations presented in the first part of the poem seems invented to "design" a void, a tauntingly indefinite reality. The multiplied conditions form stages in the mind's effort to cope with cosmic doubt. For it is not any particular man's presence or absence that gives the greatest challenge or hurt in the poems. What challenges and pains is the conflict between the need to possess, to know and believe, and the creative necessity to deny such security. To possess and know would be to give up "the tossing," to deprive consciousness of the very source of energy. To lack and desire means to open possibility. And so, rather than settle for any final solution, Dickinson dwells "in Possibility— / A fairer House than Prose—" (657).

The physical separation from the lover, the piercing virtue of renunciation in general, is made analogous to the rejection of the security of faith. Intellectual distance from specific creeds, religious or philosophical, finds metaphorical equivalents in withdrawal from emotional and sensuous gratifications in so many poems. Thus questions may be asked again and again, and imaginative confrontations may recur. Just as physical distance in encounters with the lover regulates emotional tensions, intellectual distance to experience makes balance and control possible.

How is the intellectual distance created? The strategies of looking "behind at pain" (*L*, 2:416), what David Porter calls her "afterward condition"[31] and Robert Weisbuch "a second spontaneity of an over the shoulder view,"[32] work for both emotional and intellectual perspectives. But Dickinson uses other strategies even more explicitly oriented toward intellectual distancing and discipline. Sharon Cameron has penetratingly discussed ways in which the form of definition is used in many poems to ensure distance and control.[33] The argument can be expanded to show that frequent use of the definition formula constitutes but an aspect of a larger tendency, in fact, of a consistent practice of fitting experience into molds of formal reasoning. Poem 398 (just as 511) is built on the negated syllogism: If the world were a monolithic rock, I could reach you but the world is something quite different, therefore. . . . Though not stated *expresis verbis*, the conclusion follows necessarily from the axiomatic pattern. It is the formal structure of thought into which intimate experience has been forcibly pressed that turns personal tragedy of noncommunication into law. It is the logical pattern of reasoning that articulates and shapes what threatens to become but an overflow of grief. In "I cannot live with You" (640), the circumstance of separation from the lover provokes the mind's struggle to master the predicament. The whole poem is virtually a duel during which the heartbreaking intensity of experience is fitted into a methodical pattern of reasoning. Possibilities, or rather impossibilities, of being together are considered one by one and, when all have been exhausted, the conclusion comes as much as a triumph of the disciplined mind as it remains an imposed, external circumstance. The mind succeeds in drawing a design where there was only the turmoil of pain. Once again, it manages to bring to a standstill the incredibly concentrated emotion resisting through order its destructive potential. The balance is recognized as infinitely precarious; the condensed emotion threatens at any moment to disrupt the inexorable design. And the recognition serves to render the achievement both more heroic and more exquisite.

In a related practice, Dickinson imposes conceits, images both formalized and intellectualized, upon situations which threaten to overwhelm consciousness. Approaching a poem like the widely anthologized "Because I could not stop for Death" (712), the reader is most likely to be first impressed with its ingenuity. The poem is explicitly oriented toward a shock effect. We are not expected to accept the truth of a discovery, and the image of death as a civilized gentleman calling on his lady to take her for a ride does not familiarize the thought of mortality in the same way as do Whitman's incorporations of death in the process of constant renewal of life. What we are meant to admire here is, first of all, the performance, the feat of imagination which, spurred by the terror of the moment, imposes, even if precariously, a wholly domestic order upon the ominous unknown.

In such moments, Dickinson is closest to the metaphysicals. She too relies on the conceit for intellectual control of an intensely emotional moment. Images like

> The Sweeping up the Heart
> And putting Love away
> We shall not want to use again
> Until Eternity.
>
> (1078)

or the one where the sexton is

> Putting up
> Our Life—His Porcelain—
> Like a Cup—
>
> Discarded of the Housewife—
> Quaint—or Broke—
>
> (640)

though not conceits in the sense of providing controlling images for the poems in which they appear, are oriented toward surprise and are used for their intellectual energy rather than for visual richness. They force the awesome experience of "a nearness to Tremendousness"

(963) into patterns of daily chores so familiar that they seem almost mechanical. The violence of the confrontation between the disruptive content of experience and the rigidity of patterns through which it becomes expressed makes the poems quiver at the breaking point. Similarly, in the final stanza of poem 1100 when an awful leisure comes "Belief to regulate," the vital spark of the closing image is struck between the disheveled condition of belief at this point and the stiff precision of the verb. To treat belief, however profound its disturbance, as an adjustable mechanism is, beside offering a psychological insight, to impose, impossibly and precariously, order where order has been abolished. "Faith" becomes simultaneously as solid as and nothing more than "a fine invention" (185), while the structure of thought and the linguistic design of the poem bring forth, arrange for viewing as it were, the essence of the psychic process.

Dickinson's use of conceit constitutes an important element in her strategy of "shifting grounds." It provides a way of retreating onto her own territory where the unknown can be met on the poet's terms. Poem 585, occasioned by the opening of Amherst–Belchertown Railroad (in which her father was greatly instrumental), furnishes an almost symbolic illustration of the procedure. The train's domestication (the controlling image is that of a horse) came, in a way, naturally as the new railroad's terminal was built on the Dickinson Meadow, land formerly owned by the poet's grandfather.[34] She could, indeed, feel on her own territory there. And once the initiative belonged to her, the performance demonstrating the mind's virtuosity mattered most. The more surprising her images, the more obvious the mind's control, but also the more precarious, the more provisional. She needed the tension, though, for, ultimately, it is on this paradox that the tragic dimension of her art depends—not on the exploitation of any personal disappointment.

Even in Dickinson's ostensibly "reportorial" poems it is the mental process of "arranging" experience which is brought to the foreground. I cannot think of a better way of demonstrating this than by comparing Emily Dickinson's most "imagistic" poem[35]—the one on the hummingbird—with Whitman's imagism as seen in, for example, "Cavalry Crossing a Ford":

A Route of Evanescence
With a revolving Wheel—

A Resonance of Emerald—
A Rush of Cochineal—
And every Blossom on the Bush
Adjusts it's tumbled Head—
The mail from Tunis, probably,
An easy Morning's Ride—

(1463)

If both poems are compared to pictures, Whitman's is a realistic scene executed with loving care for detail while Dickinson's is an impressionistic view in which the object becomes decomposed into elements of color and movement. The hummingbird is replaced on the canvas by the analysis of the effect produced on the artist's mind.[36] In the end the subject is dropped entirely, as the concluding two lines do not, expectedly, reassemble the object but move away from it to present the reader with a literary association. The seemingly arbitrary allusion to *The Tempest*[37] offers a synthesis of the observer's reaction in addition to juxtaposing her garden with infinite distances, and the fleeting moment of beauty with the permanence of Shakespeare's art. Again Dickinson "shifts grounds." She will not trust the scene, as Whitman does, to convey perfectly her emotional and intellectual response. Instead, she uses the scene to activate the mind and drops it when it has served the purpose by making "the leap" into infinity possible.

Viewing Dickinson's poetry as centered on the confrontation between the self's overwhelming response to experience and the imperative of consciousness to make sense of it in an act of articulation highlights the poet's compositional problems. Like Whitman's, they converge on balance. To be dramatically effective, the duel at the base of Dickinson's poems must involve equal partners: the heart's need to believe must be offset by the equally legitimate claim of the mind to comprehend; God's omnipotence must be juxtaposed with the child's trustful vulnerability; the enticing "silver call" of the lover must be counterbalanced by the physical and psychic impossibility of the union; the terror of death must be met by the mind's gallant effort to familiarize the unknown.

On the stylistic level, as David Porter noticed, "to express her vision with finality she was compelled not to make her own minute feelings reveal a general truth for others, but rather to take what others had also seen and felt and expressed (in the hymn, for example), and refine that to suit her own purposes."[38] Roland Hagenbüchle expands: "Generally speaking, some established pattern (hymn, rhyme, level of style, intellectual, social and religious structures) functions as background or expectation horizon in the reader whom Dickinson strategically disappoints in rhythmic, phonetic, semantic and even philosophical respects."[39] In other words, Dickinson relies on conventions, on "established patterns," whether philosophical, psychological, or stylistic, and sets them at odds with the uniqueness of the private vision and style. It is, I think, important to realize that the "established pattern" in Dickinson's poems does not correspond to any organic law or design. It is insistently, a man-made construct: a belief, a custom, a form of verse, a pattern of argument, or a design of language, and it derives from the intellect's "rage for order" for "Pattern is the Mind bestowed" (1223). In a Dickinson poem, the established pattern forms a hold of the known, resisting the idiosyncratic, the chaotic, the unknown. Yet the necessity of final yielding to the mystery is never lost from sight. The "established pattern" is only provisional, the exhilaration of the achievement cannot last, the triumph of order is but momentary. The instability of the achieved poise limits the commanding power of consciousness in the same degree in which existentially man is limited by the fact of his mortality (see 1238).

When the achievement came too easily, Dickinson was most likely to lapse into her sentimental and childish postures:

> I went to Heaven—
> 'Twas a small Town—
> Lit—with a Ruby—
> Lathed—with Down—
>
> Stiller—than the fields
> At the full Dew—
> Beautiful—as Pictures—
> No Man drew.
> People—like the Moth—
> Of Mechlin—frames—
> Duties—of Gossamer—
> And Eider—names—
> Almost—contended—
> I—could be—

'Mong such unique
Society—

(374, see also, e.g., 248, 413)

The facility with which imagination makes a toy out of the encounter with Heaven eliminates drama. Instead, the reader is left with a reductively precious conceit. The tension, the exhilaration of response to a challenge, the thrill of a difficult struggle, all are gone. By comparison, a poem like "Because I could not stop for Death" (712) is rescued from mere cleverness by the vivid realization that the order imposed through the extravagantly idyllic image is infinitely fragile, that "the mail of mirth" is poignantly insubstantial:

The Dews drew quivering and chill—
For only Gossamer, my Gown
My Tippet—only Tulle—

The cold shiver here is the shiver of recognition of the audacity of imagination attempting to familiarize the terror of death through sheer bravado of performance. Eventually, however, it is the panic-defying performance that allows the hope that the "Horses Heads were toward Eternity—."

Surprise with the familiar, as Charles Anderson has extensively shown,[40] is Dickinson's constant practice and a source of much delight for her readers. Images of social and domestic order extravagantly imposed upon the realm of nature abound in her poems, early and late. In "The Grass so little has to do—" (333), the controlling image is that of common grass occupied with royal activities such as threading "the Dews, all night, like Pearls." "The Day undressed—Herself—" in 716, taking off "Her Garter— . . . of Gold," "Her Petticoat—of Purple plain—," and "Her Dimities—as old / Exactly—as the World—." The bat is a "fallow Article—," "His small Umbrella quaintly halved" (1575). After the storm is over (1397), the first courageous men leave their shelters to find nature "in an Opal Apron, / Mixing fresher Air." Beyond surprise with the familiar, the images quoted (and countless others) also demonstrate the facility with which the poet imposed imaginative order upon various natural phenomena. As Maurice Gonnaud says:

Her warning to the clown . . . may very well originate in an almost irresistible inclination on her part to treat "This whole Experiment of Green— / As if it were [her] own" (1333). And the poem itself comes off because of the tension between the orthodoxy of a tradition which insists on Nature's distinct existence as a source of inspiration, and her personal experience, in which she feels that Nature responds all too submissively to her moods.[41]

Extending this observation, I'd like to suggest that generally we object to Dickinson's poems when they fail to convey the tension between the established pattern and the content of personal experience; when the difficult and precarious balance in which consciousness just manages to retain hold on experience is upset either because consciousness triumphs too easily or because the intensity of experience defies order.

When the imposition of the imaginative order comes too easily as in poem 374 quoted above and numerous others, Dickinson is most likely to pose in her coy, flirtatious, "little girl" attitudes, showing off the facility with which experience unconditionally surrenders to the caprices of imagination. Delight in the activity of the mind overshadows or removes the concern for the quality of experience. An early poem by Dickinson can look more like an exercise in stretching logic to the extremes of paradox than like an effort to articulate experience:

> If recollecting were forgetting,
> Then I remember not.
> And if forgetting, recollecting,
> How near I had forgot.
> And if to miss, were merry,
> And to mourn, were gay,
> How very blithe the fingers
> That gathered this, Today!
>
> (33, c. 1858)

The poem parades intellectual nimbleness at the cost of emotional depth. It starts and ends in showy cleverness.

On other occasions, poems dissolve into abstractions as they fail to offset the pattern created by the mind with the physical concreteness of detail and with the sense of immediacy of the experience lived through. In poem 376, the audacious gesture of the bird is made at the same time illustrative of, and distanced from, the speaker's bitterness by the recognition of its insignificance:

> Of Course—I prayed—
> And did God Care?
> He cared as much as on the Air
> A Bird—had stamped her foot—
> And cried "Give Me"—
> My Reason—Life—
> I had not had—but for Yourself—
> 'Twere better Charity
> To leave me in the Atom's Tomb—
> Merry, and Nought, and gay, and numb—
> Than this smart Misery.

Tension is created between individual rebellion projected upon the bird and the recognition of its futility. The cause of rebellion, the factual content of the experience, is not even clearly specified because it is irrelevant. Essentially the poem is organized by the contradictory pulls of emotional response to the predicament and the apprehension of its futility. They reverberate in the incongruous epithets "Merry, and Nought," "gay, and numb," and in the concluding oxymoron of "this smart Misery."

In contrast, assuming a generalized perspective, poem 377 eliminates drama. The authority of firsthand experience is replaced by the authority of laying the law. In other words, the poem fails to realize the tension between individual sensibility and general rule; abstractions take over:

> To lose one's faith—surpass
> The loss of an Estate—
> Because Estates can be
> Replenished—faith cannot—
>
> Inherited with Life—
> Belief—but once—can be—
> Annihilate a single clause—
> And Being's Beggary—

The poem is a variation on Dickinson's poem of definition. It provides the rule. Faith imaged as "Estate," belief as a title deed, and its loss as the condition of "Beggary" remain legal abstractions which fail to capture the immediate quality of experience, the personal sense of loss. Similarly, poems such as 807 or 809 operate exclusively on generalizations and end by sounding sententious. They do not have the ability of cutting to the quick which Dickinson's best poems possess so remarkably. Instead, the reader feels that the personal experience behind them offers no resistance to the generalizing mold into which it is smoothly and completely pressed. The energy of the immediate and the particular is given no chance to modify the abstract pattern.

At the other end of the spectrum, the intensity of experience can narrow the speaker's perspective, making it self-centered. Here we find Dickinson's speaker in the attitudes familiar from the "grovelling" love poems, begging for recognition as she assumes postures of conspicuous humility:

> What shall I do—it whimpers so—
> This little Hound within the Heart
> All day and night with bark and start—
> And yet, it will not go—
> Would you *untie* it, were you me—
> Would it stop whining—if to Thee—
> I sent it—even now?
>
> (186)

Poems of this type are especially prone to tones of self-pity and melodrama (see also 192, 193, 236, 248) with, occasionally, a note of vindictiveness creeping in:

> I'm banished—now—you know it—
> How foreign that can be—
> You'll know—Sir—when the Savior's face
> Turns so—away from you—
>
> (256)

They lack the stark dignity and the sense of hard-won strength of the self so characteristic of Dickinson's best poems. One feels that the speaker-persona is not equal to the demands presented by experience and retreats into the attitudes of self-abasement and self-pity.

In some poems language fails to carry the weight of experience. The second and especially the third of the "Master" letters furnish the most obvious examples, though in their extant form they are but drafts and very possibly were never sent as communications. However, poem 462, also addressed to the "Master," shows related difficulties:

> Why make it doubt—it hurts it so—
> So sick—to guess—
> So strong—to know—
> So brave upon it's little Bed
> To tell the very last They said
> Unto Itself—and smile—And shake—
> For that dear—distant—dangerous—Sake—
> But—the Instead—the Pinching fear
> That Something—it did do—or dare—
> Offend the Vision—and it flee—
> And They no more remember me—
> Nor ever turn to tell me why—
> Oh, Master, This is Misery—

The disproportion of forces between partners in this relationship is conveyed through reducing the speaker-persona to "it" (an insignificantly small creature? a thing?) while the Master figure is meant to loom larger compounded to "They." However, the "it"–"They" relation does not seem intimate enough; more, it does not feel human enough to give the last line the poignancy it should have. On the contrary, the poem sounds disjointed, an effect strengthened by the breathless syntax. The use of the "it" pronoun blurs the meaning of the poem, especially in line 10 where another "it" refers to "the Vision." Eventually, the ineffectiveness of this, presumably distancing, device breaks to the surface when, in the desperate closing lines, the "it" is abandoned in favor of the straightforward first person pronoun. The reason for the inconsistency must be that the "it" persona proved too close to playing a game and could not sustain the weight of suffering.

The whole poem 172 (c. 1862) depends on exclamations which sound more shrill than enraptured. Poem 296 fails, it seems to me, primarily on the level of incoherent language whose fragmentation obscures the essence of the experience behind it. Relying on the energy of emotions to carry a poem through is not Dickinson's province. She is at her best when she can oppose the intensity of feelings with the rigor of made forms. The poems quoted above and others of this type resemble instead Emerson's journal poem quoted on page 134. They fail to transform emotion into art and leave the reader with the sense that at some basic level the power of articulation capitulated to the overwhelming experience.

More poems can be quoted to demonstrate the failure of the structuring imagination to impose a pattern upon the raw intensities of feeling. Poem 399 attempts to define what apparently cannot be known, to articulate what defies articulation, and to design a mystery that surpasses the compass of the mind:

A House upon the Hight—
That Wagon never reached—
No Dead, were ever carried down—
No Peddler's Cart—approached—

Whose Chimney never smoked—
Whose Windows—Night and Morn—
Caught Sunrise first—and Sunset—last—
Then—held an Empty Pane—

Whose fate—Conjecture knew—
No other neighbor—did—
And what it was—we never lisped—
Because He—never told—

Critics differ rather widely in their interpretations of this poem. Brita Lindberg-Seyersted sees it as a rendering of an everyday scene (the house, the hill, the cart) beneath whose surface throb suspence and mystery.[42] For Eleanor Wilner, the poem is Dickinson's "closest approach to the idea of God,"[43] and for Inder Nath Kher, it is "an autonomous symbolic construct. . . . The house is a metaphor for art."[44] In the typical Dickinsonian manner, the poem dismisses the "what" of the experience it seeks to convey. The factual content, the "what the poem is about" disappears perhaps too easily for the reader's needs. What remains constitutes the record of the imagination's effort to cope with ultimate mystery. The attempt proceeds by negation. "A House upon the Hight" is like nothing we know; no activities known from everyday experience take place in or around it so that there is no way in which "Conjecture" about it can be visualized and articulated. The poem negates any point of comparison, any similarity between "A House upon the Hight" and our daily knowledge of houses. Consequently, there is no possibility of making the content of the experience more available. "Conjecture," even if it guesses, has no means to tell. Hence the excessive openness to a variety of readings. At the end of the poem the reader is really no closer to the nature of the experience than he was at its beginning. The poem stands still starting with the assumption that what it has to convey cannot be told, and ending with the same realization. Since its sole point seems to be to demonstrate "the Impotence to Tell" (407), it feels closer to compulsive talking from some powerful but hardly specified need than to a deliberate effort at clarifying meaning and designing an aesthetically ordered space in the expanse of the unknown.

Poem 466, in turn, attempts to visualize the experience of ultimate fulfillment which makes the speaker superior to any temptation. Four successive images of treasures (Pearles, Brooches, Gold, and Diamonds) rejected because the speaker already owns greater wealth (the "sea," "Rubies" with which "the Emperor . . . pelteth" her, gold mines, and "A Diadem to fit a Dome— / Continual upon me") are used to illustrate the general statement to be inferred from them: that no riches are tempting where extravagant wealth is already owned. In its attempt to convey supreme contentment, the poem suffers from a lack of dynamism somewhat similar to poem 399. It too ends where it starts. The images employed to illustrate the rule do not lead to its gradual inference. Instead, they restate the law in four not so very different ways; they resemble Whitman's catalogues without Whitman's sense of progression. Rather, the poem leaves the reader with the impression of the speaker groping for some final clinching image or formula and failing to find it. As in the poem on "A House upon the Hight," the ultimate cannot be finally captured. The designing consciousness gives up, incapable of structuring the superlative experience or, perhaps, withdraws for fear of diminishing it, of nullifying its superlative quality in the act of articulation.

Dickinson's poems have a concern more vital than the "flood subjects." Their ostensible themes of nature, love, death, and immortality are employed to one overwhelming purpose: they serve to map the road by which the mind travels to meet the unknown; they show how consciousness impinges on the mystery's territory, failing sometimes but also managing to exhibit "Sheets of Place—" (974) by taking constant risks in the perilous confrontation. Events along the road of experience are in the poems deliberately turned into designs of the mind since Dickinson cannot believe, as Whitman does all the time, that the idea inheres in physical reality to the point where the craft's role is simply to demonstrate that truth. She could not agree that "To elaborate is no avail, learn'd and unlearn'd feel that it is so" ("Song of Myself," *LG*, 31 : 47) because for her it is always individual consciousness "Where the Meanings, are—" (258, see also 526 and 1223). Whitman's whole art goes into a hiding technique so that the poems can participate in the spontaneity of life; Dickinson, on the other hand, consistently and deliberately, exposes her craft. For ultimately, in her vision, it is not faith but the achievement of consciousness, its actual performance in daily confrontations with experience, that measures the heroism of the self and ensures salvation. Dickinson's domain is the poem of critical confrontation between the ordering power of consciousness and the tumultuous forces of the unknown. Her failures result from the inability to adjust the balance of forces between the dueling partners. Success comes in moments of precarious poise when a frightening glimpse into the abyss of nothingness offsets the triumphant, tragic beauty of the poem as "a momentary stay against confusion."

Notes

1. John F. Lynen, "Three Uses of the Present. The Historian's, The Critic's and Emily Dickinson's," *College English* 28, no. 2 (November 1966): 134–35.

2. Robert Weisbuch, *Emily Dickinson's Poetry* (Chicago: University of Chicago Press, 1975), 10.

3. On the relation between Dickinson's ambiguous vision and aspects of her style, see also Karl Keller's "Alephs, Lahirs, and the Triumph of Ambiguity: Typology in Nineteenth-Century American Literature," in *Literary Uses of Typology from the Middle Ages to the Present*, ed. Earl Miner (Princeton: Princeton University Press, 1977), 302–14.

4. Ruth Miller, *The Poetry of Emily Dickinson* (Middletown, Conn.: Wesleyan University Press, 1968), 130.

5. David Porter talks about "the fundamental disjunction of experience into motion and stasis" in Emily Dickinson's poems (*The Art of Emily Dickinson's Early Poetry* [Cambridge, Mass.: Harvard University Press, 1966], 131). For the contrast between motion and stasis, transience and permanence in Dickinson's poetry, see esp. chap. 5 of Porter's book.

6. Brita Lindberg-Seyersted, *The Voice of the Poet: Aspects of Style in the Poetry of Emily Dickinson* (Uppsala: Almqvist and Wiksells Boktryckeri AB, 1968), 81.

7. Ibid., 89.

8. Albert Gelpi, *Emily Dickinson: The Mind of the Poet* (Cambridge, Mass.: Harvard University Press, 1965), 60; see also Richard Chase, *Emily Dickinson* (New York: William Sloane Associates, 1951), esp. chap. 5. In chapter 7 of this book, Chase makes the following statement: "It would never have occurred to Emily Dickinson that a poem might have a primarily metaphysical origin, or that anyone would write a poem out of a desire to create a finished and formal object of art" (192).

9. Roland Hagenbüchle, "Precision and Indeterminacy in the Poetry of Emily Dickinson," *Emerson Society Quarterly* 20 (1974): 38–39.

10. Miller, *The Poetry of Emily Dickinson*, 130.

11. See Richard Wilbur's beautiful essay "Sumptuous Destitution," in *Emily Dickinson: Three Views* (Amherst: Amherst College Press, 1960) reprinted in *Emily Dickinson: A Collection of Critical Essays*, ed. Richard Sewall (Englewood Cliffs, N.J.: Prentice-Hall, 1963), 127–36.

12. Thomas Johnson dates this poem c. 1860 and so does Ralph Franklin. Compare also, for example, 442, 525, 770, 1355.

13. See also Agnieszka Salska, "Emily Dickinson's Commanding Consciousness," *Acta Universitatis Lodziensis, Folia Anglica* 1, no. 20 (1976): 47–55.

14. My attention to this effort of Emerson's was drawn by remarks in the foreword to vol. 3 of William H. Gilman et al., eds., *The Journals and Miscellaneous Notebooks of Ralph Waldo Emerson* (Cambridge, Mass.: Harvard University Press, 1962), xi–xii.

15. Jay Leyda, *The Years and Hours of Emily Dickinson* (New Haven: Yale University Press, 1960), xxi; Miller, *The Poetry of Emily Dickinson*, 129–30; Weisbuch, *Emily Dickinson's Poetry*, 16.

16. See Miller, *The Poetry of Emily Dickinson*: "When she wearied of the

weight of her message, she was obliged to deliver herself of her poetry" (166). In support of the thesis, Miller quotes from Dickinson's letter to T. W. Higginson (June 7, 1862): "I felt a palsy here—the Verses just relieve."

17. See especially the chapter "A Few Herbs and Apples" In F. O. Mathiessen's *American Renaissance: Art and Expression in the Age of Emerson and Whitman* (London: Oxford University Press, 1941). See also Philip Charles Smith's "Momentary Music: The Problem of Power and Form in Emerson's Poetry" (Ph.D. diss., University of Nebraska, 1974).

18. Richard Chase, for example, comments on "There came a day at summer's full" (322): "Even this often praised poem may be somewhat weakened by a running analogy between the lovers and various phenomena associated with the Christian religion which tend to give a remoteness, an intangibility to the lovers and their feelings, and a diffuseness to the general movement of the poem" (*Emily Dickinson*, 243).

19. Adrienne Rich, "Vesuvius at Home: The Power of Emily Dickinson," *Parnassus: Poetry in Review* 5, no. 1 (Fall/Winter 1976), reprinted in *Shakespeare's Sisters: Feminist Essays on Women Poets*, ed. Sandra M. Gilbert and Susan Gubar (Bloomington: Indiana University Press, 1979), 99–121; see also Albert J. Gelpi, "Emily Dickinson and the Deerslayer: The Dilemma of the Woman Poet in America," in Gilbert and Gubar, *Shakespeare's Sisters*, 122–34.

20. See also Joanne Feit Diehl, "Dickinson and the American Self," *Emerson Society Quarterly* 26 (1980): 1–9 and *Dickinson and the Romantic Imagination* (Princeton: Princeton University Press, 1981), esp. chaps. 1 and 5. Diehl argues that Dickinson projects "the Stranger" whom in varying guises of Lover, God, Death, or the other Self she must confront in the poems. In Diehl's view this is the result of the pressures under which a woman artist worked in a patriarchal culture.

21. For a similar reading of this poem see also Porter, *The Art of Emily Dickinson's Early Poetry*, 35; and Suzanne Juhasz, *Naked and Fiery Forms* (New York: Octagon Books, 1976), 25.

22. Evan Carton maintains that Dickinson's attitude to the Divine Ideal is marked by both terror of integration and terror of detachment. Integration means loss of the self, detachment—loss of expectation. See "Dickinson and the Divine: The Terror of Integration, the Terror of Detachment," *Emerson Society Quarterly* 24 (1978): 242–52.

23. In the fascicle copy (Fascicle 32, dated by Franklin "about 1862," *The Manuscript Books of Emily Dickinson* [Cambridge, Mass.: Harvard University Press, 1981], 781), the last line reads: "Master—I've seen the face—before." It is difficult to avoid associations with the "Master letters" (*L*, 187, 233, 248). Johnson's dating of the letters (no. 187 undated, no. 233 about 1861, no. 248 early 1862?) though tentative, encourages the connection.

24. On Dickinson's "strangely abstracted images" see especially chapter 2 in David T. Porter, *Dickinson: The Modern Idiom* (Cambridge, Mass.: Harvard University Press, 1981).

25. Brian Attebery in "Dickinson, Emerson and the Abstract Concrete," *Dickinson Studies* 35 (1979): 17–22, sees the practice of treating abstract nouns as if they were things and persons as Dickinson's consistent stylistic feature, becoming in fact more striking in her later poems.

26. Enlarging consciousness through loss is the subject of Richard Wilbur's essay "Sumptuous Destitution" (*Emily Dickinson: Three Views*). The use of distance for clarity and discipline is discussed in Sharon Cameron's *The Lyric Time: Dickinson and the Limits of Genre* (Baltimore: Johns Hopkins University Press, 1979), esp. chap. 1.

27. Clarke Griffith, *The Long Shadow: Emily Dickinson's Tragic Poetry* (Princeton: Princeton University Press, 1964), 183.

28. John Cody, *After Great Pain: The Inner Life of Emily Dickinson* (Cambridge, Mass.: Harvard University Press, Belknap Press, 1971), 224.

29. "Perfectly typical of much of her love poetry is the representation of an experience which is both the spiritual reception of grace and union with the lover" (Chase, *Emily Dickinson*, 157).

30. Rich, "Vesuvius at Home"; Diehl, *Dickinson and the Romantic Imagination*, 18–19.

31. Porter, *Dickinson: The Modern Idiom*, chap. 1, "The Crucial Experience." (An earlier version of this chapter was published in *Emerson Society Quarterly* 20 [1974]: 280–90.)

32. Weisbuch, *Emily Dickinson's Poetry*, 20.

33. Cameron, *Lyric Time*, chap. 1, "Naming as History: Dickinson's Poems of Definition."

34. I am indebted to Charles Anderson's discussion of this poem in *Emily Dickinson's Poetry: A Stairway of Surprise* (New York: Holt, Rinehart and Winston, 1960), 14–16, for the information.

35. Amy Lowell quoted this poem admiringly in her lectures on imagism at The Brooklyn Institute in 1918. She regarded Dickinson as a forerunner of imagism because of her "'unrelated' method" of "describing . . . a thing by its appearance only, without regard to its entity in any other way" (*Poetry and Poets: Essays* [Boston: Houghton Mifflin, 1930], 107).

36. Although Roland Hagenbüchle (in "Precision and Indeterminacy") associates Emily Dickinson with Edgar Allan Poe because of the shared concentration on effect, it is difficult to accept the association without reservation. Dickinson's concern is with analyzing the effect of experience on the mind and psyche while Poe's emphasis rests on reproducing the desired effect.

37. Frank Davidson first noticed that the allusion is to *The Tempest*, 2:246–48 (see "A Note on Emily Dickinson's Use of Shakespeare," *New England Quarterly* 18 [September 1945]: 407–8).

38. Porter, *The Art of Emily Dickinson's Early Poetry*, 136. The "strategic" imbalance of her style was also noticed by Northrop Frye in his excellent essay "Emily Dickinson," in *Fables of Identity* (New York: Harcourt, Brace and World, 1963).

39. Hagenbüchle, "Precision and Indeterminacy," 40.

40. Anderson, *Emily Dickinson's Poetry*.

41. Maurice Gonnaud, "Nature, Apocalypse or Experiment: Emerson's Double Lineage in American Poetry," a paper delivered at the EAAS conference in Heidelberg in 1976, published in *Vistas of a Continent: Concepts of Nature in America*, ed. Teut Andreas Riese (Heidelberg: Carl Winter Universitätsverlag, 1979), Heft 136, 123–41.

42. Lindberg-Seyersted, *The Voice of the Poet*, 192–93.

43. Eleanor Wilner, "The Poetics of Emily Dickinson," *Journal of English Literary History* 38 (1971): 141.

44. Inder Nath Kher, *The Landscape of Absence: Emily Dickinson's Poetry* (New Haven: Yale University Press, 1974), 51.

6 / *The Tool: Language*

IN the much quoted section of "Nature," Emerson makes his most explicit statement about what he believes is the essence of language:

1. Words are signs of natural facts.
2. Particular words are symbols of particular spiritual facts.
3. Nature is the symbol of spirit.

(1:25)

Language, therefore, is on the one hand grounded in physical reality: "Every word which is used to express a moral or intellectual fact, if traced to its root, is found to be borrowed from some material appearance. *Right* means *straight*; *wrong* means *twisted*" (1:25). Other examples press the point. On the other hand, language participates directly in the spiritual essence of all nature, which is "put forth" by the spirit "as the life of the tree puts forth new branches and leaves" (1:64).

Fifty years later Whitman expressed a similar view,[1] and his examples show that he had kept Emerson's argument in mind:

Language in the largest sense . . . is really the greatest of studies. It involves so much; is indeed a sort of universal absorber, combiner, and conqueror. The scope of its etymologies is the scope not only of man and civilization, but the history of Nature in all departments, and of organic Universe. . . . Language, be it remember'd, is not an abstract construction of the learn'd, or of dictionary-makers, but is something arising out of the work, needs, ties, joys, affections, tastes, of long generations of humanity, and has its bases broad and low, close to the ground. Its final decisions are made by the masses, people nearest to the concrete, having most to do with actual land and sea. (*PW*, 2:572:3–8; 573:46–51)

Whitman is interested in slang because he recognizes it to be the level at which language comes closest to the elemental life force:

Slang, profoundly consider'd, is the lawless germinal element, below all words and sentences, and behind all poetry, and proves a certain perennial rankness and protestantism in speech. Slang, too, is the wholesome fermentation or eructation of those processes eternally active in language, by which froth and specks are thrown up, mostly to pass away; though occasionally to settle and permanently to chrystallize. (*PW*, 2:572:12–14; 573:26–30)

What fascinate Whitman are the qualities of language which make words share in the essence of nature: its tangibility, its sensuous richness and, above all, its primal energy.

That language, especially poetic language, not only participates but originates in the nonconscious life is Emerson's belief as well, though Emerson more explicitly joins the living base of language with rhythm:

Meter begins with pulse-beat, and the length of lines in songs and poems is determined by the inhalation and exhalation of the lungs. If you hum or whistle the rhythm of the common English meters,—of the decasyllabic quatrain, or the octosyllabic with alternate sexisyllabic, or other rhythms,—you can easily believe these meters to be organic, derived from the human pulse, and to be therefore not proper to one nation, but to mankind. . . . And human passion, seizing these constitutional tunes, aims to fill them with appropriate words, or marry music to thought, believing, . . . that for every thought its proper melody or rhyme exists. (8:46; 47)

When Emily Dickinson asked Higginson for criticism, she too wanted to know first of all if her verses "breathed" (*L*, 2:403). Language which is life is the ideal to which all three artists aspire. Where they differ is in their assumptions about how language lives.

The striking thing in the passage from "Poetry and Imagination" is that language seems to preexist not in the form of meanings from which the poet chooses, not as an intellectual system, but as sensation, as primal energy which demands wording. Words fill a preexisting rhythmic pattern. Emerson believes, at least in this essay, that in the beginning there was impulse or beat rather than word, motion rather than thought: "The nature of things is flowing, a metamorphosis. The free spirit sympathizes not only with the actual form, but with the power of possible forms" (8:71).

Since "Poetry and Imagination" is a late essay, as far as publication date is concerned,[2] it must be that Whitman arrived more or less independently at the idea or intuition that language is first of all rhythmic motion. In important studies of his prosody, Pasqualle Jannaccone and Sculley Bradley have both shown that Whitman returns in his metrical principles to the "periodic," as opposed to syllabic, rhythmic units characteristic of primitive oral poetry. Sculley Bradley concludes: "One finds that the organized rhythmic recurrence is even more fundamental and more universally applied than logical parallelism, not only in the single line, but in longer passages as well."[3] Jannaccone goes further in his recognition of the affinities of Whitman's prosody with the metrical principles of all primary poetry, such as the Bible, Greek hymns, the early poetry of India, China, and Arabia. Sound seems to this scholar the basic generative principle of Whitman's poetry: "From the repetition of verses and words, then parallelism, that is to say, the repetition of thought is generated. The analysis we have made of Whitman's poetry follows the whole progression of these forms step by step, not in the direction of evolution, however, but of involution, showing how one form attaches itself to another or is generated by it."[4] Jannaccone's findings support the argument that in his effort to renew the poetic language, Whitman instinctively recognized that the primary layer of language is sensory, and, in his prosody, attempted to penetrate to that very level.

Critics who pay less attention to the sound qualities of Whitman's poetry acknowledge too, though in more general terms, the fundamental role of the categories of motion and process for Whitman's conception of language. In a memorable statement, Charles

Feidelson insists: "His new method was predicated not only on the sense of creative vision—itself a process which renders a world in process—but also, as part and parcel of that consciousness, on the sense of creative speech." "Since Whitman regards meaning as an activity of words rather than an external significance attached to them, language . . . turns out to be a process, the pouring of the flood."[5] This observation focuses not on language as a sensuous experience but on language as energy. It is, however, important to realize that Whitman's interest in language as flow embraces both these directions. On the one hand, he stresses language as sensation, on the other—language as energy, because the energy of his language is bound inseparably with its ability to reproduce—not to report but to enact—the actual seething life: "A perfect writer would make words sing, dance, kiss, do the male and female act, bear children, weep, bleed, rage, stab, steal, fire cannon, steer ships, sack cities, charge with cavalry or infantry, or do any thing that man or woman or the natural powers can do" (*D*, 3 : 742). The postulate is grounded, of course, in the doctrine of correspondence which guarantees that "a perfect user of words uses things" (*D*, 3 : 740), and that experience brings with itself commensurate language: "Language follows events, and swallows them to preserve them.—Conquests, migration, commerce, etc. are fossilized in language" (*D*, 3 : 718).[6]

Whitman's one, and constant, worry is the "fossilizing" property of language. What is immobilized is dead and he admonishes himself: "Do not forget that what is now fixed was once floating and movable" (*D*, 3 : 720). To prevent language from "fossilizing" life the artist must rely upon the dynamics of his experience. And, for Whitman, experience is always sensual rather than conceptual:

Latent, in a great user of words, must actually be all passions, crimes, trades, animals, stars, God, sex, the past, night, space, metals, and the like—because these are the words, and he who is not these, plays with a foreign tongue, turning helplessly to dictionaries and authorities. (*D*, 3 : 742)

Ultimately, it is the quality of experience which determines the quality of language, and language is validated by its immersion in active life. In Whitman's view, the power of language is evocative and its energy—one with the life force.

Another aspect of Whitman's interest in language is his delight in words vocalized, in language as pure sensation. In crucial moments of ecstasy it is not the significance of words which is important but the primary simplicity of sound. The experience recorded in Section Five of "Song of Myself" transcends intellectual comprehension; its most treasured part is conveyed in inarticulate murmur: "Not words, not music or rhyme I want, not custom or lecture, not even the best, / Only the lull I like, the hum of your valved voice" (*LG*, 33 : 85–86).

Whitman's fascination with the sensuality of sound shows not only in his well-documented and much commented on love for the opera;[7] it is equally evident in his convalescing reports from Timber Creek, in which he comes back insistently to the delight of sounds: birds, crickets, the wind,[8] and in his comments on Tennyson's poetry.[9] But more than anywhere else, the hypnotizing power of sound, its primal appeal, is celebrated in the sea poems and in the recollections of the beach escapades of his youth.[10] And in his old age, with the senses supposedly less responsive, Whitman returns again to the magic of "the perfect human voice":

> Beyond all other power and beauty, there is something in the quality and power of the right voice (*timbre* the schools call it) that touches the soul, the abysms. It was not for nothing that the Greeks depended, at their highest, on poetry's and wisdom's vocal utterance by *tête-à-tête* lectures—(indeed all the ancients did). (*PW*, 2 : 674 : 13–17)

John Irwin's discussion of Whitman's involvement with the pictorial aspect of hieroglyphics concludes by stressing the prevalence of "the musical component of poetry" which "in Whitman's idealized conception of song . . . transforms spoken language into the audible equivalent of that original language of natural signs in which the form of the pictographic physical object was transparently its meaning."[11]

Viewed from this point, language is at its core a rhythmic continuity of sound, an elemental power which to touch means to touch the very marrow of life and, thus, to attain highest wisdom. The position may seem uncouth for a poet, but a Whitman student should be able to see beneath surfaces. As Gay Wilson Allen remarks: "Some critics have thought Whitman an atavistic savage who believed in the magic of words. Actually, however, he worships neither words nor images, but the mystic powers and relationships which they feebly signify."[12] In other words, Whitman's conception of language is at one with his religious stance. "In the ideal transparency of embodiment, the singer becomes his song, the object its meaning"[13] and there is a large dose of mystical abrogation of the self in Whitman's concept of language. At times, in fact, he is ready to yield to its power so completely that he believes himself to be only a transmitter which the divine medium uses:

> Through me the afflatus surging and surging, through me the
>   current and index.
> I speak the pass-word primeval, . . .
> . . . .
> Through me many long dumb voices,
> Voices of the interminable generations of prisoners and slaves,
> Voices of the diseas'd and despairing and of thieves and dwarfs,
> Voices of cycles of preparation and accretion,
> And of the threads that connect the stars, and of wombs and of
>   the father-stuff,
> And of the rights of them the others are down upon,
> Of the deform'd, trivial, flat, foolish, despised,
> Fog in the air, beetles rolling balls of dung.
> ("Song of Myself," *LG*, 52:505–6, 508–15)

Here, Whitman, the practicing poet, seems to realize perfectly the assertions Emerson made in the early *Journals*: "No man can write well who thinks there is any choice of words for him" (*J*, 3:270) and "No choice. Self abandonment to the truth (of things) makes words things" (*J*, 4:428).

However, Whitman could not have been the artist he was had he not possessed an experimenter's curiosity about the workings of language. His passion for collecting quaint expressions, provincialisms, particularly apt idioms and his fascination with names may be easily linked with the catalogue technique, but there is more to Whitman's interest in language than mere collector's impulse or a craftsman's anxiety to secure ample materials. His comments on grammar and his criticism of Murray's handbook make his attitude clear:

> Drawing language into line by rigid grammatical rules, is the theory of the martinet applied to processes of the spirit, and to the luxurant

growth of all that makes art. . . . The fault that he [Murray] fails to understand those points where the language [is] strongest, and where [the] developments should [be] most encouraged, namely, in being *elliptic* and *idiomatic*.—Murray would make of the young men merely a correct and careful set of writers under laws.—He would deprive writing of its life—there would be nothing voluntary and insouciant left.—(*D*, 3 : 666, 666–67)

Whitman's position here, as everywhere else, is that language is—like life—organic. In further notes we can observe the poet looking at the laws by which this organism proliferates:

pantaloons—"pants"—trowsers—breeches—
Do not these words illustrate a law of language, namely, that with the introduction of any new thing (as the pantaloons), the word, from the same land or source, is introduced with them? (*D*, 3 : 673)

Words, as it were, inhere in things and travel with them. One cannot have the thing without the word or the word without the thing. In the same *Notebook* on words the poet affirms: "Language expresses originally objects only, and leaves the understanding to supply the connecting form—afterwards facilitating and improving the connections and relations by degrees" (*D*, 3 : 721). The remark (preceded by a note "Von Humboldt") validates the theory that language grows by stringing on ever-new nouns, that the principal mechanism of its growth is accretion. On the other hand, it lends support to the "indirect" mode of writing, to metonymic expression as working *with* the primary law of language. Whitman's irritation with Murray's grammar stems from his conviction that instead of energizing the natural development of language, he would arrest its growth.

The *American Primer*[14] is not only the compilatory effort of one who needs effective words; it also reflects the not-so-modest ambition to analyze the nature of language:

A great observation will detect sameness through all languages, however old, however new, however polished, however rude.—As humanity is one, under its amazing diversities, language is one under its.—The flippant, reading on some long past age, wonder at its dead costumes, its amusements, etc.; but the master, understands well the old, ever-new, ever-common grounds, below those animal growths.—And between any two ages, any two languages and two humanities, however wide [apart?] in Time and Space marks well not the superficial shades of difference, but the mass-shades, of a joint nature. (*D*, 3:730–32)

Balancing the law of changeless unity is the weight of individual words: "To me, each word . . . has its own meaning, and does not stand for anything but itself—and there are no two words the same any more than there are two persons the same (*D*, 3:736).

The two passages from the *Primer* indicate the range of Whitman's linguistic curiosity. At the one extreme is his fascination with language as a living force whose seething energy can be penetrated to the simplicity of a primary law, as illustrated in the practices of his prosody. At the other pole is his delight in the fertility, in the inexhaustible hoard of words mirroring the inexhaustible wealth of natural forms. On this level each word is individual, unique, and stands only for itself. For, ultimately, Whitman's analysis of language does not differ from his analysis of society or of natural life. Language, too, is "democratic yet en-mass."

Whitman's ideals of poetic language form the material of "A Song of the Rolling Earth"[15] which, as a poem, is mainly interesting for just this reason. The central image of Mother Earth revolving imperturbably through Time and Space, holding a mirror to all, "inviting none, denying none," unites the two aspects of Whitman's concept of language: individual words are evocations of individual objects, and words are process, eternal motion at the core of all reality. On both levels, Whitman as poet moves in the direction of undercutting the intellectual qualities of language. When he postulates that true language is not text or conversation but pictures and gestures:

> Were you thinking that those were the words, those upright lines? those curves, angles, dots?
> No, those are not the words, the substantial words are in the ground and sea,
> They are in the air, they are in you.
>
> Were you thinking that those were the words, those delicious sounds out of your friends' mouths?
> No, the real words are more delicious than they.
>
> Human bodies are words, myriads of words,
>
> (*LG*, 219:2–7)

and when he calls for the use of such "inaudible" words in poems:

> The workmanship of souls is by those inaudible words of the earth,
> The masters know the earth's words and use them more than audible words.
>
> (*LG*, 220:15–16)

He not only argues for a poetics of images but treats words as hieroglyphics.

Whitman's conception of language was undoubtedly influenced by the wide interest in Egyptology in nineteenth-century America (and Europe, of course, as well).[16] It drew on the mystical interpretation of hieroglyphics as emblematic encodings containing the key to the knowledge of the primary simplicity of the universe.[17] The act of Adamic naming was thus viewed as penetration to the message hidden beneath the surfaces of things. Because objects were mysterious symbols, words signifying them shared in the mystery. A similar approach underlies the view of language as a continual collective utterance:

> Underneath the ostensible sounds, the august chorus of heroes, the wail of slaves.
> Persuasions of lovers, curses, gasps of the dying, laughter of young people, accents of bargainers,
> Underneath these possessing words that never fail.
>
> To her children the words of the eloquent dumb great mother never fail,
> The true words do not fail, for motion and reflection does not fail,
> Also the day and night do not fail, and the voyage we pursue does not fail.
>
> (*LG*, 221:38–43)

Beneath the surface of jarring sounds, there are depths where primary meaning resides as certain as the earth's laws of motion and reflection.

Practically, then, Whitman the poet believes that language is first of all suggestive; that its main function lies not in crystallizing meaning but in opening vistas, in leading the reader to where truth may be grasped intuitively:

The words of the true poems give you more than poems,
They give you to form for yourself poems, religions, politics, war, peace, behavior, histories, essays, daily life, and every thing else,

. . . .

Whom they take they take into space to behold the birth of stars, to learn one of the meanings,
To launch off with absolute faith, to sweep through the ceaseless rings and never be quiet again.

("Song of the Answerer," *LG*, 170 : 75–76; 82–83)

This conviction favors a conscious strategy of "indirection," that is, of using language to emphasize what is left unsaid rather than to bring into focus what is being said:

I swear I begin to see little or nothing in audible words,
All merges toward the presentation of the unspoken meanings of the earth,
Toward him who sings the songs of the body and of the truths of the earth,
Toward him who makes the dictionaries of words that print cannot touch.

I swear I see what is better than to tell the best,
It is always to leave the best untold.

("A Song of the Rolling Earth," *LG*, 224 : 98–103)

The strategy of leaving "the best untold" is justified by the recognition that words fail to convey the sensual, intuitive knowledge which gives superior wisdom:

When I undertake to tell the best I find I cannot,
My tongue is ineffectual on its pivots,
My breath will not be obedient to its organs,
I become a dumb man.

("A Song of the Rolling Earth," *LG*, 224 : 104–7)

Yet, of course, the artist has to go on attempting the impossible, uttering words in a process parallel to or identical with the eternal rolling of the earth. For, like the Great Mother, he, too, is paradoxically "eloquent and dumb." The depth of his art is inextricably bound with the depth of his reader's sympathetic insight.

The question of how to wrest power from words never seems to be among the problems Whitman might have with language. This is because Whitman seldom feels that he has to fight with language, that he must wring his meanings by force. On the contrary, he most often seems to be seeking means to intensify what he takes to be the natural operations of language. This intention, I suggest, lies behind Whitman's neologisms and his somewhat notorious borrowings from other languages. Words like "camerado," "libertad," "originatress," "eclaircise" do not appear in their contexts because no other word can express quite the same meaning; "liberty" and "libertad" have, after all, almost the same sound value, not to mention identity of meaning. Such words are borrowed or made up because language is creative and absorbant, "a sort of universal combiner and conqueror," because words multiply, sounds fascinate, and the growth can never be stopped. Some of Whitman's coinages are awkward, some are awful, but the poet is not afraid of gaucherie. Language, like nature, cleans itself. Words die, other words come into use; the organism perpetually renews itself, throwing up "froth and specks" in healthy fermentation.

Without being as picturesque as Whitman, Emerson observes the same process: "Every age gazettes a quantity of words which it has used up. We are now offended with 'Standpoint', 'Myth', 'Subjective', 'the Good and the True' and 'the Cause'" (12:293). The organic ability of language to regulate its growth encourages the artist's linguistic freedom. The medium itself provides the creative impulse.

If, for comparison, we look at Dickinson's coinages, the first surprising discovery is that they are comparatively few. Dickinson's reputation as an idiosyncratic poet cannot be supported by claims to unusual vocabulary. William Howard's helpful investigation shows that "at least two thirds of the words in the Dickinson vocabulary were sufficiently common to be used by one or more of three poets who were approximately contemporary with her (i.e., Keats, Lanier, and Emerson)."[18] Eventually, Howard finds that out of her total vocabulary, only 159 words are not recognized by the dictionaries of her time:

Seven of these are Verbs formed with the prefix re-, e.g., redeck, rewalk; 9 are adjectives formed with the prefix a-, e.g., achirrup, a'lull, asailing; 19 are words formed with the prefix un-, e.g., unbared, unerudite, unpretension; 34 are words of her own coining, e.g., addings, gianture, heres, incognite, optizan, russetly; 43 are compound words, e.g., by-thyme, co-eternity, egg-life, goer-by, To Come, wizzard fingers; and 47 are adjectives formed with the suffix -less, e.g., arrestless, conceiveless, findless, latitudeless, reportless, vital-less.

The counting permits Howard to conclude that, because in fact coinages account for only slightly more than 2 percent of Dickinson's total vocabulary, they must be considered a minor rather than a major characteristic of her language.[19]

Howard's findings remain in keeping with Dickinson's general tendency to base on conventions, and to work out her meanings by playing off the familiarity of an "established form" against the unexpected "slant" she gives it.[20] A further look at Dickinson's neologisms reveals that more often than not she coins her own word where language does not supply one, a practice quite consistent with the laws of morphology. Among her neologisms the prevalence of words formed with the usual prefixes and suffixes is striking. As for her own coinages, such as "gianture," the context shows how she made the word because she needed an abstract noun to correspond to the concrete one:

> Size circumscribes—it has no room
> For petty furniture—
> The Giant tolerates no Gnat
> For Ease of Gianture—
>
> (641)

Similarly, when she turns the adverb *here* into a plural noun: "Here!" There are typic "Heres"— / Foretold Locations—(1515), the generative mechanism seems to be the need for a generalization corresponding to the concrete word.

Some of Dickinson's liberties with grammar illustrate the same process. "I often wish I was a grass," she wrote to Mrs. Holland (*L*, 2 : 324), and repeated the indefinite article with a collective noun in the poem on grass: "The Grass so little has to do / I wish I were a Hay" (333). The two formulations do not occur close enough in time to suggest that she merely repeated a surprising word combination because the effect pleased her. Johnson dates the letter January 1856 and the two existing manuscripts of the poem early 1862. In both contexts, however, the writer is preoccupied with the possibility, or rather impossibility, of reconciling organic life, like that of grass, with the fact of self-consciousness. The striking grammatical "error" serves as an appropriate linguistic rendering of the main philosophical paradox of her times.

Even such a limited look at Dickinson's linguistic inventiveness confirms the impression that her language follows rather than generates thought. Moreover, she repeatedly admits to an acute sense of separation between thought and language. While Whitman fears, first of all, the "fossilizing" of life through language, Dickinson worries over the inadequacy of words to the processes of the mind. Thoughts and words appear autonomous and show a frustrating tendency to go their separate ways. "I hardly know what I have said—my words put all their feathers on—and fluttered here and there" (*L*, 2 : 336). "The old words are *numb*—and there *a'nt* any *new* ones—Brooks—are useless—in *Freshet-time*" (*L*, 2 : 395). "While my thought is undressed—I can make the distinction, but when I put them in the Gown—they look alike, and numb" (*L*, 2 : 404). All three observations, made to the Hollands, to Samuel Bowles, and to Higginson respectively, focus on the difficulty of making language adequate to the vividness, intensity, or clarity of mental experience. Somewhat like Whitman, who feels that language cannot ultimately do justice to the variety and profundity of experience, Emily Dickinson finds that words fail in confrontation with the depth of emotion: "If I could tell how glad I was / I should not be so glad" (1668, see also 1750). At the same time, however, she tries again and again to "tell" how it felt to have been pained beyond words because articulation controls intensity. Although the intensity of experience defies language and "It is the Ultimate of Talk / The Impotence to Tell" (407, see also 581), the relation is one of loss and gain. In the process of "telling how it felt," lost is the most intimate core of experience, gained is the power of control. Articulation saves the artist from drowning in her own intensities.[21]

In several poems Dickinson takes the attitude of an observer of her own mental processes, and the poems reflect on the bewildering necessity of having to admit the inscrutable autonomy of the life of the mind:

A Thought went up my mind today—
That I have had before—

. . . .

It just reminded me—'twas all—
And came my way no more—

(701)

Between these ostensibly quiet statements, the poem contemplates the mystery of the origin and the seeming lack of direction in the processes of the mind:

Nor where it went—nor why it came
The second time to me—
Nor definitely, what it was—
Have I the Art to say—

The poet takes us to the very brink of subconsciousness and leaves us there to face yet another aspect of "the challenging unknown." For the essence of thought, like the essence of nature, remains a mystery:

The Capsule of the Wind
The Capsule of the Mind

Exhibit here, as doth a Burr—
Germ's Germ be where?

(998)

If the processes of thought show disquieting autonomy, language in its own right possesses equal independence. First of all, it does not inhere in the variety of natural forms, as it ideally does for Emerson and Whitman. Words are not things or gestures but inhabit "an autonomous symbolic realm."[22] Interested as Dickinson was all her life in birds, bees, flowers, and seasons, they never ceased to be her "competeless show" (290). For words to deal with the spectacle she went to her lexicon (see *L*, 2 : 404) and "searched Philology" (1126). This does not mean that she viewed language as a dry convention; on the contrary, language was or should be "vital" (see 883, 1039). The first question she put to Higginson was: "Are you too deeply occupied to say if my Verse is alive?" (*L*, 2 : 403). And to Samuel Bowles she remarked: "Some phrases are too fine to fade—and Light but just confirms them—" (*L*, 2 : 419). When she considered the pleasures of reading an old book, she personified the volume as a gentleman with whom her mind could be shared:[23]

> Facts Centuries before
>
> He traverses—familiar—
> As One should come to Town—
> And tell you all your Dreams—were true—
> He lived—where Dreams were born—
>
> (371)[24]

In another poem (1212) she claims that only articulated language can really live, that is—endure. The power of words to stay fascinated Dickinson (see 1467) and the hope she expressed in a letter to Higginson that "If fame belonged to me, I could not escape her—" (*L*, 2 : 408) must have been based on her belief in the permanence of language.[25]

The enduring and nourishing (see 1587) power of language is offset for Dickinson by its destructive potential. Words are not to be treated lightly and their resilience to time makes linguistic choice a matter of grave responsibility. Words do harm (see 479) and "infect" across "centuries" (1261). Quoting poem 1537, Charles Anderson observes that "false words are 'inequity,' both in the theological sense of wickedness and in the Latin root sense of being 'unequal' to the meaning they intend to convey. For a poet the latter is indeed original sin."[26] But beyond those questions of the writer's craft and ethics, language constitutes a threat to the artist's very existence. Dickinson asks Higginson to tell her frankly her fault "for I had rather wince, than die" (*L*, 2 : 412) and the death she wants to escape with his help is clearly artistic death from faulty language. In one of the Master letters so charged with emotion that the language nearly breaks down completely, she becomes frightened of the destructiveness of words: "You say I do not tell you all—Daisy confessed—and denied not. Vesuvius dont talk—Etna—dont—one of them—said a syllable—a thousand years ago, and Pompeii heard it, and hid forever—" (*L*, 2 : 374). Thoughts, experience in general, are made final by language, and the finality terrifies: "And so Around the Words I went— / Of meeting them afraid—" (734). In this sense language may be as overwhelming as emotions let loose. She fears being flooded by words as she fears drowning in the wild sea of her emotional intensity. The poet Dickinson would not let language speak for her, something Whitman is sometimes too willing to do. Instead, she concentrates on choosing the proper word and is likely to overburden it with concentrated meaning.

Dickinson's central problem with language is one of power and form,[27] which is also the central problem in "Experience" and the main concern of Emerson the poet.[28] In the poems and, to a lesser extent, in letters we see Dickinson struggling for the most precise rendering of thought. She is not eager to inquire into the nature of language. In fact, she is quite prepared to declare it a divine mystery. What interests her is how to win for herself the blessing of the angel, how to "distill" personal meanings from the established medium. Neither new experience nor new reality can redeem language for Dickinson as they promise to do for Whitman. Language can only be redeemed through a new use of it. She may have found her attitude confirmed in "The Poet":

> Why covet a knowledge of new facts? Day and night, house and garden, a few books, a few actions, serve us as well as would all trades and all spectacles. We are far from having exhausted the significance of the few symbols we use. We can come to use them yet with a terrible simplicity. It does not need that a poem should be long. Every word was once a poem. Every new relation is a new word. (3 : 18)[29]

The problem is not one of cumulative effect but of power through compression. The mastery of language holds for Dickinson the promise of mastering experience. For Whitman, the promise lies in the prospect of regaining the unfallen condition of harmony with the universe.

All through Dickinson's correspondence with Higginson the question of control, of acquiring perspective on her own work, runs like the main color thread in a weaver's design:

> The Mind is so near itself—it cannot see distinctly—(*L*, 2 : 403)
>
> You think my gait "spasmodic"—I am in danger—Sir.
> You think me "uncontrolled"—I have no Tribunal!
> . . . .
> If I might bring you what I do— . . . and ask if I told it clear—
> 'twould be control, to me. (*L*, 2 : 409)
>
> I had no Monarch in my life, and cannot rule myself. (*L*, 2 : 414)

On the other hand, even as she asks Higginson's advice, the poet makes it known that she will not take anyone's word and must find out for herself:

> When much in the Woods as a little Girl, I was told that the Snake would bite me, that I might pick a poisonous flower, or Goblins kidnap me, but I went along and met no one but Angels, who were far shyer of me, than I could be of them, so I haven't that confidence in fraud which many exercise. (*L*, 2:415)

The childhood recollection is preceded by an impatient remark in answer to Higginson's query about the meaning of her poems: "All men say What to me, but I thought it a fashion—" and followed by the complying assurance "I shall observe your precept—though I don't understand it, always." Thus, by August 1862 (and their correspondence began in April of that year) Dickinson seems to have sensed that although she indeed needed Higginson, she wanted from him mainly an opportunity to clarify her own standards. Perspective was crucial for control, as she confided to Bowles: "It is easier to look behind at pain . . ." (*L*, 2:416). And, as Emerson, too, realized in "Fate":

> The whole circle of animal life—tooth against tooth, devouring war, war for food, a yelp of pain and a grunt of triumph, until at last the whole menagerie, the whole chemical mass is mellowed and refined for higher use—pleases at a sufficient perspective. (6:36)

Dickinson's ideal poet compresses everyday "meanings" into "Attar so immense. . . . We wonder it was not Ourselves / Arrested it—before—" (448). What strikes the reader as natural only seems natural. Poems do not bud "as unerringly and loosely as lilacs or roses on a bush" (*LG*, 714:192–93); they are not "expressed by Suns—alone" but are "the gift of Screws" as well (675). If the ideal poetic effect is that of stunning revelation:

> To pile like Thunder to it's close
> Then crumble grand away
> While Everything created hid
> This—would be Poetry—
>
> (1247)

he who would produce such powerful impression must masterfully calculate his strategies:

> He fumbles at your Soul
> As Players at the Keys
> Before they drop full Music on—
> He stuns you by degrees—
> Prepares your brittle Nature
> For the Etherial Blow
> By fainter Hammers—further heard—
> Then nearer—Then so slow
> Your Breath has time to straighten—
> Your Brain—to bubble Cool—
> Deals—One—imperial—Thunderbolt—
> That scalps your naked Soul—
>
> When Winds take Forests in their Paws—
> The Universe—is still—
>
> (315)

The last two lines of the poem offer analogy between the effect of a conscious performance and that of an elemental upheaval. Both exhibit extremities of power but there the similarity ends. How nature produces her effect cannot be known. How the master performer achieves his is analyzed in detail so that the full range of his calculating craftsmanship may be admired. It is how things are said that makes them significant (cf. 1545).

"Nature is a Haunted House—but Art—a House that tries to be Haunted" (*L*, 2:554). Dickinson's poetry aspires to be like nature only in the intensity of its effect; it is the procedures of trying to be "haunted" which concern the poet most. Dickinson is not really interested in documenting the proposition that the principles of nature and the principles of language are identical. Nor does she want to devise strategies by which to intensify the assumed organic workings of language. Her question is how to achieve effects comparable to those of the natural phenomena with the tool taken out of her dictionary; how to evoke sensations using an intellectual medium. She knows, in other words, that the power of her language must be transformative.

Whitman's (and Emerson's) marriage of thought and object involves a return to natural innocence, to the unfallen condition of language and of man.[30] It is a reattaching of words to their primary sources, an "involution" as Jannacone puts it. Dickinson's marriage of thought and word is a sudden influx of grace, a revelation. Her images for such a union are invariably sacramental: of communion (see 1452) and illumination (see 1126, 1581). The quest for the right word becomes identical with the religious quest for the state of Grace. When Dickinson talks about it, her metaphors employ images of clothing (as in the letters to the Hollands and to Higginson quoted above) because in the union of thought and word the spirit takes on visible form. "She insists here [*L*, 2:460—"A Letter always feels to me] upon the reifying capacity of words, and readers as a result would do well to disengage themselves from the notion that specific Dickinson poems spring from precise and proximate circumstances in her life and to recognize the priority of language in her poetry."[31] Emerson also thought of the language of his poems as "the clothing of ideas" but with him, when the linear drive of the "meter-making argument" toward revelation—which in itself could furnish a shape and a form, as Whitman recognized—was further constrained by a self-conscious literary form, the result was "devitalized thoughts" and diluted strength.[32] Dickinson's position is different in that her vision offered no sense of direction or form; it was, in fact, anarchic. She needed, therefore, the discipline of thought patterns, hymnal forms, and scrupulous word choices as the necessary clothing for the chaos of the mind's "naked" response to experience.

When the poet succeeds in marrying thought to the proper word, two distinct natures become one and the miracle for Dickinson is comparable only to Divine Incarnation:

> A Word that breathes distinctly
> Has not the power to die
> Cohesive as the Spirit
> It may expire if He—
> "Made Flesh and dwelt among us
> Could condescension be
> Like this consent of Language
> This loved Philology
>
> (1651)

The miracle brings into existence a realm out of time, self-sufficient and secure in its permanence. Poems become "a fearless, sleepless, deathless progeny, which is not exposed to the accidents of the weary kingdom of time" (3:23).

> There is a Zone whose even Years
> No Solstice interrupt—
> Whose Sun constructs perpetual Noon
> Whose perfect Seasons wait—
>
> Whose Summer set in Summer, till
> The Centuries of June
> And Centuries of August cease
> And Consciousness—is Noon.
>
> (1056, see also 657)

Linguistic and, generally, aesthetic excellence comes so close to immortality of the soul that the two can no longer be distinguished.

"All experience, and meaning if it existed," observes David Porter, "for this poet was to be found in the solitary sufferer. That extraordinary transfer of Christian parable into personal affairs had produced a private typology of affairs."[33] It also produced, I would like to add, that extraordinary combination of modernity and backwardness in her poems; the combination that permits one to claim Dickinson for the postmodern mind, as Porter himself does, or with equal validity to reflect on her intimate links with the Puritan tradition, as does Karl Keller.[34] The combination manifests itself vividly in Dickinson's conception of language. While on the one hand she struggles, in an almost modernist way, to establish the linguistic construct of the poem as autonomous of any creed, even of a recognizable frame of reference, on the other hand, with the same or greater conviction, she insists on talking about language and the creative process in words and metaphors which her Puritan forefathers used only about God and His mysteries. In other words, intuiting or perhaps recognizing that language was in fact a convention, Dickinson, with poignant emphasis, keeps endowing this construct of the mind with attributes of godhead. Writing poems became for her not the quest for the saving truth, which it still was for Emerson and Whitman, but radically, itself the very act of salvation.

Dickinson shares with Emerson, Whitman, and other Romantics the conviction that art's ultimate dimension is religious, but she removes nature from the center of her aesthetic considerations. Although it depends on nature for providing the standard of achievement, a Dickinson poem becomes an intellectual and linguistic performance whose order is not verifiable by the order of nature. The effects, too, though comparable, are hardly identical, as she warns herself (and the reader) in, for example, the poem on the splendors of an aurora borealis:

> Of Bronze—and Blaze—
> The North—Tonight—
> So adequate—it forms—
> So preconcerted with itself—
> So distant—to alarms—
> An Unconcern so sovereign
> To Universe, or me—
> . . . .
> My Splendors, are Menagerie—
> But their Competeless Show
> Will entertain the Centuries
> When I am long ago,
> An Island in dishonored Grass—
> Whom none but Daisies, know.
>
> (290)

Both the aurora borealis and the poet's "menagerie" are spectacles, performances to be admired. While nature's production impresses with its "sovereign" self-sufficiency and its majestic "Unconcern," the poet's "Show" possesses a uniqueness of its own. Presumably less autonomous as well as subject to "alarms," the poet's art resists time more effectively than the supreme but brief spectacle of the northern lights.

Whitman's language is generated by sensory experience preceding thought, and aims at taking words back to where they touch a primary, "unfallen" reality. Despite the declaration to Traubel that he thought *Leaves of Grass* "only a language experiment,"[35] the existence of his poems as purely linguistic constructs seemed to him at all times less vital than the need to make poems partners in living relationships. The hope that "distance avails not, and place avails not" and "who knows but I am as good as looking at you now" motivated his self-revelations to a large extent. Moreover, the disconsolate stanzas of "As I Ebb'd with the Ocean of Life" as well as the remark in "A

Backward Glance O'er Travel'd Roads" that "the actual living light of poems is always curiously from elsewhere" (*LG*, 565 : 128) show how, in a moment of doubt whether language indeed participated in the primary reality, he also had to doubt the relevance of his art.

Dickinson's words neither start with objects nor aim at them as their final destination. The creative impulse, "Germ's Germ," is contained in "the Capsule of the Mind." All activity starts with thought:

> A Deed knocks first at Thought
> And then—it knocks at Will—
> That is the manufactoring spot
> And Will at Home and well
>
> It then goes out an Act
>
> (1216)

At the other end of their journey words take off into "circumference" and move toward abstraction[36] as the poet attempts to wrest "staying power" from the perishable forms of experience. Gestures and objects come into Dickinson's poems instrumentally, because they serve in that more important quest for a "House of Possibility" (657), for "Estate perpetual" (855). When words are no longer validated by physical reality, language, freed from its representational function, becomes a "condition of being"[37] rather than a means by which man may repossess his place within the harmonies of the universe. "The telling of the tale" remains as the only salvation available.

Notes

1. In "Slang in America," *North American Review* 141 (November 1885): 431–35.

2. Published in *Letters and Social Aims* (Boston: Osgood, 1876), but written between 1870 and 1872 from earlier manuscript notes. See note on the essay in Edward Waldo Emerson, ed., *The Complete Works of Ralph Waldo Emerson*, Centenary ed. (Boston: Houghton Mifflin, 1903–4), 8 : 357–58.

3. Sculley Bradley, "The Fundamental Metrical Principle in Whitman's Poetry," *American Literature* 10 (January 1939): 447–48.

4. Pasqualle Jannaccone, *Walt Whitman's Poetry and the Evolution of Rhythmic Forms*, trans. Peter Militineos (Washington, D.C.: NCR Micro-

card, 1973), 104. The astonishing thing about Jannaccone's study is that it first appeared in 1898 (*La Poesia di Walt Whitman e L'evoluzione delle forme ritmiche*), and yet in many ways its perceptions went deeper than the argument of most later American critics who ascribed Whitman's parallelisms to the influence of rhetorics or of oratory and saw them primarily in logical terms. Other studies of Whitman's prosody are: Fred Newton Scott, "A Note on Whitman's Prosody," *Journal of English and Germanic Philology*, 7 (1908); R. M. Weeks, "Phrasal Prosody," *English Journal* 10 (January 1923); Autrey Neil Wiley, "Reiterative Devices in Leaves of Grass," *American Literature* 1 (May 1929): 161–70.

5. Charles Feidelson, *Symbolism and American Literature* (Chicago: University of Chicago Press, 1953), 18, 20. On language as process in Emerson, see Roland Hagenbüchle, "Sign and Process: The Concept of Language in Emerson and Dickinson," *Emerson Society Quarterly* 25 (1979): 137–55, also in *Proceedings of a Symposium on American Literature* (Poznań: Universytet Adema Mickiewicza, 1979), 59–88.

6. On Emerson's preoccupation with nature as text, see Sacvan Bercovitch, "Emerson the Prophet: Romanticism, Puritanism, and Auto-American-Biography," in *Emerson: Prophecy, Metamorphosis and Influence*, ed. David Levin (New York: Columbia University Press, 1975), 1–27; and Hagenbüchle, "Sign and Process."

7. See especially Robert D. Faner, *Walt Whitman and Opera* (Philadelphia: University of Pennsylvania Press, 1951).

8. In "Specimen Days."

9. "To me, Tennyson shows more than any poet I know (perhaps has been a warning to me) how much there is in finest verbalism. There is such a latent charm in mere words, cunning collocations, and in the voice ringing them, which he has caught and brought out, beyond all others—" (*PW*, 2:571).

10. One thinks first of all, of course, about "Out of the Cradle" and "As I Ebb'd with the Ocean of Life" but see also reminiscences in "Specimen Days" and "A Backward Glance O'er Travel'd Roads."

11. John T. Irwin, *American Hieroglyphics: The Symbol of the Egyptian Hieroglyphics in the American Renaissance* (New Haven: Yale University Press, 1980), 39–40.

12. Gay Wilson Allen, *Walt Whitman Handbook*, reprint ed. (New York: Hendricks House, 1962), 432.

13. Irwin, *American Hieroglyphics*, 40.

14. I quote from the manuscript version of "The Primer of Words for American Young, Men, and Women, For Literats, Orators, Teachers, Musicians, Judges, Presidents etc.," in vol. 3 of William White, ed., *Daybooks and Notebooks* (New York: New York University Press, 1978). The Primer was edited by Horace Traubel and published posthumously as *An American Primer by Walt Whitman, with Facsimiles of the Original Manuscript* (Boston: Small, Maynard, 1904).

15. First published in the 1856 edition of *Leaves of Grass* as "Poem of The Sayers of The Words of The Earth," the poem underwent no significant revisions except for the changes in title.

16. Floyd Stovall presents evidence of Whitman's interest in ancient Egypt and Egyptology (*The Foreground of Leaves of Grass* [Charlottesville: University of Virginia Press, 1974], 161–64).

17. See Irwin, *American Hieroglyphics*, 3–14, where the historical, intellectual, and literary context of the interest is presented.

18. William Howard, "Emily Dickinson's Poetic Vocabulary," *PMLA* 72 (March 1957): 229–30.

19. Ibid., 230.

20. See, for example, David T. Porter's article "Emily Dickinson: The Poetics of Doubt," *Emerson Society Quarterly* 60 (Summer 1970): 86–93, where the author demonstrates how Dickinson's poems open with confident, almost complacent repetitions of established beliefs which are then subtly subterfuged.

21. Compare Chapter 3 and Chapter 5, where the conception of poetry as release and the problem of balance and control are discussed.

22. See Hagenbüchle, "Sign and Process," in *Proceedings of a Symposium on American Literature*, esp. 63–73.

23. Compare Emerson's statement in "Nominalist and Realist": "The modernness of all good books seems to give me an existence as wide as man" (3 : 233) and the journal entry made in 1839: "Plutarch fits me better than Southey or Scott, therefore I say, there is no age to good writing. Could I write as I would, I suppose the piece would be no nearer Boston in 1839 than to Athens in the fiftieth Olympiad. Good thought, however expressed, saith to us 'Come out of time; come to me in the Eternal!'" (quoted in 3 : 346, n. 1 to 233). Characteristically, Emerson makes no distinction between writing and thinking. Good writing has no age and good thought is eternal. Dickinson shows much more awareness that how things are said makes an essential difference.

24. The phrasing of the stanza quoted (Johnson's dating–c. 1862) echoes a comment Emily Dickinson is reported to have made on Emerson's visit to Amherst in December 1857: "It must have been as if he had come from where dreams are born!" (*L*, 3). There is no evidence that the poet either heard Emerson lecture or met him when he stayed at the Austin Dickinsons'.

25. Emerson commented on the permanence and autonomy of language as well. And he noticed that words offer resistance to the efforts of an innovator: "Language is a quite wonderful city, which we all help to build. But each word is like a work of nature, determined a thousand years ago, and not alterable. We confer and dispute and settle the meaning so or so, but it remains what it was in spite of us. The word beats all the speakers and definers of it and stands to their children what it stood to their fathers" (*J*, 11 : 232).

26. Charles R. Anderson, "The Conscious Self in Emily Dickinson's Poetry," *American Literature* 31 (November 1959): 294.

27. See Adrienne Rich, "Vesuvius at Home: The Power of Emily Dickinson," *Parnassus: Poetry in Review* 5, no. 1 (Fall/Winter 1976): 49–74, reprinted in Sandra M. Gilbert and Susan Gubar, eds., *Shakespeare's Sisters: Feminist Essays on Women Poets* (Bloomington: Indiana University Press, 1979), 99–121. Also John Mann in "Emily Dickinson, Emerson, and the Poet as Namer," *New England Quarterly* 51 (December 1978): 467–88, succeeds in bringing Emerson and Dickinson together mainly with a view to their shared interest in power through language.

28. "Human life is made up of two elements, power and form" (3:65). On Emerson's theory of poetry, see Charles Philip Smith, "Momentary Music: The Problem of Power and Form in Emerson's Poetry" (Ph.D. diss., University of Nebraska, 1974).

29. Jack Capps finds that this passage was pencil-marked in the Dickinson family copy of *Essays: Second Series.* Jack L. Capps, *Emily Dickinson's Reading* (Cambridge, Mass.: Harvard University Press, 1966), 116.

30. See "Nature" (1:29–32).

31. Porter, "Emily Dickinson: The Poetics of Doubt," 88.

32. See David T. Porter, *Emerson and Literary Change* (Cambridge, Mass.: Harvard University Press, 1978), 25–26.

33. David T. Porter, *Dickinson: The Modern Idiom* (Cambridge, Mass.: Harvard University Press, 1981), 167.

34. Karl Keller, "Alephs, Lahirs, and the Triumph of Ambiguity: Typology in Nineteenth-Century American Literature," in *Literary Uses of Typology*, ed. Earl Miner (Princeton: Princeton University Press, 1977), 274–314.

35. See Traubel's foreword to *An American Primer by Walt Whitman*, viii.

36. Among the critics who notice how Dickinson's language moves away from the concrete object are: Roland Hagenbüchle (see especially "Precision and Indeterminacy in the Poetry of Emily Dickinson," *Emerson Society Quarterly* 20 [1974]: 33–56), Robert Weisbuch, and Sharon Cameron. This is Sharon Cameron's comment on poem 675: "Essential Oils—are wrung—Whether the oils are perfume from the rose or speech from the lyric, to arrive at their essence, life must be pressed to the thinness of its own immemorial finish, must be condensed and, in the condensation, lost to the extract that will symbolize it." (*Lyric Time: Dickinson and the Limits of Genre* [Baltimore: Johns Hopkins University Press, 1979], 195.)

37. The phrase comes from Adrienne Rich's tribute to Emily Dickinson: "you, woman, masculine / in single-mindedness, / for whom the word was more / than a symptom— / a condition of being." (See Marguerite Harris, ed., *Emily Dickinson: Letters from the World* [Corinth, 1970].)

7 / Conclusion

DESPITE their ostensibly opposing positions as "public" and "private" poets,[1] Whitman and Dickinson respond fundamentally to the same philosophical and aesthetic problems. Emerson provides the frame of reference for both when he postulates the ideal of "the whole soul"[2] and struggles to maintain "the equilibrist perspective."[3] For, as Jonathan Bishop observes, Emerson's "whole soul" is much more "a criterion for judgment than a description of a possible protagonist. It can never be seen in its entirety except through instances that symbolically demonstrate the style of the whole in one or another partial context."[4] This aspect of Emerson's vision provides the key to both Whitman's and Dickinson's style. Because totality can only manifest itself in fragments and under aspects, metonymy becomes the chief characteristic of style. "The raid on the inarticulate" is only possible through focusing on the partial, a method that constitutes common ground for both Whitman and Dickinson.

To demonstrate further the inclusive power of the soul Emerson avails himself of the strategy of polarity: "'Polarity' allows Emerson to stress first one aspect of the Soul and then another, the pair appearing, to the understanding mutually opposite but, to the reason, complementary parts of a whole."[5] Similarly, Whitman uses the partial in the faith that the cumulative effect of stringed details will make the flowing unity accessible to reason—that is, to intuitive or imaginative comprehension. By making the inclusive unity his ideal Whitman is released from the necessity to probe its nature. Instead, his main concern remains with multiplying particular instances in which totality manifests itself. Thus, for example, aspects of the self proliferate endlessly in "Song of Myself" while the self's essence resides in its very ability to sympathetically enter "the not me." The partial images are analogical and aim at revealing identity beneath diversity of and continuity beneath apparent fragmentation.

However if reason finds itself unable to transcend the perceptions of understanding, there is a yawning discontinuity in the polarized pattern—a fact which with time became more and more disturbing to Emerson himself. For Dickinson, the particular and the fragmentary are the only unquestionable data. The rest is "conjecture" (see 399, 1128, 1221). In Dickinson's vision, perceptions of understanding do not, as a rule, coalesce into unity by virtue of reason's superior insight. Instead, they are patterned into designs by the mind's method. It is an imperative of the mind that the nature of the whole be mapped, just as it is part of the nature of "the not me" to defy total comprehension. The two are thus locked in perpetual confrontation and the mind multiplies meanings as it strives to reach "circumference." Individual perceptions serve as anchoring, concretizing illustrations in the process of progressive abstraction.

Both Whitman and Dickinson insist, as does Emerson, on "seeing the universe in the light of human needs";[6] both posit the centrality of the artist's consciousness. The difference is that Whitman's projection is affective and sympathetic. He is Adam naming for himself a whole new world into being. Dickinson has experienced the intellectual fall. She can but watch herself create a world of meanings. Constructing analogies, detecting correspondences are the ways of both human perception and human emotional need while the "Single Hound" of consciousness must forever question the truths of its own making.

The common ground and the divergence between the two poets may be further determined by considering the way in which each concentrates on the illuminating experience. Both acknowledge the immense importance of such a moment yet for Whitman it is usually located in the future, always to be reached. The moment when doubt is transcended constitutes the poem's destination. Experiences along the way are treated as instrumental in bringing about the final insight. The intense moment comes as a climax to the preparatory efforts. In this respect Whitman's poems repeat the essential structure of all religious meditations, with the reservation that his preparatory strategies emphasize sensual and affective rather than intellectual receptivity. This basic pattern, repeated sequentially as in "Song of Myself" or abbreviated to the lucid moment itself as in the imagistic poems, conveys a sense of form as inherent in experience and opens up the poem's temporal frame. Whitman is the poet of the present tense in whose works the perspective always opens expectantly into the future, even in such despondent poems as "Prayer of Columbus."

For Dickinson the inspiring moment is invariably located in the past. An experience as brief as it was powerful, it is viewed as both stimulating and shattering, essentially creative and potentially destructive. The past moment, lost but present as the memory of a ravishing visitation, challenges the mind. Thus, poems permeated with the sense of loss move away from the actual experience into the regions of abstraction: "But are not all Facts Dreams as soon as we put them behind us?" (*L*, 3:915). Again and again we find Dickinson's speaker positioned after the major event. After death, after pain, after summer, after the lovers' meeting—in so many poems she tries to make sense of her "afterward" condition.[7] The act of creation becomes radically split into the initial inspiring experience and the later process of "ex-pressing" its essence. Dickinson's poems show how the mind feeds on what has already occurred and finds meaning not in the experience itself but in the very process of analyzing it. Her intense moment, though charged with potential significance, does not disclose it. Order has to be "distilled" in the later process of looking back on the lost moment and arranging it in a design which permits only tentative inference of the general law from the particular event.

While for Whitman the intense moment clarifies meaning, for Dickinson it supplies the necessary energy; it activates the mind. Her vision is characterized by polarities ("the me" versus "the other," heart versus mind, inspiration versus conscious craftsmanship) which are not dialectically resolved within an inclusive wholeness of the soul or the universe, but are held suspended for contemplation. Ultimately, their resolution is transferred onto the symbolic plane. In other words, they are resolved by her faith in language and in the power of art to establish an autonomous realm where immortality is possible.[8]

In his discussion of Emerson's crucial position as a poet at the time of "literary change," David Porter finds that, ironically, Emerson the poet achieved aesthetic liberation only in the essays of the period immediately following *Nature*. In the poems, his expansive vision demanding liberation from conventional constraints is stubbornly pressed into excessively rational philosophical formulas and strict metrical forms. Emerson thus denies his vision the kind of liberty that would truly make it a meter-making argument. The vision is crippled by his practical inability to yield to its associative, irrational impulses from which new poetic forms could arise.[9]

Both Whitman's and Dickinson's work can be usefully viewed in relation to the tension between Emerson's vision and method as outlined by Porter. When Porter argues that Emerson's poems are built, as a rule, on a pattern of "the formulaic transition from ignorance to clarity,"[10] we recognize that, basically, this is Whitman's journey as well. But Whitman at his best can abandon himself to "the nature of things." His sensuous mysticism rescues his poetry with the conviction that the power of experience and the power of language derived from it must of themselves furnish direction and form. Whitman's delight in himself and the world around him is so strong that he only needs to worry how to enhance his vision with "natural" forms. In other words, Whitman resolves Emerson's problem of the conflict between the liberating vision and constraining form by working out modes of expression organic to the vision.

Dickinson is different because her vision contains no liberating or even reconciliatory message. Deprived of the certainty and optimism of faith, her vision needs strict forms to keep the poems from total disintegration. And many of Dickinson's poems fail precisely because of insufficient structuring.[11] Her failures, however, need not concern us here. It seems only fair that, in a study like this, the two poets should be compared on the basis of their best work. Dickinson's superficial likenesses to Emerson—"formal brevity, partial rhymes, stock ideas of compensation, and shared tropes"[12]—result, I believe, from a more fundamental affinity of poetic method. They originate in the shared clinging to rationalized, conventional, and frequently narrow forms. Dickinson avoids the contradiction of the liberating vision thrust into confining form because in her most powerful poems the vision contains no revelation. Its freedom is the freedom of agnosticism. Her poems, then, abandon the search for the saving message and confront the bleak expanse of the unknown. Their cutting edge is the outcome of the essentially agnostic vision played off against conventions of thought and custom and against tight linguistic patterns. The patterns are not meant to corroborate the message (which is Whitman's solution), but, on the contrary, to resist it, to provide anchorage for the vision's instability. The poem becomes, purely and painfully, an act of the mind, a linguistic performance, offering no words of wisdom but demonstrating instead the heroic struggle of consciousness to resist chaos.

The extent of Dickinson's faith in language in this struggle is perhaps best indicated by her use of the word "experiment." One of the most strikingly employed terms in her vocabulary, in its contexts the word always refers to natural and existential phenomena: Faith is "The Experiment of Our Lord" (300); nature—"This whole Experiment of Green—" (1333, see also 1080, 1084); "Experiment to me / Is every one I meet / If it contain a Kernel?" (1073, see also 902). Death, too, presents itself as the "most profound experiment / Appointed unto Men—" (822, see also 1770). It is experience, not language, which seems problematic to Dickinson. Experience is experiment, language—finality.

The word "experiment" is not one of Whitman's favorites in the poems. Eby's *Concordance to Leaves of Grass* lists "experiments" only once, used in the sense of a method for scientific investigation: "The past entire, with all its heroes, histories, arts, experiments," (*LG*, 512, "To-day and Thee"). The words "experiment," "experiments," "experimental" appear more frequently in the prose writings. In "Democratic Vistas" they refer to the novelty of the American political system:

For my part, I would alarm and caution even the political and business reader, and to the utmost extent, against the prevailing delusion that the establishment of free political institutions, and plentiful intellectual smartness, with general good order, physical plenty, industry, etc., (desirable and precious advantages as they are) do, of themselves, determine and yield to our experiment of democracy the fruitage of success. (*PW*, 2 : 369 : 225–30, see also *PW*, 2 : 380 : 577 and *PW*, 2 : 387 : 778)

In the preface to "As a Strong Bird on Pinions Free" (1872), Whitman asks, somewhat like Emily Dickinson: "But what is life but an experiment? and mortality but an exercise?" (*LG*, 740 : 13). And, by the time he was writing the 1876 preface, his poems too appeared to him first of all experimental:

The arrangement in print of Two Rivelets—the indirectness of the name itself, (suggesting meanings, the start of other meanings, for the whole Volume)—are but parts of the Venture which my Poems entirely are. For really they have been all Experiments, under the urge of powerful, quite irresistible, perhaps wilful influences, (even escapades), to see how such things will eventually turn out—and have been recited, as it were, by my Soul, to the special audience of Myself, far more than to the world's audience. (*LG*, 749–50 : 99–105)

In "A Backward Glance" the view of his work as basically "an experiment" is confirmed: "Behind all else that can be said, I consider 'Leaves of Grass' and its theory experimental—" (*LG*, 562 : 39–40).

The above quotations show how, in the course of time, Whitman's sense of reality as tentative expanded to include ultimately his own art. This never happened with Dickinson. Having committed herself to writing poetry, she never came to question its absolute reality. Resolutely, she went on about her business of "singing" (*L*, 2 : 413) regardless of Higginson's uneasy comments and his evasive opinion that she should "delay to publish" (*L*, 2 : 408). Because poetry was her one raison d'être, she elevated language, or, more generally, the symbolic realm of the poem to the status of transcendent reality. Her faith in "the sufficiency of the creative word," as Roland Hagenbüchle has observed, saved her from a despair comparable to Melville's.[13]

The last recognition leads, in turn, to questions about Whitman's and Dickinson's place in literary history. Acknowledging for both poets Emerson's role as precursor, it seems justifiable to claim that while Whitman asserts Transcendental faith with a radicality surpassing that of Transcendentalism's chief exponent, Dickinson, in Glauco

Cambon's terms, presents her reader with a later phase, with "a kind of critical Transcendentalism" which followed "Puritan rigor" and "Transcendentalist exuberance."[14] The historical development providing Cambon's chronological criterion is that of the disintegration of institutionalized religion and, with it, of orthodox belief. Indeed, in Dickinson's vision faith is but "the Pierless Bridge / Supporting what We see / Unto the Scene that We do not—" (915), unless it is the faith in the mind's creative power.

A similar interpretation of literary history underlies Bernard Duffey's *Poetry in America*. Duffey divides the history of American poetry into three principal stages determined by progressive questioning of coherence in reality and its transference to the mind. Duffey, however, fails to see Dickinson's poems as more than "terminations" to the Whitmanian stage, which he calls "Fictions of Incoherence."[15]

Roland Hagenbüchle, on the other hand, argues:

> If one agrees that discontinuity is at the very roots of modernity, then it is not Emerson and Whitman who stand at the threshold of modern poetry, but Dickinson. . . . While Emerson . . . should be read within the Romantic tradition, Dickinson—although profoundly indebted to Romanticism—can fully be understood as a post-Romantic whose anti-lyrical poetry springs from the very experience of disharmony and loss.[16]

Dickinson does posit a fragmented universe. Just how far her sense of incoherence takes her is easily seen when Whitman's declaration opening the Lincoln elegy, "I mourn'd, and yet shall mourn with ever returning spring," is juxtaposed with a Dickinson poem on spring's return:

> When they come back—if Blossoms do—
> I always feel a doubt
> If Blossoms can be born again
> When once the Art is out—
>
> When they begin, if Robins may,
> I always had a fear
> I did not tell, it was their last Experiment
> Last Year,

When it is May, if May return,
Had nobody a pang
Lest in a Face so beautiful
We might not look again?

For Whitman, the lilac blossoms returning every year have a secure place within the immemorial cycle of nature. For Dickinson no continuity is certain. The advent of spring has to be confirmed each time by personal experience. Thus she ends the poem:

If I am there—One does not know
What Party—One may be
Tomorrow, but if I am there
I take back all I say—

(1080)

Dickinson's awareness that continuity and direction, even if they do reside in the universe or the mind, are no longer available through either faith or cognition is counterbalanced in the poems by sometimes pathetic clinging to conventions. I hope that enough has been said on the subject, especially in Chapter 5, to justify the conclusion that she clings to them for life and that, much of the time, she is aware of the fact. For what is at stake for her is nothing less than the possibility of form itself. In a world more unstable than Whitman's, Dickinson clutches at mind-made patterns because they provide the only stays against confusion. They are her substitutes for personal fulfillment, for orthodox religious faith, and for the immortality of the soul. They do not always sustain her, but when they do the triumph of "Costumeless Consciousness" (1454) makes up for the loss of "Crowns of Life" (1357).

To make Dickinson altogether our contemporary, to emphasize too strongly the postmodern dimension of her mind, is to overlook the powerful religious motivation behind her art. Ultimately, poetry, the art of writing itself, holds for her the promise of personal salvation very much the way orthodox creeds did for her Puritan forefathers. There is a "backward looking" impulse[17] in her poetry with which she strives to balance her sense of experience gone chaotic. The biographical fact of the withdrawal into her father's house, the habit of pressing her thoughts into familiar hymnal forms, the extent to which she relied on the standard emotional and intellectual attitudes[18] of her day, even the exorbitant demands she made on words and syntax in her poems, should, I believe, be viewed as aspects of the same process of desperate clinging to what she perceived as harbors of stability in the unsettled universe.

Dickinson's personal and historical position made her uniquely suited for entertaining the "Compound Vision": "Back—toward Time— / and forward— / Toward the God of Him—" (906). Historically, she is an artist at the critical point when the forces of emotional and intellectual change hung in uncertain balance and the vista opened both ways: into the past with longing and an acute sense of loss and into the future, with exhilaration and fear. The position enlarged consciousness or at least she had to believe it did. But it also barred her from the kind of sustained achievement that only comes with a secure position from which to view experience.

However, there also exists a synchronic dimension to the Whitman–Dickinson relationship, proved by the fact that both have been invoked as parent figures of modern poetry. Without producing tedious lists of names, among affinities claimed for Dickinson are those with existentialism, with the symbolists, and with such American modernists as Wallace Stevens.[19] Whitman has been claimed for the twentieth century by a number of practicing poets: William Carlos Williams, Hart Crane, Allan Ginsberg, to name only the most conspicuous instances of kinship. Also, scholars and critics have been conscious of Whitman's "long shadow," especially over American epic poetry.[20]

The synchronic relation depends crucially on asserting one or the other of the traditionally recognized aspects of the creative process—that is, intuition or composition. Upholding nonconscious principles of creativity leads to the assumption that form inheres in reality. Whichever aspect of reality the artist chooses to focus upon: the inclusive wholeness of the universe, the subconscious psychic processes, or some biological life force, he will expect its inherent laws to provide the formal principles of his art. Thus Whitman shows affinities with Bergson,[21] with the vitalists,[22] expressionists, and surrealists as well as with the projectivists.[23] On the other hand, if the emphasis is transferred to deliberate composition, the order the poem reveals belongs to the mind. The poem is organized by imagination alone and must be viewed solely as "the act of mind." Its order can supply little help in showing man his place in reality and—even less in rendering it cognizable.

The two principles of creativity have been variously stressed in the twentieth century, both in American poetry and in Western literature in general. Thus, the respective "modernity" of Whitman and Dickinson depends, and will perhaps always depend, on which emphasis is at the moment dominant. For although the terms of the discourse have changed many times, the dilemma of the modern mind which lay at the heart of Emerson's writings is still very much with us.

Notes

1. See Ed Winfield Parks, "The Public and the Private Poet," *South Atlantic Quarterly* 56 (1957): 480–95; and Louis L. Martz, "Whitman and Dickinson: Two Aspects of the Self," in *The Poem of the Mind* (New York: Oxford University Press, 1966).

2. See Jonathan Bishop, *Emerson on the Soul* (Cambridge, Mass.: Harvard University Press, 1964), 77–81.

3. Richard Allyn Yoder, "The Equilibrist Perspective: Toward a Theory of American Romanticism," *Studies in Romanticism* 12, no. 4 (Fall 1973): 705–40.

4. Bishop, *Emerson on the Soul*, 80.

5. Ibid., *passim*.

6. Sherman Paul, *Emerson's Angle of Vision: Man and Nature in American Experience* (Cambridge, Mass.: Harvard University Press, 1952), 2. See also the concluding chapter, "Prospects."

7. See David Porter, *Dickinson: The Modern Idiom* (Cambridge, Mass.: Harvard University Press, 1981), chap. 1, published earlier as "The Crucial Experience in Emily Dickinson's Poetry," *Emerson Society Quarterly* 20 (1974): 280–90. Similarly, Sharon Cameron concludes: "Language is what has the power of being in the absence of being—that which can still stand for something in the empty space whose task it is to sound with the inscrutable sweetness of its plain meanings" (*Lyric Time: Dickinson and the Limits of Genre* [Baltimore: Johns Hopkins University Press, 1979], 200).

8. On Dickinson's strategy of opposing time through art, see especially Cameron, *Lyric Time*.

9. David Porter, *Emerson and Literary Change* (Cambridge, Mass.: Harvard University Press, 1978): "No matter what Emerson's theoretical protestations were concerning a meter making organicism, the narrow path of

this revelation-seeking impulse determines both the philosophical and structural formulas of the poem" (33).

10. Ibid., 36.

11. See especially Porter, *Dickinson: The Modern Idiom*, chap. 5.

12. Ibid., 171.

13. Roland Hagenbüchle, "Sign and Process: The Concept of Language in Emerson and Dickinson," in *Proceedings of a Symposium on American Literature*, ed. Marta Sienicka (Poznań: Universytet Adema Mickiewicza, 1979), 81. The article in *Proceedings* differs slightly from the version printed in the *Emerson Society Quarterly* 25 (1979).

14. Glauco Cambon, "Emily Dickinson and the Crisis of Self-Reliance," in *Transcendentalism and Its Legacy*, ed. Myron Simon and Thornton H. Parsons (Ann Arbor: University of Michigan Press, 1966), 132.

15. Bernard Duffey, *Poetry in America: Expression and Its Values in the Times of Bryant, Whitman and Pound* (Durham, N.C.: Duke University Press, 1978).

16. Hagenbüchle, "Sign and Process," in *Proceedings*, 83.

17. Robert Daly's discussion of the death poems of Edward Taylor, especially of "Upon Wedlock and the death of Children" and of the elegy on his wife (*God's Altar: The World and the Flesh in Puritan Poetry* [Berkeley: University of California Press, 1978], 163–69), points to the tension between the worldly metaphor and the sense of loss which it seeks to relieve and control. Of course Taylor is both emotionally and intellectually compelled to stay within orthodoxy. The compulsion, as Daly demonstrates, determines the way in which his metaphors work. The tensions latent in Taylor's use of metaphor became focal in Dickinson's poetry. Though she certainly feels the need for faith, she no longer finds it intellectually honest. Tensions between unstable vision and stabilizing form become the organizing center of her work.

18. See especially Nina Baym, "God, Father, and Lover in Emily Dickinson's Poetry," in *Puritan Influences in American Literature*, ed. Emory Elliott, Illinois Studies in Language and Literature, vol. 65 (Urbana, Ill.: University of Illinois Press, 1979), 195–209. Baym argues that "Dickinson's poetry illustrates a residual traditionalism rather than a thoroughgoing rebellion against a set of unacceptable religious beliefs" (206).

19. See especially Zacharias Thundyil, "Circumstance, Circumference, and Center: Immanence and Transcendence in Emily Dickinson's Poems of Extreme Situations," *Hartford Studies in Literature* 3 (1971): 73–92; and Inder Nath Kher, *The Landscape of Absence: Emily Dickinson's Poetry* (New Haven: Yale University Press, 1974). Kurt Oppens's "Emily Dickinson: Überlieferung und Prophetie," *Merkur* 14 (January 1960): 17–40, contains an extensive comparison of Dickinson and Rilke. On Dickinson and Stevens, see especially Harold Bloom, *Wallace Stevens: The Poems of Our Climate* (Ithaca: Cornell University Press, 1977), chap. 1; and David Porter, "Emily Dickinson: The Poetics of Doubt," *Emerson Society Quarterly*, no. 60 (Sum-

mer 1970): 86–93. Porter also relates her to Hart Crane. Dickinson's most unambiguous affinity seems to be that with Robert Frost (significantly, another poet at the turning point); see, e.g., George Monteiro, "Emily Dickinson and Robert Frost," *Prairie Schooner* 51 (Winter 1977/78): 369–86; chap. 10 in Karl Keller's *The Only Kangaroo Among the Beauty: Emily Dickinson and America* (Baltimore: Johns Hopkins University Press, 1979); and William Mulder, "Seeing 'New Englandly': Planes of Perception in Emily Dickinson and Robert Frost," *New England Quarterly* 52 (1979): 550–59.

20. See especially Roy Harvey Pearce, *The Continuity of American Poetry* (Princeton: Princeton University Press, 1961), chap. 3; and James Edwin Miller, *The American Quest for a Supreme Fiction: Whitman's Legacy in the Personal Epic* (Chicago: University of Chicago Press, 1979).

21. See Steven Foster, "Bergson's Intuition and Whitman's 'Song of Myself,'" *Texas Studies in Literature and Language* 6 (Autumn 1964): 376–87.

22. The two Polish poets who most strikingly represented the trend in Polish poetry of the 1920s—Wierzyński and Tuwim, both expressed their admiration and acknowledged their debt to Whitman.

23. See Marta Sienicka, *The Making of a New American Poem* (Poznań: Universytet Adema Mickiewicza, 1972).

Selected Bibliography

General

Abrams, Meyer Howard. *The Mirror and the Lamp*. London: Oxford University Press, 1960.

———. *Natural Supernaturalism: Tradition and Revolution in Romantic Literature*. New York: W. W. Norton, 1971.

Anderson, Quentin. *The Imperial Self*. New York: Random House, 1971.

Bercovitch, Sacvan. *The Puritan Origins of the American Self*. New Haven: Yale University Press, 1975.

Bloom, Harold. *The Ringers in the Tower: Studies in Romantic Tradition*. Chicago: University of Chicago Press, 1971.

———. "American Poetic Stances: Emerson to Stevens." In *Wallace Stevens: The Poems of Our Climate*, 1–26. Ithaca: Cornell University Press, 1977.

———, ed. *Romanticism and Consciousness*. New York: W. W. Norton, 1970.

Bové, Paul A. *Destructive Poetics: Heidegger and Modern American Poetry*. New York: Columbia University Press, 1980.

Brooks, Van Wyck. *The Flowering of New England*. New York: E. P. Dutton, 1936.

Buell, Lawrence. "Transcendentalist Catalogue Rhetoric: Vision versus Form." *American Literature* 40 (1968): 325–39.

———. *Literary Transcendentalism: Style and Vision in the American Renaissance*. Ithaca: Cornell University Press, 1973.

Cambon, Glauco. *The Inclusive Flame: Studies in American Poetry*. Bloomington: Indiana University Press, 1963.

Charvat, William. *The Origins of American Critical Thought, 1810–1835*. 1936. Reissued. New York: Barnes, 1961.

Coffman, Stanley K. *Imagism: A Chapter for the History of Modern Poetry*. Norman: University of Oklahoma Press, 1951.

Collins, Christopher. *The Uses of Observation: A Study of Correspondential Vision in the Writings of Emerson, Thoreau and Whitman*. The Hague: Mouton, 1971.

Daly, Robert. *God's Altar: The World and the Flesh in Puritan Poetry*. Berkeley: University of California Press, 1978.

Donoghue, Denis. *Connoisseurs of Chaos*. London: Faber and Faber, 1965.

Duffey, Bernard. *Poetry in America: Expression and Its Values in the Times of Bryant, Whitman and Pound*. Durham, N.C.: Duke University Press, 1978.

Elliott, Emory, ed. *Puritan Influences in American Literature*. Illinois Studies in Language and Literature, vol. 65. Urbana: University of Illinois Press, 1979.

Ellmann, Richard, and Robert O'Clair, eds. *The Norton Anthology of Modern Poetry*. New York: W. W. Norton, 1973.

Feidelson, Charles. *Symbolism and American Literature*. Chicago: University of Chicago Press, 1953.

Fluck, Winfried, Jürgen Peper, and Willi Paul Adams, eds. *Forms and Functions of History in American Literature: Essays in Honor of Ursula Brumm*. Berlin: Erich Schmidt Verlag, 1981.

Frye, Northrop. *Fables of Identity: Studies in Poetic Mythology*. New York: Harcourt, Brace and World, 1963.

Fussell, Edwin. *Lucifer in Harness: American Meter, Metaphor and Diction*. Princeton: Princeton University Press, 1973.

Gelpi, Albert. *The Tenth Muse: The Psyche of the American Poet*. Cambridge, Mass.: Harvard University Press, 1975.

Gilbert, Sandra M., and Susan Gubar, eds. *The Madwoman in the Attic: The Woman Writer and the Nineteenth-Century Imagination*. New Haven: Yale University Press, 1979.

———. *Shakespeare's Sisters: Feminist Essays on Women Poets*. Bloomington: Indiana University Press, 1979.

Hartman, Geoffrey. *Beyond Formalism: Literary Essays, 1958–1970*. New Haven: Yale University Press, 1970.

Homans, Margaret. *Women Writers and Poetic Identity*. Princeton: Princeton University Press, 1980.

Horton, Rod W., and Herbert W. Edwards. *Backgrounds of American Literary Thought*. New York: Appleton-Century-Crofts, 1967.

Irwin, John T. *American Hieroglyphics: The Symbol of the Egyptian Hieroglyphics in the American Renaissance*. New Haven: Yale University Press, 1980.

James, Henry. *The Art of the Novel: Critical Prefaces with an Introduction by R. P. Blackmur*. New York: Charles Scribner's Sons, 1962.

Jones, Howard Mumford. *Revolution and Romanticism*. Cambridge, Mass.: Harvard University Press, Belknap Press, 1974.

Keller, Karl. "Alephs, Lahirs, and the Triumph of Ambiguity: Typology in Nineteenth-Century American Literature." In *Literary Uses of Typology from the Middle Ages to the Present*, edited by Earl Miner, 274–314. Princeton: Princeton University Press, 1977.

Lewis, Richard Warrington Baldwin. *The American Adam*. Chicago: University of Chicago Press, 1955.

Lovejoy, Arthur O. "On the Discriminations of Romanticisms." *PMLA* 39 (1924): 229–53. Enlarged and reprinted in *Essays in the History of Ideas*. Baltimore: Johns Hopkins University Press, 1948.

Lowance, Mason I. *The Language of Canaan*. Cambridge, Mass.: Harvard University Press, 1980.

Lowell, Amy. *Poetry and Poets: Essays*. 1930. Reprint. New York: Biblo, Tannen, 1971.

Lynen, John F. *The Design of the Present: Essays on Time and Form in American Literature*. New Haven: Yale University Press, 1969.

Mabbott, Thomas Ollive, ed. *Collected Works of Edgar Allan Poe*. 3 vols. Cambridge, Mass.: Harvard University Press, Belknap Press, 1969.

Martz, Louis L. *The Poem of the Mind*. London: Oxford University Press, 1966.

Mathiessen, F. O. *American Renaissance: Art and Expression in the Age of Emerson and Whitman*. London: Oxford University Press, 1941.

Miller, James Edwin. *The American Quest for a Supreme Fiction: Whitman's Legacy in the Personal Epic*. Chicago: University of Chicago Press, 1979.

Miller, Perry. *The New England Mind: From Colony to Province*. Cambridge, Mass.: Harvard University Press, 1953.

Parrington, Vernon L. *Main Currents in American Thought*. 3 vols. in 1. New York: Harcourt, Brace, 1930.

Pearce, Roy Harvey. *The Continuity of American Poetry*. Princeton: Princeton University Press, 1961.

Poirer, Richard. *The World Elsewhere*. London: Oxford University Press, 1966.

Pound, Ezra. *Literary Essays*. Edited with an Introduction by T. S. Eliot. New York: New Directions, 1968.

Riese, Teut Andreas, ed. *Vistas of a Continent: Concepts of Nature in America*. Heidelberg: Carl Winter Universitätsverlag, 1979.

Salska, Agnieszka. *Wczesna poezja amerykańska na tle dazenia do niepodległości*. Łódź: Uniwersytet Łódzki, 1972.

———. "Puritan Poetry: Its Public and Private Strain." *Early American Literature*. Fall 1984.

Sienicka, Marta. *The Making of a New American Poem*. Poznań: Uniwersytet Adama Mickiewicza, 1972.

Simon, Myron, and Parsons Thornton, eds. *Transcendentalism and Its Legacy*. Ann Arbor: University of Michigan Press, 1966.

Spencer, Benjamin T. *The Quest for Nationality: An American Literary Campaign*. Syracuse: Syracuse University Press, 1957.

Spiller, Robert E. *The American Literary Revolution (1783–1837)*. New York: New York University Press, 1969.

———, et al., eds. *Literary History of the United States*. 1946. 4th ed. rev. New York: Macmillan, 1974.

Waggoner, Hyatt H. *American Poets: From the Puritans to the Present*. Boston: Houghton Mifflin, 1968.

———. *American Visionary Poetry*. Baton Rouge: Louisiana State University Press, 1982.

Wellek, René. "The Concept of 'Romanticism' in Literary History." *Comparative Literature* 1 (1949): 1–33, 147–72.

———. *Confrontations*. Princeton: Princeton University Press, 1965.

Yoder, Richard Allyn. "The Equilibrist Perspective: Toward a Theory of American Romanticism." *Studies in Romanticism* 12, no. 4 (Fall 1973): 705–40.

Emerson

Texts

Emerson, Edward Waldo, ed. *The Complete Works of Ralph Waldo Emerson*. Centenary Edition. Boston: Houghton Mifflin, 1903–4.

Ferguson, Alfred, and Joseph Slater, gen. eds. *The Complete Works of Ralph Waldo Emerson*. Cambridge, Mass.: Harvard University Press, 1971—. Volumes published to date include: *Nature, Addresses and Lectures* (vol. 1); *Essays, First Series* (vol. 2); *Essays, Second Series* (vol. 3).

Gilman, William H., et al., eds. *The Journals and Miscellaneous Notebooks of Ralph Waldo Emerson*. 16 vols. Cambridge, Mass.: Harvard University Press, 1960–82.

McGiffert, Arthur C., Jr., ed. *Young Emerson Speaks*. Boston: Houghton Mifflin, 1938.

Rusk, Ralph L., ed. *The Letters of Ralph Waldo Emerson*. 6 vols. New York: Columbia University Press, 1939.

Slater, Joseph, ed. *The Correspondence of Emerson and Carlyle*. New York: Columbia University Press, 1964.

Whicher, Stephen E., and Robert E. Spiller, eds. *The Early Lectures of Ralph Waldo Emerson*. 3 vols. Cambridge, Mass.: Harvard University Press, 1959.

Criticism

Allen, Gay Wilson. *Waldo Emerson*. New York: Viking Press, 1981; Penguin Books, 1982.

Bishop, Jonathan. *Emerson on the Soul*. Cambridge, Mass.: Harvard University Press, 1964.

Carpenter, Frederic Ives. *Emerson and Asia*. Cambridge, Mass.: Harvard University Press, 1930.
———. *Ralph Waldo Emerson*. New York: American Book Co., 1934. (Contains bibliography with emphasis on the period 1917–34.)
———. *Emerson Handbook*. New York: Hendricks House, 1953.
Emerson Society Quarterly. Publishes Emerson bibliography since 1955.
Gonnaud, Maurice. *Individu et société dans l'oeuvre de Ralph Waldo Emerson. Essai de biographie spirituelle*. Paris: Didier, 1964.
Hagenbüchle, Roland. "Sign and Process: The Concept of Language in Emerson and Dickinson." *Emerson Society Quarterly* 25 (1979): 137–55. Also in *Proceedings of a Symposium on American Literature*, edited by Marta Sienicka, 59–88. Poznań: Uniwersytet Adama Mickiewicza, 1979.
Hopkins, Vivian C. *Spires of Form: A Study of Emerson's Aesthetic Theory*. Cambridge, Mass.: Harvard University Press, 1951.
Konvitz, Milton, ed. *Emerson: A Collection of Critical Essays*. Englewood Cliffs, N.J.: Prentice-Hall, 1963.
Levin, David, ed. *Emerson: Prophecy, Metamorphosis and Influence*. New York: Columbia University Press, 1975.
Loving, Jerome. *Emerson, Whitman, and the American Muse*. Chapel Hill: University of North Carolina Press, 1982.
McIntosh, James. "Emerson's Unmoored Self." *The Yale Review* 65, no. 2 (1975): 232–40.
Paul, Sherman. *Emerson's Angle of Vision: Man and Nature in American Experience*. Cambridge, Mass.: Harvard University Press, 1952.
Porte, Joel. *Emerson and Thoreau: Transcendentalists in Conflict*. Middletown, Conn.: Wesleyan University Press, 1966.
———. "Emerson, Thoreau and the Double Consciousness." *New England Quarterly* 41 (1968): 40–50.
Porter, David. *Emerson and Literary Change*. Cambridge, Mass.: Harvard University Press, 1978.
Rountree, Thomas, ed. *Critics on Emerson*. Readings in Literary Criticism, no. 20. Coral Gables, Fla.: University of Miami Press, 1973.
Rusk, Ralph L. *The Life of Waldo Emerson*. New York: Charles Scribner's Sons, 1949.
Smith, Philip Charles. "Momentary Music: The Problem of Power and Form in Emerson's Poetry." Ph.D. dissertation, University of Nebraska, 1974 (Ann Arbor, Mich.: Xerox University Microfilms, 1975).
Sowder, William J. *Emerson's Reviewers and Commentators: A Biographical and Bibliographical Analysis of Nineteenth-Century Periodical Criticism with a Detailed Index*. Hartford: Transcendental Books, 1968.
Staebler, Warren. *Ralph Waldo Emerson*. The Great American Thinkers Series. New York: Twayne Publishers, 1973.
Stovall, Floyd, ed. *Eight American Authors*. New York: Modern Language Association, 1956. Contains a chapter by the editor reviewing "research and criticism" of Emerson.

Wagenknecht, Edward Charles. *Ralph Waldo Emerson: Portrait of a Balanced Soul*. New York: Oxford University Press, 1974.
Waggoner, Hyatt H. *Emerson as Poet*. Princeton: Princeton University Press, 1974.
Whicher, Stephen E. *Freedom and Fate: An Inner Life of Ralph Waldo Emerson*. Philadelphia: University of Pennsylvania Press, 1953.
Yoder, Richard Allyn. *Emerson and the Orphic Poet in America*. Berkeley: University of California Press, 1978.

Whitman

Texts

Blodgett, Harold, and Sculley Bradley, eds. *Leaves of Grass. Comprehensive Reader's Edition*. New York: New York University Press, 1965. Reprinted in paperback by W. W. Norton, 1973.
Bradley, Sculley, Harold W. Blodgett, Arthur Golden, and William White, eds. *Leaves of Grass: A Textual Variorum of the Printed Poems*. 3 vols. New York: New York University Press, 1980.
Brasher, Thomas L., ed. *Walt Whitman: The Early Poems and the Fiction*. New York: New York University Press, 1963.
Bucke, Richard M., ed. *Notes and Fragments*. London: privately printed, 1899.
Cowley, Malcolm, ed. *Walt Whitman: Leaves of Grass*. 1855. Reprint. New York: Viking Press, 1959.
Ghodes, Clarence, and Rollo Silver, eds. *Faint Clews and Indirections: Manuscripts of Walt Whitman and His Family*. 1949. Reprint. New York: Ams Press, 1965.
Holloway, Emory, ed. *The Uncollected Poetry and Prose of Walt Whitman*. 2 vols. 1921. Reprint. Gloucester, Mass.: Peter Smith, 1972.
———, ed. *I Sit and Look Out: Editorials from the Brooklyn Daily Times*. New York: Columbia University Press, 1932.
———, ed. *Walt Whitman: Complete Poetry and Selected Prose and Letters*. London: Nonesuch Press, 1936.
Miller, Edwin Haviland, ed. *The Correspondence of Walt Whitman*. 6 vols. New York: New York University Press, 1961–77.
Pearce, Roy Harvey, ed. *Leaves of Grass by Walt Whitman*. Facsimile edition of the 1860 text. Ithaca: Cornell University Press, 1961.
Stovall, Floyd, ed. *Walt Whitman: Representative Selections*. New York: Hill and Wang, 1961.
———, ed. *Walt Whitman: Prose Works*. 2 vols. New York: New York University Press, 1963.

White, William, ed. *Walt Whitman: Daybooks and Notebooks.* 3 vols. New York: New York University Press, 1978.
Whitman, Walt. *Leaves of Grass.* Facsimile of 1855 edition. San Francisco: Chandler Publishing Co., 1968.

Criticism

Allen, Gay Wilson. *Walt Whitman Handbook.* 1946. Reprint. New York: Hendricks House, 1962.
———. *The Solitary Singer: A Critical Biography of Walt Whitman.* 1955. Revised. New York: New York University Press, 1967.
———. *Walt Whitman as Man, Poet and Legend: With a Check List of Whitman Publications, 1945–1960.* Carbondale: Southern Illinois University Press, 1961.
———. *A Reader's Guide to Walt Whitman.* New York: Farrar, Strauss, Giroux, 1970.
———, ed. *Walt Whitman Abroad.* Syracuse: Syracuse University Press, 1955.
———, and Charles T. Davis, eds. *Walt Whitman's Poems: Selections with Critical Aids.* New York: New York University Press, 1955.
Asselineau, Roger. *The Evolution of Walt Whitman.* 2 vols. Cambridge, Mass.: Harvard University Press, Belknap Press, 1960–62.
Black, Stephen A. *Whitman's Journeys into Chaos: A Psychoanalytic Study of the Poetic Process.* Princeton: Princeton University Press, 1975.
Blodgett, Harold. *Walt Whitman in England.* Ithaca: Cornell University Press, 1934.
Bowers, Fredson, ed. *Whitman's Manuscripts: Leaves of Grass: 1860.* Chicago: University of Chicago Press, 1955.
Bradley, Sculley. "The Fundamental Metrical Principle in Whitman's Poetry." *American Literature* 10 (January 1939): 437–59.
Carlisle, E. Fred. *The Uncertain Self: Whitman's Drama of Identity.* East Lansing: Michigan State University Press, 1973.
Carpenter, Edward. *Days with Walt Whitman.* London: George and Unwin, 1906.
Chari, V. K. *Whitman in the Light of Vedantic Mysticism.* Lincoln: University of Nebraska Press, 1964.
Chase, Richard. *Walt Whitman Reconsidered.* New York: William Sloane Associates, 1955.
———. "Out of the Cradle as a Romance." In *The Presence of Walt Whitman,* edited by R. W. B. Lewis. New York: Columbia University Press, 1962.
Coffman, Stanley K. "Crossing Brooklyn Ferry: A Note on the Catalogue Technique in Whitman's Poetry." *Modern Philology* 51 (1954): 225–32.
———. "Form and Meaning in Whitman's Passage to India." *PMLA* 70 (June 1955): 337–49.
Coleman, Philip Y. "Walt Whitman's Ambiguities of 'I'." In *Studies in Ameri-*

can Literature in Honor of Robert Dunn Faner, edited by Robert Partlow. Carbondale: Southern Illinois University Press, 1969.

Cowley, Malcolm. *Introduction to Leaves of Grass: The First (1855) Edition*. Reprinted in *Walt Whitman*, edited by Francis Murphy. Harmondsworth, Penguin Critical Anthologies, 1969; and in *Whitman's Song of Myself—Origin, Growth, Meaning*, edited by James E. Miller. New York: Dodd, Mead, 1964.

Crawley, Thomas Edward. *The Structure of Leaves of Grass*. Austin: University of Texas Press, 1970.

DelGreco, Robert David. *Whitman and the Epic Impulse*. Ph.D. diss., University of Illinois at Urbana-Champaign, 1975 (Ann Arbor, Mich.: Xerox University Microfilms, no. 48106).

Donoghue, Denis. "Walt Whitman." In *Connoisseurs of Chaos*, 23–51. London: Faber and Faber, 1965. Reprinted in *Walt Whitman*, edited by Francis Murphy. Harmondsworth: Penguin Critical Anthologies, 1969.

Eby, Edwin Harold. *A Concordance of Walt Whitman's Leaves of Grass and Selected Prose Writings*. Seattle: University of Washington Press, 1955.

Faner, Robert D. *Walt Whitman and Opera*. Philadelphia: University of Pennsylvania Press, 1951.

Forster, Steven. "Bergson's Intuition and Whitman's Song of Myself." *Texas Studies in Literature and Language* 6 (Autumn 1964): 376–87.

Frank, Armin Paul. "The Long Withdrawing Roar: Eighty Years of the Ocean's Message in American Poetry." In *Forms and Functions of History in American Literature: Essays in Honor of Ursula Brumm*, edited by Winfried Fluck, Jürgen Peper, and Willi Paul Adams, 71–90. Berlin: Erich Schmidt Verlag, 1981.

Fussell, Paul. "Whitman's Curious Warble: Reminiscence and Reconciliation." In *The Presence of Walt Whitman*, edited by Richard Warrington Baldwin Lewis, 28–51. New York: Columbia University Press, 1962.

Goodale, David. "Some of Walt Whitman's Borrowings." *American Literature* 10 (May 1938): 202–13.

Hagenbüchle, Roland. "Whitman's Unfinished Quest for an American Identity." *Journal of English Literary History* 40 (1973): 428–78.

Hensler, Donna L. "The Voice of the Grass Poem 'I': Whitman's 'Song of Myself.'" *Walt Whitman Review* 15 (March 1969): 26–32.

Hindus, Milton, ed. *Leaves of Grass: One Hundred Years After*. Stanford, Calif.: Stanford University Press, 1955.

———, ed. *Walt Whitman: The Critical Heritage*. London: Routledge and Kegan Paul, 1971.

Hungerford, Edward. "Walt Whitman and His Chart of Bumps." *American Literature* 2 (January 1931): 350–84.

Hyman, Ronald. *Arguing with Whitman: An Essay on His Influence on 20th Century American Verse*. London: Covent Garden Press, 1971.

Jannaccone, Pasqualle. *Walt Whitman's Poetry and the Evolution of Rhythmic Forms*. Translated from the Italian by Peter Mitilineos. Washington, D.C.: NCR Microcard Edition, 1973.

Jarrell, Randall. "Some Lines from Whitman." In *Poetry and the Age*. New York: Alfred A. Knopf, 1953.
Kepner, Diane. "From Spears to Leaves: Walt Whitman's Theory of Nature in Song of Myself." *American Literature* 51, no. 2 (May 1979): 179–204.
Lawrence, David Herbert. "Whitman." In *Studies in Classic American Literature*, 163–177. New York: Boni and Liveright, 1923.
Lewis, Richard Warrington Baldwin. "Walt Whitman: Always Going out and Coming in." In *Trials of the Word: Essays in American Literature and the Humanistic Tradition*, 3–35. New Haven: Yale University Press, 1965.
———, ed. *The Presence of Walt Whitman*. New York: Columbia University Press, 1962.
Lynen, John F. "The Poetry of the Present and the Form of the Moment: Walt Whitman." In *The Design of the Present: Essays on Time and Form in American Literature*, 273–339. New Haven: Yale University Press, 1969.
McElderry, Bruce R., Jr. "Personae in Whitman (1855–1860)." *American Transcendental Quarterly* 12 (1971): 25–32.
Marks, Alfred H. "Whitman's Triadic Imagery." *American Literature* 23 (1951): 99–126.
Marx, Leo, ed. *The Americanness of Walt Whitman*. Boston: D. C. Heath, 1960.
Miller, Edwin Haviland. *Walt Whitman's Poetry: A Psychological Journey*. New York: New York University Press, 1968.
———, ed. *A Century of Whitman Criticism*. Bloomington: University of Indiana Press, 1969.
Miller, James E., Jr. *A Critical Guide to Leaves of Grass*. Chicago: University of Chicago Press, 1957.
———, ed. *Whitman's Song of Myself—Origin, Growth, Meaning*. New York: Dodd, Mead, 1964.
Mirsky, D. "Poet of American Democracy." In *Walt Whitman*, edited by Francis Murphy. Harmondsworth: Penguin Critical Anthologies, 1969.
Murphy, Francis, ed. *Walt Whitman*. Harmondsworth: Penguin Critical Anthologies, 1969.
Musgrove, Sydney. *T. S. Eliot and Walt Whitman*. New York: Columbia University Press, 1953.
Pearce, Roy Harvey, ed. *Whitman: A Collection of Critical Essays*. Englewood Cliffs, N.J.: Prentice-Hall, 1962.
Rubin, Joseph Jay. *The Historic Whitman*. University Park: Pennsylvania State University Press, 1973.
Schyberg, Frederic. *Walt Whitman*. Translated from the Danish by Evie Allison Allen. New York: Columbia University Press, 1951.
Smuts, Jan Christian. *Walt Whitman*. Detroit: Wayne State University Press, 1973.
Snyder, John. *The Dear Love of Man: Tragic and Lyric Communion in Walt Whitman*. The Hague: Mouton, 1975.

Spitzer, Leo. "Explication de Texte Applied to Walt Whitman's Poem 'Out of the Cradle Endlessly Rocking.'" *Journal of English Literary History* 16 (September 1949): 229–49.

Stovall, Floyd. *The Foreground of Leaves of Grass*. Charlottesville: University of Virginia Press, 1974.

Strauch, Carl. "The Structure of Walt Whitman's Song of Myself." *English Journal* 27 (September 1938): 597–607. Reprinted in *Whitman's Song of Myself—Origin, Growth, Meaning*. Edited by James E. Miller. New York: Dodd, Mead, 1964.

Swayne, Mattie. "Whitman's Catalogue Rhetoric." *University of Texas Studies in English*, no. 21 (1941): 162–78.

Tanner, James T. F. *Walt Whitman: A Supplementary Bibliography: 1961–1967*. Kent, Ohio: Kent State University Press, 1968.

Traubel, Horace. *With Walt Whitman in Camden*. Vols. 1–2, New York: Appleton, 1908. Vol. 3, Philadelphia: University of Pennsylvania Press, 1953. Vol. 4, Carbondale: Southern Illinois University Press, 1964.

Trilling, Lionel. "Sermon on a Text from Whitman." In *Walt Whitman*, edited by Francis Murphy. Harmondsworth: Penguin Critical Anthologies, 1969.

Warfel, Harry R. "Whitman's Structural Principles in 'Spontaneous Me.'" *College English* 18 (1957): 190–95.

Waskow, Howard. *Whitman: Explorations in Form*. Chicago: University of Chicago Press, 1966.

Wells, Carolyn, and Alfred F. Goldsmith. *A Concise Bibliography of the Works of Walt Whitman*. New York: Burt Franklin, 1922. Reprinted 1968.

White, William. "Whitman: A Current Bibliography." *Walt Whitman Review* (continuing).

Wiley, Autrey Neil. "Reiterative Devices in Leaves of Grass." *American Literature* 1 (May 1929): 121–70.

Willard, Charles B. *Whitman's American Fame: The Growth of His Reputation in America after 1892*. Providence: Brown University Press, 1950.

Dickinson

Texts

Franklin, Ralph William, ed. *The Manuscript Books of Emily Dickinson*. Cambridge, Mass.: Harvard University Press, 1981.

Johnson, Thomas H., ed. *The Poems of Emily Dickinson*. 3 vols. Variorum Edition. Cambridge: Harvard University Press, Belknap Press, 1955.

———, ed. *The Complete Poems of Emily Dickinson*. Boston: Little, Brown, 1960.

———, ed. *Final Harvest: Emily Dickinson's Poems*. Boston: Little, Brown, 1961.
———, ed. *Emily Dickinson: Selected Letters*. Cambridge, Mass.: Harvard University Press, Belknap Press, 1971.
———, and Theodora Ward, eds. *The Letters of Emily Dickinson*. 3 vols. Cambridge, Mass.: Harvard University Press, Belknap Press, 1958.

Criticism

Anderson, Charles R. "The Conscious Self in Emily Dickinson's Poetry." *American Literature* 31 (November 1959): 290–308.
———. *Emily Dickinson's Poetry: A Stairway of Surprise*. New York: Holt, Rinehart and Winston, 1960.
Attebery, Brian. "Dickinson, Emerson and the Abstract Concrete." *Dickinson Studies* 35 (1979): 17–22.
Banzer, Judith. "Compound Manner: Emily Dickinson and the Metaphysical Poets." *American Literature* 32 (1961): 417–33.
Baym, Nina. "God, Father, and Lover in Emily Dickinson's Poetry." In *Puritan Influences in American Literature*, edited by Emory Elliott, 193–209. Illinois Studies in Language and Literature, vol. 65. Urbana: University of Illinois Press, 1979.
Bianchi, Martha Dickinson. *Emily Dickinson Face to Face: Unpublished Letters with Notes and Reminiscences*. Boston: Houghton Mifflin, 1932.
Bingham, Millicent Todd. *Ancestors' Brocades: The Literary Debut of Emily Dickinson*. New York: Harper and Brothers, 1945.
———. *Emily Dickinson: A Revelation*. New York: Harper and Brothers, 1954.
———. *Emily Dickinson's Home: Letters of Edward Dickinson and His Family*. New York: Harper and Brothers, 1955.
Blake, Caesar R., and Carlton F. Wells, eds. *The Recognition of Emily Dickinson: Selected Criticism since 1890*. Ann Arbor: University of Michigan Press, 1964.
Buckingham, Willis J. *Emily Dickinson: An Annotated Bibliography*. Bloomington: Indiana University Press, 1970.
———. "Emily Dickinson Bulletin Index, 1968–1974." *Emily Dickinson Bulletin* 28 (1975): 79–106.
Cambon, Glauco. "Violence and Abstraction in Emily Dickinson." *Sewanee Review* 68 (July/September 1960): 450–64.
———. "Emily Dickinson and the Crisis of Self-Reliance." In *Transcendentalism and Its Legacy*, edited by Myron Simon and Thornton H. Parsons, 123–33. Ann Arbor: University of Michigan Press, 1966.
Cameron, Sharon. *Lyric Time: Dickinson and the Limits of Genre*. Baltimore: Johns Hopkins University Press, 1979.
Capps, Jack L. *Emily Dickinson's Reading*. Cambridge, Mass.: Harvard University Press, 1966.

Carton, Evan. "Dickinson and the Divine: The Terror of Integration, the Terror of Detachment." *Emerson Society Quarterly* 24 (1978): 242–52.

Chase, Richard. *Emily Dickinson.* New York: William Sloane Associates, 1951.

Childs, Herbert E. "Emily Dickinson and Sir Thomas Browne." *American Literature* 22 (1951): 455–65.

Cody, John. *After Great Pain: The Inner Life of Emily Dickinson.* Cambridge, Mass.: Harvard University Press, Belknap Press, 1971.

Davidson, Frank. "A Note on Emily Dickinson's Use of Shakespeare." *New England Quarterly* 18 (September 1945): 407–8.

Diehl, Joanne Feit. *Dickinson and the Romantic Imagination.* Princeton: Princeton University Press, 1981.

Donoghue, Denis. "Emily Dickinson." In *Connoisseurs of Chaos.* Chap. 4. London: Faber and Faber, 1965.

———. *Emily Dickinson.* Pamphlets on American Writers, no. 81. Minneapolis: University of Minnesota Press, 1969.

Duchac, Joseph. *The Poems of Emily Dickinson: An Annotated Guide to Commentary Published in English, 1890–1977.* Boston: Hall, 1979.

Emily Dickinson: Three Views. Amherst, Mass.: Amherst College Press, 1960.

Ferlazzo, Paul J. *Emily Dickinson.* Boston: Twayne, 1970.

Franklin, Ralph William. *The Editing of Emily Dickinson: A Reconsideration.* Madison: University of Wisconsin Press, 1967.

Frye, Northrop. "Emily Dickinson." In *Fables of Identity: Studies in Poetic Mythology.* New York: Harcourt, Brace and World, 1963.

Gelpi, Albert J. *Emily Dickinson: The Mind of the Poet.* Cambridge, Mass.: Harvard University Press, 1965.

———. "Emily Dickinson and the Deerslayer: The Dilemma of the Woman Poet in America." In *Shakespeare's Sisters: Feminist Essays on Women Poets,* edited by Sandra M. Gilbert and Susan Gubar, 122–34. Bloomington: Indiana University Press, 1979.

Gonnaud, Maurice. "Nature, Apocalypse or Experiment: Emerson's Double Lineage in American Poetry." In *Vistas of a Continent: Concepts of Nature in America,* edited by Teut Andreas Riese, 123–41. Heidelberg: Carl Winter Universitätsverlag, 1979.

Griffith, Clark. *The Long Shadow: Emily Dickinson's Tragic Poetry.* Princeton: Princeton University Press, 1964.

Hagenbüchle, Roland. "Precision and Indeterminacy in the Poetry of Emily Dickinson." *Emerson Society Quarterly* 20 (1974): 33–56.

Haiskänen-Mäkelä, Sirka. *In Quest of Truth: Observations on the Development of Emily Dickinson's Poetic Dialectic.* Jyväskylä, Finland: K. J. Gummerns Osakeyhtiön Kirjapainossa, 1970.

Harris, Marguerite, ed. *Emily Dickinson: Letters from the World.* Corinth, 1970.

Higgins, David. *Portrait of Emily Dickinson: The Poet and Her Prose.* New Brunswick: Rutgers University Press, 1967.

Howard, William. "Emily Dickinson's Poetic Vocabulary." *PMLA* 72 (March 1957): 225–48.
Johnson, Thomas H. *Emily Dickinson: An Interpretive Biography*. Cambridge, Mass.: Harvard University Press, Belknap Press, 1955.
Keller, Karl. *The Only Kangaroo Among the Beauty: Emily Dickinson and America*. Baltimore: Johns Hopkins University Press, 1979.
Kher, Inder Nath. *The Landscape of Absence: Emily Dickinson's Poetry*. New Haven: Yale University Press, 1974.
Leyda, Jay. *The Years and Hours of Emily Dickinson*. New Haven: Yale University Press, 1960.
Lindberg-Seyersted, Brita. *The Voice of the Poet: Aspects of Style in the Poetry of Emily Dickinson*. Uppsala: Almqvist and Wiksells Boktryckeri AB, 1968.
Lubbers, Klaus. *Emily Dickinson: The Critical Revolution*. Ann Arbor: University of Michigan Press, 1968.
Lynen, John F. "Three Uses of the Present: The Historian's, the Critic's and Emily Dickinson's." *College English* 28, no. 2 (November 1966): 126–36.
Miller, James E. "Emily Dickinson: The Thunder's Tongue." *Minnesota Review* 2 (Spring 1962): 289–304.
Miller, Ruth. *The Poetry of Emily Dickinson*. Middletown, Conn.: Wesleyan University Press, 1968.
Moldenhauer, Joseph J. "Emily Dickinson's Ambiguity: Notes on Technique." *Emerson Society Quarterly*, no. 44 (1966): 35–44.
Morey, Frederic L. "Hundred Best Poems of Emily Dickinson." *Emily Dickinson Bulletin* 27 (1975): 4–43.
Mulder, William. "Seeing 'New Englandly': Planes of Perception in Emily Dickinson and Robert Frost." *New England Quarterly* 52 (1979): 550–59.
Oppens, Kurt. "Überlieferung und Prophetie." *Merkur* 14 (January 1960): 17–40. Contains an extensive comparison of Dickinson and Rilke.
Patterson, Rebecca. *Emily Dickinson's Imagery*. Amherst: University of Massachusetts Press, 1979.
Pollak, Vivian. "Thirst and Starvation in Emily Dickinson's Poetry." *American Literature* 51 (1979): 33–49.
Porter, David T. *The Art of Emily Dickinson's Early Poetry*. Cambridge, Mass.: Harvard University Press, 1966.
———. "Emily Dickinson: The Poetics of Doubt." *Emerson Society Quarterly* 60 (Summer 1970): 86–93.
———. *Dickinson: The Modern Idiom*. Cambridge, Mass.: Harvard University Press, 1981.
Rich, Adrienne. "Vesuvius at Home: The Power of Emily Dickinson." *Parnassus: Poetry in Review* 5, no. 1 (Fall/Winter 1976): 49–74. Reprinted in *Shakespeare's Sisters: Feminist Essays on Women Poets*, edited by Sandra M. Gilbert and Susan Gubar, 99–121. Bloomington: Indiana University Press, 1979.

Rosenbaum, Stanford Patric. *A Concordance to the Poems of Emily Dickinson.* Ithaca: Cornell University Press, 1964.

Sewall, Richard. *The Life of Emily Dickinson.* New York: Farrar, Strauss, Giroux, 1974.

———, ed. *Emily Dickinson: A Collection of Critical Essays.* Englewood Cliffs, N.J.: Prentice-Hall, 1963.

Sherwood, William R. *Circumference and Circumstance: Stages in the Mind and Art of Emily Dickinson.* New York: Columbia University Press, 1968.

Thundyil, Zacharias. "Circumstance, Circumference, and Center: Immanence and Transcendence in Emily Dickinson's Poems of Extreme Situations." *Hartford Studies in Literature* 3 (1971): 73–92.

Todd, John Emerson. *Emily Dickinson's Use of the Persona.* The Hague: Mouton, 1973.

Ward, Theodora. *The Capsule of the Mind: Chapters in the Life of Emily Dickinson.* Cambridge, Mass.: Harvard University Press, Belknap Press, 1961.

Weisbuch, Robert. *Emily Dickinson's Poetry.* Chicago: University of Chicago Press, 1975.

Wells, Henry W. *Introduction to Emily Dickinson.* Chicago: Hendricks House, 1947.

Whicher, George Frisbie. *This Was a Poet: A Critical Biography of Emily Dickinson.* Ann Arbor: University of Michigan Press, 1957. First published New York: Charles Scribner's Sons, 1939.

Wilbur, Richard. "Sumptuous Destitution." In *Emily Dickinson: Three Views.* Amherst, Mass.: Amherst College Press, 1960. Reprinted in *Emily Dickinson: A Collection of Critical Essays*, edited by Richard Sewall. Englewood Cliffs, N.J.: Prentice-Hall, 1963.

Williams, JoAnne De Lavan. "Spiders in the Attic: A Suggestion of Synthesis in the Poetry of Emily Dickinson." *Emily Dickinson Bulletin* 29 (1976): 21–29.

Wilner, Eleanor. "The Poetics of Emily Dickinson." *ELH* 38 (1971): 126–54.

Whitman–Dickinson Comparisons

Diggory, Terence. "Armored Women, Naked Men: Dickinson, Whitman and Their Successors." In *Shakespeare's Sisters: Feminist Essays on Women Poets*, edited by Sandra M. Gilbert and Susan Gubar, 135–50. Bloomington: Indiana University Press, 1979.

Eitner, Walter H. "Emily Dickinson's Awareness of Walt Whitman: A Reappraisal." *Walt Whitman Review* 22 (September 1976): 111–15.

Gelpi, Albert. "Walt Whitman: The Self as Circumference" and "Emily Dickinson: The Self as Center." Chapters 5 and 6 in *The Tenth Muse: The*

Psyche of the American Poet. Cambridge, Mass.: Harvard University Press, 1975.

Hagenbüchle, Roland. "Whitman's Unfinished Quest for an American Identity." *Journal of English Literary History* 40 (1973): 428–78. Refers comparatively to Emily Dickinson.

Keller, Karl. "The Sweet Wolf Within: Emily Dickinson and Walt Whitman." In *The Only Kangaroo Among the Beauty: Emily Dickinson and America*, 251–93. Baltimore: Johns Hopkins University Press, 1979.

Lynen, John F. "Three Uses of the Present: The Historian's, the Critic's and Emily Dickinson's." *College English* 28 (November 1966): 126–36. Contains a contrastive analysis of Dickinson's and Whitman's sense of time.

Marcus, Mordocai. "Walt Whitman and Emily Dickinson." *Personalist* 43 (1962): 497–514.

Martz, Louis L. "Whitman and Dickinson: Two Aspects of the Self." In *The Poem of the Mind*. New York: Oxford University Press, 1966.

Nist, John. "Two American Poets and a Spider." *Walt Whitman Birthplace Bulletin* 4 (January 1961): 8–11.

Parks, Ed Winfield. "The Public and the Private Poet." *South Atlantic Quarterly* 56 (1957): 480–95.

Index